D1604238

SACRAMENTO PUBLIC LIBRARY

Foundation

SACRAMENTO PUBLIC LIBRARY

Schelling's Game Theory

Schelling's Game Theory

How to Make Decisions

ROBERT V. DODGE

OXFORD
UNIVERSITY PRESS

Oxford University Press, Inc., publishes works that further
Oxford University's objective of excellence
in research, scholarship, and education.

Oxford   New York
Auckland   Cape Town   Dar es Salaam   Hong Kong   Karachi
Kuala Lumpur   Madrid   Melbourne   Mexico City   Nairobi
New Delhi   Shanghai   Taipei   Toronto

With offices in
Argentina   Austria   Brazil   Chile   Czech Republic   France   Greece
Guatemala   Hungary   Italy   Japan   Poland   Portugal   Singapore
South Korea   Switzerland   Thailand   Turkey   Ukraine   Vietnam

Published by Oxford University Press, Inc.
198 Madison Avenue, New York, New York 10016
www.oup.com

Oxford is a registered trademark of Oxford University Press

Library of Congress Cataloging-in-Publication Data
Dodge, Robert, 1945-
Schelling's game theory : how to make decisions / Robert V. Dodge.
p. cm.
Includes bibliographical references and index.
ISBN 978-0-19-985720-3 (cloth : alk. paper)
1. Schelling, Thomas C., 1921-   2. Economists–United States–Biography.   3. Political scientists–
United States–Biography.   4. Nobel Prize winners–United States–Biography.   5. Game theory.
I. Title.
HB119.S28D628 2012
330.092–dc23
[B]
2011018453

9 8 7 6 5 4 3
Printed in the United States of America
on acid-free paper

For Pat Stocker, sister and friend

CONTENTS

ACKNOWLEDGMENTS

I would like to express my gratitude to Thomas Schelling for making available personal materials for me to use in the preparation of this book and for his continued support. Special thanks goes to my longtime friend, Alice Olson, for the considerable amount of time she put in reading and editing drafts of the manuscript before it was submitted for publication. My gratitude is expressed to the many notable people who allowed me to include their work and who contributed original work to illuminate the ideas included in this book. Thanks to Catherine Rae and Terry Vaughn at Oxford University Press for bringing this to the public and Molly Morrison of Newgen for her technical skills.

FOREWORD

Thomas C. Schelling

My last year at Harvard I had a Kennedy School student who took my course in Conflict, Cooperation, and Strategy, and did exceptionally well. He was a midcareer student, Robert Dodge, a high school teacher at a private school in Singapore. He decided to write a book suitable for high school students and, hopefully, a general public, based on my course. He went home thoroughly capable of presenting it to high schoolers. Over the years he put together this reader-friendly exposition of what I used to teach. Bob wanted it to be a textbook for high school students; I want it to be an exciting set of ideas for the general public. He got sidetracked into writing a professional biography of me (*The Strategist: The Life and Times of Thomas Schelling*, 2006) but returned to his original project.

This is not the book I would have written, but then I probably would never have written it. Bob has done it, and while there are things I might have included that are not here, there are things I would never have thought of that are here. I'm happy to endorse this compendium of a course (always in flux) that I taught for both graduates and undergraduates at Harvard for thirty years and at the University of Maryland for fifteen.

Some readers may know that in 2005 I received a Nobel Prize for "having enhanced our understanding of conflict and cooperation through game-theory analysis" and will wonder whether the subject of this book is "game theory." The answer is both yes and no. There are two definitions of game theory, a "soft" one and "hard" one. The soft one depicts game theory as the study of situations in which two or more entities—persons, organizations, governments, businesses, teams, couples—might rationally reach decisions in situations in which the outcome for both parties depends on the decisions both make. Nobody can choose what to do without considering what the other will choose to do. This means anticipating what the other anticipates what oneself will do, or what the other anticipates oneself to anticipate, and so forth.

The hard definition, as presented in my dictionary, is "the study of mathematical models of conflict and cooperation between rational-decision makers." You won't find any mathematics, beyond simple arithmetic, in this book. We might say that this book is in the spirit of game theory, whether or not it is game theory.

What I can assure you is that this book is fun. I always enjoyed teaching the subject, and so does Bob. He has made it all intellectually accessible, with a little hard thinking, and I'm sure you will be glad that after all these years he finally got it into shape for a book. I'm glad too.

CHAPTER 1

Thomas Schelling and His Signature Course on Strategic Thinking

His acute understanding of game theory has propelled advances in the field and *contributed to our hope for greater safety in the world.* —William C. Kirby, Harvard Business School

Tom Schelling has perhaps the most brilliant and interesting mind I've had the *privilege to encounter.* —William Ury, Founder, Senior Fellow, Harvard Negotiation Project

As much as any social scientist alive, Tom Schelling's work shows that ideas matter. —Richard Zeckhauser, JFK School of Government, Harvard University

In Japan Thomas Schelling would be named a national treasure. —Paul Samuelson, Nobel Laureate, Economics

Tom Schelling is a titan, and it is not the slightest exaggeration to say that his *remarkable scholarship has made the world a safer and better place.* —David T. Ellwood, Dean, JFK School of Government, Harvard University

In October of 2005 Thomas Schelling was named Nobel Laureate in Economics "for having enhanced our understanding of conflict and cooperation through game-theory analysis." The accolades above, by elite scholars, are not hyperbole; they describe a remarkable man. Though he remains less well known than his impact warrants, Schelling's work is the ultimate in rational strategic analysis. He identified and developed skills for making imaginative choices in diverse situations with an understanding of what the results of those choices will be. This is a book about his approach to decisions and to understanding what decisions mean; his work's purpose is to foster intelligent decision-making.

Schelling is primarily a product of the Cold War. He left Harvard Graduate School in 1948 to work in the Marshall Plan in Europe, where he witnessed economic recovery through cooperation. Next he went into the Truman administration in work related to NATO. He remained at the White House when Eisenhower became president, and then entered the academic world as a professor of economics at Yale.

Schelling's work on bargaining theory attracted attention, and he spent the summer of 1957 at the RAND Corporation in California. It was at this think tank, with its military associations, that he developed an interest in thermonuclear strategic planning. The Soviet Union sent up Sputnik that fall, and Schelling returned for a full year at RAND, emerging as one of the organization's foremost strategists.

By the fall of 1960, when Schelling was teaching in the Economics Department and at the Center for International Affairs at Harvard, his strategic achievements were considerable. He had given nuclear deterrence an intellectual framework, most notably with his influential book *The Strategy of Conflict*[1] and his explanation of the deadly balance of Mutually Assured Destruction (MAD). He was called on to do more.

He advised John Kennedy during the Berlin crisis of 1961. He proposed the hotline as a means of direct communication between U.S. and Soviet leaders in the event of an accidental nuclear launch. Using war games he had developed, he conducted training for Henry Kissinger and Robert Kennedy, among others, for dealing with crisis situations. There is disagreement over his impact on the decision to bomb North Vietnam, but general acknowledgment of his influence on the achievement of arms control agreements. He did studies on how segregation takes place, and was one of a small group responsible for the creation of a new graduate school at Harvard for teaching governance, the John F. Kennedy School of Government. Global warming, organized crime, and addictive behavior were among the topics that caught his attention and for which he proposed rational explanations.

When Schelling first came to Harvard he was asked to develop a course based on his experience in bargaining and strategy. The course came to be called Conflict, Cooperation, and Strategy, and Schelling would teach this course on rational choice until his retirement forty-five years later. He taught for thirty years at Harvard until mandatory retirement age and then for fifteen years at the University of Maryland. Many public servants and academics from around the world came to learn his rational, imaginative approach to problem solving.

This book seeks to make the methods and skills Schelling has offered at an elite level available to a general audience. The substance remains the same, but the readings have been selected not for Harvard graduate students, but for anyone interested in understanding rational choice. Professor Schelling has made all of his teaching materials from over the years available for the preparation of this book, which closely follows two syllabi (2003 and 1990). Additional explanation and skills practice is included along with supplemental materials from a variety of sources to reinforce the ideas and processes explored here.

What follows is the course about methods of thinking clearly and being aware of the outcome of decisions one makes as it was taught by Thomas Schelling. Problems from the course are used to initiate thinking and discussion of methods of strategic analysis. The general approach is descriptive of the points made in readings and class presentation. This material has been taught as an elective course to students 16 to 18 years of age at Singapore American School and is sensitive to different levels of understanding. The thinking skills from the Harvard graduate course apply and, while some of the problems used in Schelling's course are included, there is additional explanatory material. There also are less challenging problems that present the same concepts and skills, and supplemental materials to put the ideas in a broad context.[2]

Supplement: Steven Levitt on Thomas Schelling

The following column is from the *New York Times*, October 20, 2005, by *Freakonomics*[3] and *Superfreakonomics*[4] coauthor Steven Levitt on his memories of being a student in Schelling's course. Levitt is William B. Ogden Distinguished Service Professor of Economics at the University of Chicago, and in 2006 he was named one of *Time* magazine's "100 People Who Shape Our World."

"Nobel Prize Winner Thomas Schelling" by Steven Levitt

I've changed addresses 10 times since I graduated from college. And each time I've moved, I've looked at the battered old box of college notebooks and debated whether it was time to throw the box out. After all, it has been more than 15 years and the box has never once been opened.

> Thomas Schelling winning the Nobel Prize in economics finally gave me a reason to open the box. My sophomore year in college I took Econ 1030 from Schelling. I believe the course was entitled something like "Conflict and Strategy." I still have vivid memories of the course. A crew-cut Schelling paced back and forth across the stage (never with any notes, if I remember correctly), spewing forth story after story that illuminated the application of simple game theory concepts in every day life. The pauses between the stories were long enough that I had the impression he was coming up with them on the spot, although my own experience as a teacher makes me think otherwise.
>
> For me, this first introduction to game theory was inspirational. For someone who thinks strategically, or would like to think strategically, the basic tools of game theory are essential. The beauty of Schelling's class was how easy the math was and how readily it applied to real world

settings. The topics of the course were basic: the Prisoner's Dilemma in lecture 1, Schelling's own "tipping point" model in lectures 2&3, the tragedy of the commons and public goods games after that, then commitment devices, credible and non-credible threats, and the strategy and tactics of controlling one's own behavior.

(For those who are unaware, Schelling coined the term "Tipping Point" thirty years before Gladwell made it popular.)

Any economist could have taught the subjects in the class, but no one would have taught it like Schelling did. Each concept was accompanied by a barrage of examples. My notes are so poorly done—I would write down only a few key words—that now I can only guess at what the story was behind the words: when Rhodesia became Zimbabwe, VHS vs. Beta, the quality of play in bridge leagues, choosing colleges, Dulles vs. National airport, Bear Bryant should not have voted for USC, good weatherman takes fair bets, tailgating, Landon vs. Roosevelt, randomly flushing the toilet, etc.

I even remember attempting to put the lessons Schelling was teaching me immediately into practice. People who know me know that I can fall asleep anywhere, anytime. I would guess that I slept through some portion of 90 percent of my college classes. So when Schelling taught us about commitment, I decided I would start sitting in the front row of class as a way of committing myself not to sleep. Unfortunately, the urge to sleep often proved all too powerful. If Schelling were to remember me, it would be as the only kid in the first row who always fell asleep.

To my mind, Schelling represents the very best of game theory. He was a pioneer in the field, a man of ideas. Unfortunately for game theory, the simple ideas that are so alluring were quickly mined. What followed was less interesting. Modern game theory has become extremely mathematical, notation heavy, and removed from everyday life. Many of my colleagues would not agree with me, but I think game theory has failed to deliver on its enormous initial promise. I'm not the only one who feels this way. I was recently speaking with a prominent game theorist. He told me that if he knew what he knew and he were just getting started in the profession today, no way would he be a game theorist.

Schelling was an early inspiration to me. His course and writings were one of the big influences pushing me towards economics. My approach to economics shares much with his approach. I was saying this to one of my colleagues last year, who happened to run into Schelling and told Schelling he should count me as one of his students. Schelling was unmoved.

(Used with permission from Steven Levitt.[5])

Notes

1. Thomas C. Schelling, *The Strategy of Conflict* (Cambridge MA: Harvard Press, 1960).
2. For readers interested in Schelling's biography and achievements, see Robert Dodge, *The Strategist* (Hollis, NH: Hollis; and Singapore: Marshall Cavendish, 2006).
3. Steven Levitt and Stephen Dunbar, *Freakonomics* (New York: Morrow, 2005).
4. Steven Levitt and Stephen Dunbar, *Superfreakonomics* (New York: Morrow, 2009).
5. Steven Levitt, e-mail to Robert Dodge, July 2, 2009.

THE SCHELLING APPROACH TO STRATEGIC THINKING AND DECISION-MAKING

CHAPTER 2

Introduction to Strategic Thought

This is a book about decisions. It involves understanding the consequences of choices and, given that foresight into outcomes, deciding between alternatives rationally. The title of the course it outlines is descriptive: Conflict, Cooperation, and Strategy encompasses a spectrum of interactions. Choice is involved in all three. Looking at situations strategically and making intelligent choices is obviously valuable, but often not simple. Methods and skills to improve the ability to make intelligent choices will be introduced through explanation and through cases and problems. This is a theoretical study. It looks at schematic analyses of conflict and cooperation; bargaining, negotiation, and collective decisions; incentives and information; rules and enforcement; secrecy and deceit; threats and promises; interactive and interdependent behavior.

Often some introductory material will be followed by an abstract puzzle or problem. When this is investigated or solved and the abstraction explored, the next step will be to identify activities and real problems that share the structure of the abstraction. Our purpose will be to discover and come to recognize recurring and universal situations, behaviors, and problems. Techniques of blackmail differ in the criminal world, in family management, among nuclear powers, and in law enforcement, but they also have much in common. A threat to a child that there will be no television if his homework is not finished may avail itself of the same analysis as a threat to a country there will be a trade boycott if it exports nuclear technology. Individuals' decisions on whether to live in segregated or integrated neighborhoods may have the opposite effect than they intend when combined with decisions by others with motives who have similar preferences. Insight into this seemingly counterintuitive result is provided by a simple Schelling game and analysis. We seek practical understanding of these things.

Strategic analysis is central to this presentation. Strategy is involved when we seek to influence or adapt to the behavior that others have adopted or are expected to adopt. Strategic analysis is about situations, not personalities. Situations can be analyzed separately from individuals and their personalities, so connections with virtue and evil are not involved. Situation analysis is neutral and from a disinterested point of view, and keeping analysis focused and detached is critical to success.[1]

While studies related to strategic analysis are often highly technical and involve advanced mathematics, Schelling's methods are based on reasoning and uncluttered logic. Explanations are often developed by analogies or by observation of phenomena and historical events. Caesar in Gaul, thermonuclear showdowns, and experiences raising small children all equally provide material for Schelling's strategic insights. Certain mathematical skills and tools are included, and several explanations involve algebra, but the manipulation of numbers often requires only simple arithmetic. The course was designed by a man whose work is embodied in the comment made by billionaire investor Walter Buffett in his annual report to his shareholders following the economic downturn of 2008: "Our advice: Beware of geeks bearing formulas."[2]

Strategic thought has been analyzed since ancient times, and some early insights hold true. Xenophon, a general and historian in ancient Greece, had a clear understanding of strategic analysis. With his army preparing to face the massive Persian enemy, his concern was that they not recognize the enemy's superiority and flee. To get them to cooperate in fighting, he placed them with their backs to a gulley so they had no retreat. Only victory would provide safety. He realized this approach worked both ways. When he confronted small forces of Persians, Xenophon allowed his enemy a way of escape when he attacked, so they would not band together and fight with greater strength and determination. Another Greek historian and general, Thucydides, led Athens in the Peloponnesian Wars and observed that looking at the problems from the other person's perspective and identifying his opportunities and interests was central to strategy. Diplomats, lawyers, and chess players traditionally practice such analysis.

A strategic move usually must impact the expectations of another. If it is wise for me to prove that I will not hurt you, I disarm myself. If I want to prove that I will not testify against you because I see something you are doing, I blind myself in your presence while you are in the act. If I want to prove I will not retreat, I chain myself to my post. Each such gratuitous impairment or sacrifice has value only in how it has influence on your behavior. Gaining someone's trust in how you will act may involve some overt strategic signal. In some past societies the strategic choice was to give the best jobs to eunuchs because of the confidence their employers had in what they could not do.

What people do affects what others do. How well people accomplish what they want to accomplish depends on what others are doing. When one raises his voice to be heard, it often adds to the total noise of the voices as others do the same, and they negate each other. Soldiers doing riot control wear gas masks to hide the fear in their faces as well as to protect themselves from possible exposure to teargas.

Strategic thought is vicarious problem solving. It involves looking at a situation from the point of view of the other person and using as much as is known about his preferences to decide what the other would do, given his goals and values and the choices he faces. Then, having an idea what the other will decide, one makes a decision that best suits one's own goals and values. Both parties go through the same process.

The number of interacting decision units in strategic analysis is typically small, so an individual's influence is of sufficient consequence that he must take into account what others are doing and expect him to do. If one typical investor decides to withdraw cash from his account, it has little impact on the financial system. However, if one withdraws cash for reasons that induce others to do so and this action encourages others, whose responses also encourage others, who encourage many more, something strategic has taken place that can be analyzed.

Strategies can be complex, as in congressional negotiations, or simple, as when a child pretends not to hear a command from his parents to wash up and come to dinner. The underlying assumption remains the same: the decision makers are rational. It can be argued that the assumption of rationality negates the value of and study of strategic thought and rational choice. Real decision makers may mis-perceive options, have prejudices that interfere with their reasoning, or choose to maximize some value that others do not recognize. Yet the assumption of rational thought provides a baseline or benchmark, and irrational behavior and decisions can be measured against it. Irrational behavior can be analyzed rationally in some cases, and the methodology is systematic.

The incompatibility between individual rationality that is based on promoting self-interest and rationality that is based on cooperation that serves the interests of the group is a pervasive problem in modern society and is examined at length. This conflict is explored thoroughly in several chapters that revolve around the best-known problem in strategic thought, "the prisoner's dilemma." Not only an academic problem but also a social and political one, the prisoner's dilemma has appeared in many forms in popular culture. Typical is the *Law and Order, Criminal Intent* story "Tomorrow"[3] in which Detective Goren can not prove whether one or both related nannies in the same building are guilty of a triple murder. He gets them in separate rooms and tells each she will be convicted of all three murders; he gets both to confess to being involved. In film, prisoner's dilemma situations often cre-ate dramatic stress. The 2008 Batman movie *The Dark Night*[4] includes a tense scene where the Joker has hostages and is taking control of the city of Gotham. The city is being evacuated, with prominent citizens on one ferry and dangerous convicts, whom the city fears the Joker plans to set free, on another. Each ferry is loaded with explosives, and the trigger to detonate each is on the other ferry. The Joker informs both groups that the only way for them to save themselves is to set off the explosives on the opposite ferry, and if neither side does so, he will destroy both at midnight. The Joker is operating on the individual rational assumption that each side will value its survival above the other and it will be a race between the upstand-ing and the criminal element to be first to push the button. It turns out both have concerns about the other, and their dilemma gives Batman time to discover the Joker's location and foil his insidious plot. So group interest with the major "exter-nality" of Batman carries the day over individual interest in *The Dark Night*.

Wanting to do what is best for oneself is the underlying assumption of free market economics and much social theory; but the shattering logic of the simple prisoner's dilemma game is that doing "what's best for yourself" is sometimes achieved by doing what is also best for others.

There are specific skills and behavior patterns set out in this presentation, but the central approach will be to explicate how some game theory assumptions function in rational, imaginative decision-making. The framework of seeing problems and choices in these terms can be helpful in becoming aware of what your decisions mean. Decisions operate differently on the individual, or micro, level than they do on the larger, or macro, level; and people's choices may not produce the results they thought they were effecting.

Models, or metaphors that represent human interaction, will be introduced to make this more apparent, and simple interactions will be presented to make more complex situations easier to recognize and evaluate. Learning of the "divided self" rational approach to the present you and the untrustworthy you of the future offers guidance for strategic approaches to controlling behaviors in which you fear you will indulge, such as overeating or drinking. The book is broken down into a series of sections that introduce concepts that affect us. They are generally grouped but not progressive.

These concepts, understood, will enable the reader to begin to think strategically with a Schelling foundation and to understand decision-making better. There are no claims that this is an elixir, a solution for all difficult problems, but it introduces a framework for analysis. As Schelling states, "I would not pretend that a strategic analysis...discovers cheap and easy tactics for solving our problems. I do suggest that in many of these enterprises there are strategic aspects that can be brought under systematic analysis and can help us identify critical requirements and vulnerabilities in the enterprise. Depending on the enterprise, we can then try to support or collapse it, tilt it to our advantage one way or the other, exploit it for our own benefit, or just understand what makes it work."[5]

Notes

1. Readers seeking an in-depth examination of Schelling's views should look to Thomas C. Schelling, *The Strategy of Conflict* (Cambridge, MA: Harvard University Press, 1960), *Micromotives and Macrobehavior* (New York: Norton, 1978), and *Choice and Consequence* (Cambridge, MA: Harvard University Press, 1984). All three works feature prominently in this book. An additional advanced source dedicated to Schelling is the collection of chapters about his ideas by distinguished scholars: Richard J. Zeckhauser, ed., *Strategy and Choice* (Cambridge, MA: MIT Press, 1991).
2. David Segal, "In Letter, Warren Buffett Concedes a Tough Year," *New York Times*, March 1, 2009, A16.
3. "Tomorrow," season two of *Law and Order, Criminal Intent*, originally aired November 10, 2002.
4. *Batman: The Dark Night*, Warner Brothers Pictures, 2008.
5. Schelling, *Choice and Consequence*, 212.

Vicarious Thinking

The essential frame of mind to adopt for strategic thinking is to view interactions vicariously when making a decision or solving a problem. This is critical: put yourself in the other's place and anticipate the solution from his position. It is the first step to seeing how your choice will affect the choice of the person or group with which you are interacting.

At times when you might be attempting to agree but are unable to communicate directly, you must rely on thinking vicariously. Such is the not uncommon case of the husband and wife separated in a supermarket, wondering how to find each other. They could each think, "Where would he/she most likely go for us to meet?" That might work. Their chances improve when they also think, "Where would he/she think that I would think he/she would think we would go?" That is vicarious thinking. Such thinking was dramatically portrayed in the fantasy film *The Princess Bride*.[1] The evil Sicilian kidnapper Vizzini was confronted by the heroic Man in Black, who set out two wine goblets, one of which apparently contained an odorless, deadly poison. The Man in Black said, "All right. Where is the poison? The battle of wits has begun. It ends when you decide and we both drink, and find out who is right and who is dead." Vizzini had to think as his opponent, stating: "Now, a clever man would put the poison into his own goblet, because he would know that only a great fool would reach for what he was given. I'm not a great fool, so I can clearly not choose the wine in front of you. But you must have known I was not a great fool; you would have counted on it, so I can clearly not choose the wine in front of me."[2]

This chapter presents part of a questionnaire (called here Questionnaire A) that has been used many times since it first appeared years ago in the inaugural issue of the *Journal of Conflict Resolution*.[3] It measures this basic skill and was originally sent to forty-two individuals. Their responses were matched after they had completed it on their own. To be of use, your answers must be compared with those of someone else. For instructional purposes the "someone else" is this book and "someone else's" answers appear in the appendix.

Answer Questionnaire A, following the Schelling instruction, "What would I do if I were playing this game?" Do not look at the answers in the appendix until you complete all eighteen responses. The analysis in the appendix is based on years of using this activity with students. Answers and the reasons for them are derived from what has been most successful. They represent how students have most often thought the people they were paired with would answer and what answer, then, would be to their best advantage.

A second option for doing this questionnaire is available. Immediately following Questionnaire A is a blank Questionnaire B, which could be answered by a second person. The results might be somewhat different if this is done with a partner one knows, since it makes thinking as the other thinks a little more specific. It also allows an opportunity to compare answers along the way. Learning could then occur, as recurring patterns may suggest answers to future questions that involve coordinating decisions; for example, couples might succeed in finding each other in shopping malls or areas of markets by recalling where they had met on previous occasions. When the exercise is done in pairs and players' values conflict, if answers are exchanged after each question, trade-offs and turn-taking can occur, though this approach is not common. Such behavior indicates vicarious thinking, which is the essential point in doing the exercise. However, vicarious thinking can be tested equally well by measuring success in answering and then comparing with the answers in the appendix.

To answer the questions, you try to adapt your choices to the choices of another with whom you cannot communicate. The "other" is a composite of former students who have communicated with some success over the years. If you tear out the B questionnaire and do this exercise with another person, it is that person's answers with which you are attempting to adapt your own, and that person is trying to adapt his choices to yours. Success is determined by how well you actually succeed in accommodating your answers to the answers given by another with a counterpart questionnaire. Thus the "right" answer for you depends on how the other fills out his or her questionnaire. And the same is true for the other.

In some problems, such as the first pure tacit collaboration is required. Your interest coincides exactly with that of your partner, and you win together only if you succeed in making identical choices without communicating. In other problems your interests will partly coincide and partly diverge; you may need to align your actions for mutual benefit, but there will be alternative beneficial choices that discriminate between the outcomes for you and your partner where one can benefit to a greater degree than the other.

In these problems the success of your answer depends on your guess as to what your partner will be putting on his questionnaire, knowing that he is trying to guess what you will be expecting him to do. Note that in many of these problems you can win only if you do what others expect you to do, just as they can win only by doing what you expect them to do. The object is usually not to "outsmart" the other person, though there are problems that involve strategic anticipation that benefits you to a greater extent than your partner. If you attempt to "outsmart" your partner, you often outsmart yourself at the same time. However much your interests may conflict, in most, but not all, of the problems you can both win only if each of you does what the other expects you to do, and a wrong guess loses for both of you. Remember, your goal in making your choice is to think as you think your partner would think.

The questionnaire follows:

Questionnaire A

1. Write down any number. You win if you write the same number your partner does.

    Your number _____

2. Choose heads or tails. You win if you chose the same as your partner.

    Heads_____ Tails _____

3. Circle one of the x's. If you circle the same x as your partner, you both win.

    x x x x

    x x x x

    x x x x

    x x x x

4. You are to meet somebody in New York City at a stated time. You have not been instructed where to meet, have no way of communicating, and neither of you lives there, has relatives there, or attends school there. You will have to guess where to meet, and hope your friend guesses the same.

    Where will you meet? _____

5. The situation is the same as in problem 4, but in this case you were told the location, but not a time to meet. Neither of you is allowed to wait for the other for more than five minutes. All you can do is hope you both guess the same time to meet.

    What time will you meet your partner? _____

6. Everyone has to choose heads or tails. You both win if you both make the same choice. However, if both choose heads, the person designated A wins $2, while the person designated B wins $1. If both choose tails, the person designated A wins $1, while the person designated B wins $2.

    Choose heads or tails. _____

7. Write down any positive number. If the numbers you write differ by more than 1, or if the numbers are the same, you both lose. If the numbers differ by exactly 1—that is, if the two numbers written by you and your partner are consecutive—you both win. The smaller number of the two wins $2, and the larger wins $1.

    Write your number here: _____

8. A and B are to choose heads and tails. If both choose heads, both get $2. If both choose tails, both get $1. If A chooses tails and B heads, A gets $3, and B gets nothing. If A chooses heads and B tails, neither gets anything.

    Mark your choice: Heads _____ Tails _____

9. There is $100 to be divided between you and your partner according to the following procedure: You each claim some amount not greater than $100. You will receive an amount equal to the smaller of a) the amount you claim and b) $100 minus the amount your partner claims.

   Write down your claim. _____

10. Name any president of the United States, living or dead. If you both write the same name you both win, otherwise you both lose.

    Write down a president's name _____

11. Imagine you have an income of $50,000. Assume you are paired with a person whose income is $80,000. You both know each other's income. A tax of $130 is levied on the two of you combined. You may divide the tax any way you please. Each of you is to volunteer, by writing down an amount of money, the share of tax you are willing to pay. If your answers add up to $65 or more, you will pay the amount that you wrote down. If your two shares add up to less than $130, each of you will be taxed $130, for a total of $260. To repeat, your income is $50,000 and the other person's is $80,000.

    What tax do you propose to pay? _____

12. You are to choose heads or tails. If you both choose heads, you get nothing. If you both choose tails, you get $1 each. If one chooses heads and the other tails, the one who chooses heads gets $2 and the one who chooses tails gets $1.

    Your choice is: Heads _____ Tails _____

13. You are to circle one of the two-digit numbers in the square array below. These numbers were picked from a table of random digits. Your partner also has a square array of 16 two-digit numbers, but his were picked from another table of random digits and bear no relation to yours. He is to circle one of his numbers. If you both circle numbers in the same position, you both get the number of dollars given by the numbers you circle. If you do not circle numbers in exactly the same position, neither of you gets anything.

    Circle a number:

    41 62 84 03
    23 78 37 59
    99 16 68 26
    30 45 08 87

14. You and your partner each receive piles of money of $1,000. You are to divide the amount you received into piles labeled A and B. If you divide the money in exactly the same way, you will each receive $1,000. If your amounts differ, you receive nothing.

    Your division is: Pile A _____ Pile B _____

15. If you both choose heads, you get nothing. If you both choose tails, you get $1 each. If one chooses heads and the other tails, the one who chooses heads gets $2, and the one who chooses tails pays the other $1.

    Your choice is: Heads _____ Tails _____

16. For this problem, A questionnaires are NORTH and B questionnaires are EAST. If you are A, you are initially assigned the seat labeled NORTH at the rectangular table illustrated below. B is assigned the seat marked EAST at that table. Now that you have been assigned a seat, you are free to pick any seat at the table. The scoring system is as follows: If you pick the same seat the other person chooses, neither of you wins anything. If you pick seats opposite each other, neither of you wins anything. If you pick adjacent seats, you both win. The one who sits to the other's right wins $3 and the one who sits to the other's left wins $1.

    Mark the seat you choose on the diagram.

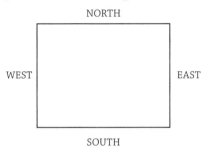

17. Name any person you both know (any person you both know of, if you are doing this with a stranger). If you both write down the same name, you both win. If you write different names, you both lose.

    Name: _____

18. Write down any positive number. If the numbers you write are consecutive, you both win, otherwise you both lose. The larger of the two wins $5, and the smaller wins $1. It is suggested that those of you designated A write 33, and those of you designated B write 32, but that is only a suggestion.

    What number do you choose? _____

Questionnaire B

1. Write down any number. You win if you write the same number your partner does.

    Your number _____

2. Choose heads or tails. You win if you chose the same as your partner.

    Heads _____ Tails _____

3. Circle one of the x's. If you circle the same x as your partner, you both win.

    x x x x

    x x x x

    x x x x

    x x x x

4. You are to meet somebody in New York City at a stated time. You have not been instructed where to meet, have no way of communicating, and neither of you lives there, has relatives there, or attends school there. You will have to guess where to meet, and hope your friend guesses the same.

   Where will you meet? _____

5. The situation is the same as in problem 4, but in this case you were told the location, but not a time to meet. Neither of you is allowed to wait for the other for more than five minutes. All you can do is hope you both guess the same time to meet.

   What time will you meet your partner? _____

6. Everyone has to choose heads or tails. You both win if you both make the same choice. However, if both choose heads, the person designated A wins $2, while the person designated B wins $1. If both choose tails, the person designated A wins $1, while the person designated B wins $2.

   Choose heads or tails. _____

7. Write down any positive number. If the numbers you write differ by more than 1, or if the numbers are the same, you both lose. If the numbers differ by exactly 1—that is, if the two numbers written by you and your partner are consecutive—you both win. The smaller number of the two wins $2, and the larger wins $1.

   Write your number here: _____

8. A and B are to choose heads and tails. If both choose heads, both get $2. If both choose tails, both get $1. If A chooses tails and B heads, A gets $3, and B gets nothing. If A chooses heads and B tails, neither gets anything.

   Mark your choice: Heads _____ Tails _____

9. There is $100 to be divided between you and your partner according to the following procedure: You each claim some amount not greater than $100. You will receive an amount equal to the *smaller* of a) the amount you claim or b) $100 minus the amount your partner claims.

   Write down your claim. _____

10. Name any president of the United States, living or dead. If you both write the same name you both win, otherwise you both lose.

    Write down a president's name: _____

11. Imagine you have an income of $50,000. Assume you are paired with a person whose income is $80,000. You both know each other's income. A tax of $130 is levied on the two of you combined. You may divide the tax any way you please. Each of you is to volunteer, by writing down an amount of money, the share of tax you are willing to pay. If your answers add up to $65 or more, you will pay the amount that you wrote down. If your two shares add up to less than $130, each of you will be taxed $130, for a total of $260. To repeat, your income is $50,000 and the other person's is $80,000.

    What tax do you propose to pay? _____

12. You are to choose heads or tails. If you both choose heads, you get nothing. If you both choose tails, you get $1 each. If one chooses heads and the other

tails, the one who chooses heads gets $2 and the one who chooses tails gets $1.

Your choice is Heads _____ Tails

13. You are to circle one of the two-digit numbers in the square array below. These numbers were picked from a table of random digits. Your partner also has a square array of 16 two-digit numbers, but his were picked from another table of random digits and bear no relation to yours. He is to circle one of his numbers. If you both circle numbers in the same position, you both get the number of dollars given by the numbers you circle. If you do not circle numbers in exactly the same position, neither of you gets anything.

Circle a number:

53 18 49 82
02 34 67 79
94 21 09 50
12 97 45 26

14. You and your partner each receive piles of money of $1,000. You are to divide the amount you received into piles, labeled A and B that divide the money. If you divide the money in exactly the same way, you will each receive $1,000. If your amounts differ, you receive nothing.

Your division is: pile A _____ pile B _____

15. If you both choose heads, you get nothing. If you both choose tails, you get $1 each. If one chooses heads and the other tails, the one who chooses heads gets $2, and the one who chooses tails pays the other $1.

Your choice is: Heads _____ Tails _____

16. For this problem, A questionnaires are NORTH and B questionnaires are EAST. If you are A, you are initially assigned the seat labeled NORTH at the rectangular table illustrated below. B is assigned the seat marked EAST at that table. Now that you have been assigned a seat, you are free to pick any seat at the table. The scoring system is as follows: If you pick the same seat the other person chooses, neither of you wins anything. If you pick seats opposite each other, neither of you wins anything. If you pick adjacent seats, you both win. The one who sits to the other's right wins $3, and the one who sits to the other's left wins $1. Mark the seat you choose on the diagram.

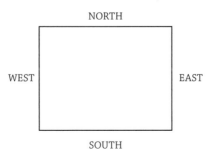

17. Name any person you both know (any person you both know of, if you are doing this with a stranger). If you both write down the same name, you both win. If you write different names, you both lose.

    Name: _____

18. Write down any positive number. If the numbers you write are consecutive, you both win, otherwise you both lose. The larger of the two wins $5, and the smaller wins $1. It is suggested that those of you designated A write 33, and those of you designated B write 32, but that is only a suggestion.

    What number do you choose? _____

Now compare your answers with Player B's answers that are in the appendix following the chapter or, if you have had someone else complete the Player B questionnaire, compare answers with that person before proceeding. Once you have noted the results (questions where you matched answers when instructed to or had consecutive answers when that was the task) and you have calculated what your results on the partially cooperative and noncooperative problems are, read the following commentary about the problems.

Questionnaire Analysis and Commentary

For questions 1, 2, 3, 4, 5, 10, 13, 14, and 17, you could win only if your answers were coordinated and identical. If they were not, you failed to gain anything. Only consider your answer for Question 4 to be correct if you named a specific location. Central Park, Times Square, or the Statue of Liberty might be starting points but are not guaranteed meeting locations for a specific time, since each offers many possible meeting locations. No cell phones allowed. If you achieved some success, such as five matches on these nine problems, you are likely making an effort to think vicariously and to choose as you think your partner is likely to think. If you could see one or two where the response seemed apparent, but the others were just guesses, there are subtle clues that you may be missing that are simple elements in strategic thinking. The remaining problems also require vicarious thought, but the payoffs are unequal, and you can begin to see something of strategic thinking in an effort to gain advantage or to exploit a partner in these.

Success on the pure coordination problems, the nine that required identical answers where both players either succeed or fail, is a clear measure, but the problems with interests somewhat at conflict are more difficult to evaluate if both players think vicariously and strategically. Sometimes the strategies involved in playing for extra points by outsmarting your opponent can interfere with achieving the best point score. What matters is that the efforts to gain an advantage are based on vicarious views of how the partner will play. This process will be a continuing theme.

A look at the last problem on the questionnaire demonstrates the strategic process involved in vicarious thinking, so first consider what takes place in answering it for both players. The question asks you to write a positive number, and the only way you win anything is if you and your partner write consecutive numbers. Writing consecutive numbers had been asked previously, but this is different. The larger of the two numbers will win $5, while the smaller receives $1. Then there is the "suggestion" that those who were designated A should write 33, and those designated B write 32. So, as a reader, you were an A and you wrote? Writing consecutive numbers without conferring is an exercise that generally fails and attempts to do so result most often in the participants receiving no points. Having numbers suggested to you is a significant clue to help you achieve a response that would reward you both. Perhaps that means the obvious choice is to write 33 on your Questionnaire A as the problem suggested. That comes with a bonus, because it is the higher number, which means it wins $5, and B receives only $1. But then you might (should?) think, "We both have this recommendation. If I were B and were given this advice, what would I do? I'd know A is going to write 33, because I, as B, am supposed to write 32. But if A is going to write 33, I'd be better off if I wrote 34. Then we would be writing consecutive, but mine would be higher. I would get the $5, while A gets $1."

To a rational A it becomes apparent that his rational partner, B, is going to write 34 instead of 32. In that case, A's best move is to write 35 instead of 33. That keeps his number higher. But if B is equally rational, he knows A thinks strategically and has figured B would switch his number from 32. B would have concluded A was going to select 35, and he would slip past him by going to 36. A might have thought B was going to try to slip past him, and would write 37. This is difficult, because they both know that unless their numbers are consecutive, they both fail to win anything, so just writing a large number is not a good choice, since it likely means both end with zero.

This circular reasoning is difficult, and some students completing the questionnaire in pairs have gone along with the suggested 32 and 33, while others have been successful with consecutive numbers at 38 and 39. Whenever B answers 32, the first question is "Why?" B has nothing to lose by going to 34 because if A follows the suggestion that would have been a winner, it just changes his payoff from $1 to $5. Where should the players stop? There is no single answer for that, as other factors enter such as whether this is a one-off encounter. As well, the individuals' priorities are to maximize their individual payoffs, but maximizing may mean knowingly settling for less rather than ending up with nothing based on previous encounters or determining where the balance lies between increasing the number and unrealistic guessing. When such problems are transformed to real world situations the reasoning can at times become extremely serious, but the process is identical.

This introductory questionnaire offers you the opportunity to get an idea of how successful you are at thinking vicariously—essential to strategic analysis. If you find this process evident, much of what follows will appear reasonable and apparent. The strategies necessary for success with the questionnaire along with Schelling's concepts of prominence and focal points, which will be addressed in later chapters, were the inspiration for this exercise.

These questions show that the problem solving involved in coordinating answers or anticipating a partner's answer involves logic, but success in vicarious thinking is also a product of imagination. Knowing your partner's decision before making your choice gives you an advantage in achieving your goals.

An introductory analysis of the questionnaire provides some hints for success in vicarious problem solving. Vicarious thinking problems are often solved fairly successfully because of convention, a critical strategic thinking idea. Conventions are commonly accepted methods of agreeing on a solution that has more than one option. Many of these problems have some signaling quality to them, what Schelling would label a focal point, which attracts both participants to make the same selection. The first question is often accurately answered with the number one, a matter of the convention of starting at the beginning. Occasionally people are successful with some other number if they know each other. Teammates on a school team might select the jersey number of one of them, or a couple who both know one has a favorite, lucky number might choose it. In the second question it is the convention of the common word order used in "heads or tails" being the normal expression has led to "heads" being chosen—likely the question answered successfully most often. The following question, with the sixteen x's in a rectangle, has been successful with the greatest frequency when partners selected the upper left x, positioned where one would begin reading a page. The position has a certain distinction that sets it apart from the others and focuses attention on it, as though it identifies the "first" x in the figure.

Question 4 has special significance in the story of how Thomas Schelling was drawn into the study of strategic thinking. Its background goes back to the summer of 1940 after his first year as a student at Berkeley. He and two friends set out for a summer road trip and when they were in Texas, they lost each other for some time. When they finally reconnected, they decided to think of how they would meet if they were separated in some other city and had no way of communicating. The three decided on some guidelines, and then each thought about a spot that would work best. Their guidelines were that it should be at some place that was unique in the city and could be found by asking any policeman or fireman. An additional desirable quality was that it be on some public transportation line. All three came up with the same solution. The meeting point they all independently named was the General Delivery window of the city's main post office. That very successfully met the issues of isolating a spot and their individual thinking focused on it.

The friends' agreement was not tested on the remainder of that trip, but what brought them to the same conclusion would be part of what he was testing when he designed this questionnaire. He had his own test years after his traveling companions had all gone their separate ways and Schelling had a visit scheduled for New York. He arrived in the City and was to visit Tom Ludwig, one of his road trip companions, but realized he did not have Ludwig's address. He thought that if Ludwig realized the situation and remembered the road trip of their younger days, a solution might be possible. The General Delivery window had made sense in 1940, but had become a thing of the past. Western Union was the closest thing he could think of to General Delivery, so Schelling called them. He asked, "Do you have a way that I can leave a message for a person who may call in for a message?" The operator answered, "Yes, what is your name?" "Schelling," he replied, and the operator said, "Oh, we have a message for you from Mr. Ludwig." The road trip lesson and vicarious thinking had been retained and successfully adapted.[4]

Question 5, seeking a meeting time, has been answered successfully with 12:00 noon more than with any other answer. Again, participants who take this questionnaire and know each other might successfully select a different time, based on previous experiences and plans; but for strangers with no other information 12:00 noon has a singular quality to it, while other times are more random.

Questions 6, 8, 12, and 15 are similar questions that offer strategic options. Making choices for these questions is simplified considerably with the use of an elementary and basic tool, the 2×2 matrix, which will be explained in Chapter 4. These problems have no correct answers, but seeing them on a payoff matrix makes the choice visual and vicarious considerations apparent. Again, these are problems where strategies might differ if you are answering the question once or expect repeated encounters. When answers are compared after each question, new strategies will apply. Players consider how their partner answered previously, and on occasions one sees responses emerge that demonstrate willingness to share for both to win or to attempt "taking turns" in winning the larger amount.

In Question 7 the most successful answer has been 1, 2 as consecutive. These choices embody the convention of starting at the beginning and the real question becomes who will write which number. One possible approach is to recognize that the numbers must be consecutive and the letters of the questionnaires are consecutive. Answering Questionnaire A with 1 and Questionnaire B with 2 matches tasks, since going in order from the beginning is the convention, and applying it to both assigned question sheet and number coordinates an answer.

The most frequent answer to Question 9 has been $50 for both players. This may suggest notions of fairness and also of coordination, as thinking of claiming more makes one think of the other player claiming more. You both know one of the two options is $100 less than the amount your opponent selected and also understand that you can only receive your claim if it is equal to or larger than the amount your amount your opponent selects.

As to naming the same president, in current times the focus of attention has been overwhelmingly on Barack Obama. This question has been more demanding in other years, but without some knowledge of the other player's priorities that would lead to a different choice, such as being partnered with a strong Republican who still looks back longingly to Ronald Reagan, at this time Obama's name is probable.

The tax question is commonly answered correctly with A offering to pay $50 and B offering to pay $80 (this question has been altered by doubling the amounts from Schelling's original 1950s salaries). They both knock the three zeros off of their income and the offer to pay the exact tax of $130. Again we have something where it can be seen as fair by both sides and the numbers work out correctly. Here the powers of suggestion are obvious in the numbers. Splitting the tax could have been a solution. If this is so obvious, is a perfectly proportional income tax obvious? If the problem had been worded that both parties were to pay a $130 tax and a $130 refund was available if they could agree on how it should be divided, would it be an identical problem? Is this consistent with the idea of a graduated income tax that is the accepted norm, and if not, why is it so frequently answered correctly? Such policy issues are generated from strategic analysis of situations, as shall be seen throughout the book.

Question 14 was much like the earlier problem of circling the matching x on a rectangular pattern of 16 x's. It is obscured with the inclusion of considerable distracting information that can entice a choice with hope of achieving a higher score, but with no additional information that coordinates the players in making their decisions. Thinking of how you can make the same decision as your partner is still the issue, and the convention of starting at the beginning and getting something still has a focal quality, which makes it likely to be the position that is most often selected. At times students focus on the final number and happen to match, but it is less common. If the answers had been seen on the question with the x's there might be some mutual thinking that the players would follow in this case, but otherwise, the numbers are a distraction and the position is the only vicarious thinking involved.

Question 16 gave each player a specific place at the table, though it was not an assigned seat. If you simply followed the directions you were given as a label for sitting at the table, the A Questionnaire wins three to the B Questionnaire's one because the player is to the right. Both would win something, which becomes less likely if they move. B has less at stake in moving. By changing from East to West, B would remain adjacent to A and would be on his opponent's right, reversing the payoffs to three to one in his favor. Of course, A is aware this is possible. If he is sure, he will move from North to South, and this is another situation that can carry on circularly. B could be aware that A knows he is likely to change from East to West and will change from North to South to remain on the right. Knowing that, he will remain at East, and let A move to South and grant him the higher score. Or A could conclude that is what would happen and return to his original position, where the thinking could carry on. All of this changing of positions and getting back to the original point where it could always go just one step further would be played out in the minds of A and B. They would only do the one simple thing required, which is to take a seat at the table. This problem illustrates how a seemingly simple choice can involve interactive possibilities and vicarious thinking can make one aware of the complexities and necessities for strategic intervention.

On Question 17 the appendix to the chapter answered "Thomas Schelling" as the person both would name for readers who were using the book as player B. It could have been President Obama again, Oprah Winfrey, or Glenn Beck, depending on whom it was thought might actually be buying this book, but the book is about Thomas Schelling's ideas and he has been mentioned frequently.

There is more to be learned from these questionnaires by examining strategic options, communication and its value to which player, dominant choices and other topics. A separate chapter on coordination with reference to this questionnaire is included (Chapter 14). At this point the questionnaire has the very important role of introducing the idea of looking at problems vicariously, and that is an idea essential for understanding the next chapter.

Chapter 3 Appendix: Questionnaire B—to be matched with Reader answering

Questionnaire A

Note: These are not "the correct" answers to these questions. In most cases there was a reason for selecting them, but see the explanation and factors involved in the analysis and commentary above.

1. Write down any number. You win if you write the same number your partner does.
   Your number: **1**
2. Choose heads or tails. You win if you chose the same as your partner.
   Heads __**X**__ Tails _____
3. Circle one of the x's. If you circle the same x as your partner, you both win.

   (**x**) x x x

   x x x x

   x x x x

   x x x x
4. You are to meet somebody in New York City at a stated time. You have not been instructed where to meet, have no way of communicating, and neither of you lives there, has relatives there, or attends school there. You will have to guess where to meet, and hope your friend guesses are the same.
   Where will you meet? **Last position in line to get into Empire State Building**
5. The situation is the same as in problem 4, but in this case you were told the location, but not a time to meet. Neither of you is allowed to wait for the

other for more than five minutes. All you can do is hope you both guess the same time to meet.

What time will you meet your partner? **12:00 (noon)**

6. Everyone has to choose heads or tails. You both win if you both make the same choice. However, if both choose heads, the person designated A wins $2, while the person designated B wins $1. If both choose tails, the person designated A wins $1, while the person designated B wins $2.

Choose heads or tails: **Heads**

7. Write down any positive number. If the numbers you write differ by more than 1, or if the numbers are the same, you both lose. If the numbers differ by exactly 1—that is, if the two numbers written by you and your partner are consecutive—you both win. The smaller number of the two wins $2, and the larger wins $1.

Write your number here: **2**

8. A and B are to choose heads and tails. If both choose heads, both get $2. If both choose tails, both get $1. If A chooses tails and B heads, A gets $3, and B gets nothing. If A chooses heads and B tails, neither gets anything.

Mark your choice: Heads __**X**__ Tails _____

9. There is $100 to be divided between you and your partner according to the following procedure: You each claim some amount not greater than $100. You will receive an amount equal to the *smaller* of (a) the amount you claim, (b) $100 minus the amount your partner claims.

Write down your claim: **$50**

10. Name any president of the United States, living or dead. If you both write the same name you both win, otherwise you both lose.

Write the name of a president: **Obama**

11. Imagine you have an income of $50,000. Assume you are paired with a person whose income is $80,000. You both know each other's income. A tax of $130 is levied on the two of you combined. You may divide the tax any way you please. Each of you is to volunteer, by writing down an amount of money, the share of tax you are willing to pay. If your answers add up to $65 or more, you will pay the amount that you wrote down. If your two shares add up to less than $130, each of you will be taxed $130, for a total of $260. To repeat, your income is $50,000 and the other person's is $80,000.

What tax do you propose to pay? **$50**

12. You are to choose heads or tails. If you both choose heads, you get nothing. If you both choose tails, you get $1 each. If one chooses heads and the other tails, the one who chooses heads gets $2 and the one who chooses tails gets $1.

Your choice is: Heads __**X**__ Tails _____

13. You are to circle one of the two-digit numbers in the square array below. These numbers were picked from a table of random digits. Your partner

also has a square array of 16 two-digit numbers, but his were picked from another table of random digits and bear no relation to yours. He is to circle one of his numbers. If you both circle numbers in the same position, you both get the number of dollars given by the numbers you circle. If you do not circle numbers in exactly the same position, neither of you gets anything.

> **(53)** 18 49 82
> 02 34 67 79
> 94 21 09 50
> 12 97 45 26

14. You and your partner each receive piles of money of $1,000. You are to divide the amount you received into piles, labeled A and B that divide the money. If you divide the money in exactly the same way, you will each receive $1,000. If your amounts differ, you receive nothing.

    Your division is: Pile A: **$500**; Pile B: **$500**

15. If you both choose heads, you get nothing. If you both choose tails, you get $1 each. If one chooses heads and the other tails, the one who chooses heads gets $2, and the one who chooses tails *pays* the other $1.

    Your choice is: Heads ___**X**___ Tails _____

16. For this problem, A questionnaires are NORTH and B questionnaires are EAST. If you are A you are initially assigned the seat labeled NORTH at the rectangular table illustrated below. B is assigned the seat marked EAST at that table. Now that you have been assigned a seat, you are free to pick any seat at the table. The scoring system is as follows: If you pick the same seat the other person chooses, neither of you wins anything. If you pick seats opposite each other, neither of you wins anything. If you pick adjacent seats, you both win. The one who sits to the other's right wins $3 and the one who sits to the other's left wins $1. Mark the seat you choose on the diagram.

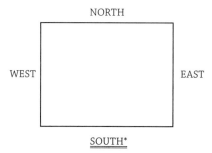

17. Name any person you both know (any person you both know of, if you are doing this with a stranger). If you both write down the same name, you both win. If you write different names, you both lose.

    Name: **Schelling**

18. Write down any positive number. If the numbers you write are consecutive, you both win, otherwise you both lose. The larger of the two wins $5, and the smaller wins $1. It is suggested that those of you designated A write 33, and those of you designated B write 32, but that is only a suggestion.

What number do you choose? **36**

Notes

1. *The Princess Bride*, Act III Communications, 1987.
2. "Princess Bride, The Script at IMSDb," http://www.imsdb.com/scripts/Princess-Bride,-The.html.
3. Thomas C. Schelling, "Bargaining, Communication, and Limited War," *Journal of Conflict Resolution*, Vol. 1, No. 1 (March 1957), 19–36.
4. Thomas Schelling, interviewed by Robert Dodge, June 8, 2000.

CHAPTER 4

Game Theory

It was 1944 when economist Oskar Morgenstern and mathematical wizard John von Neumann released *The Theory of Games and Economic Behavior*[1] and the new methodology was formalized. Game theory is not a theory of anything, but an approach to analyzing situations. The name was a result of the authors' observations of characteristics of parlor games like checkers and chess. The games had rules and scoring systems, and the amount of information available to each player was specified at every point. Most importantly, the decisions players made were interdependent. Making a wise move in chess depended on the moves one's opponent made or was likely to make, and both players would try to think as their opponent was thinking before deciding on a play. The authors thought there were similar situations in economics and set out to make mathematical models of conflict and cooperation that would determine expectations game players could have about each other's choices.

While game theory is most commonly studied in economics, it has long since branched out to find application across the social sciences and in the natural sciences as well. It has become a discrete mathematics topic that has made many strides, while mathematicians and social scientists advance different frontiers in its progress. Nobel Laureate Robert Aumann pointed this out, writing,

> "Interactive Decision Theory" would perhaps be a more descriptive name for the discipline usually called Game Theory. This discipline concerns the behaviour of decision makers (players) whose decisions affect each other. As in non-interactive (one person) decision theory, the analysis is from a rational, rather than a psychological or sociological viewpoint. The term "Game Theory" stems from the formal resemblance of interactive decision problems (games) to parlour games.... The term also underscores the rational, "cold," calculating nature of the analysis.[2]

He went on to say that it has become an umbrella, or "unified field" in social sciences that applies to economics, political science, tactical and strategic problems, evolutionary biology, and computer science and also social psychology and branches of philosophy such as epistemology.[3]

Simply stated, game theory is the study of interactive decision-making by rational decision makers. It is a formal study of vicarious thinking as introduced in the previous chapter. To transform social encounters into situations with predictable outcomes requires several assumptions, agreement on definitions and, normally, the conversion of decisions into numbers. The individuals or groups involved are commonly called "players." A "game" is any social interaction involving two or more players, and the outcome for each depends not only on one player's choice, but also on what the other chooses. A player is assumed to be a "rational actor." This means the player is intelligent and understands the interaction and outcomes of his decision. Another critical aspect of being rational is that the player will make decisions that are in his or her own interest. Players will operate by choosing to maximize their personal "payoff," or achieve the result best for themselves personally. A player is concerned with his own payoff, not concerned with "beating" the other player. That is a point frequently mistaken; perhaps calling it a "game" contributes to this common initial error.

A common method in game theory for evaluating the outcome of games and determining whether the interactive behavior has been successful is whether the result has achieved equilibrium. As in nature, in game theory equilibrium exists when an interactive situation is in balance. In game theory terms, an outcome of a game is in equilibrium if there is no incentive to "defect," or no party has any incentive to change his decision. A stable equilibrium is one in which an altered "externality," or outside disruption to the equilibrium, would be followed by a return to the original equilibrium solution. If the equilibrium is unstable, a disruption will result in movement farther from the equilibrium solution.

While stability is a highly desired outcome in decision-making, Schelling is less fascinated with outcomes at equilibrium than are many other game theorists and sees the equilibrium solution idea as an oversimplification that neglects processes of adjustment or exaggerates the prevalence of equilibrium by neglecting shifts in factors that determine it. While not rejecting equilibrium analysis, he warns of the danger that, by recognizing that something is in equilibrium, people will have acknowledged that the outcome is satisfactory or that it could not be better. As an example, he comments that a hanged man's body is in equilibrium when it stops swinging, but that does not mean the man is all right.[4]

The assumption of rational actors making perfectly logical choices has raised questions about the usefulness of game theory in solving any real world problems, but it manages to remain helpful. There are difficulties in knowing what values each player is attempting to maximize, and not all players are completely logical, but it is a constructive starting point for many problems and they can be modified to accommodate the irrational. Game theory sometimes offers answers that provide surprisingly counterintuitive insights into what a rational answer is, and has been of considerable value in times of the greatest dangers.

The following chapter will introduce the form of game theory analysis Schelling employed most often, the two-by-two matrix, and further explore some basic concepts, especially those he employed.[5]

Supplement: A History and Explanation of Game Theory from *The Logic of Life*, by Tim Harford

The following supplement is a brief history of game theory and its basic underlying ideas, viewed through the prism of two influential game theorists. This is an edited version of a chapter from *The Logic of Life* by Tim Harford (London: Little, Brown, 2008). Harford writes "Dear Economist" and "Undercover Economist" columns for the *Financial Times* of London and is a presenter on the BBC2 series *Trust Me, I'm an Economist*.

Las Vegas: The Edge of Reason

THE RIO HOTEL, LAS VEGAS, NEVADA

It is hard to say where the check-in queue ends and the casino begins. Even in the quiet midmorning hours, as the guests sleep off the night's excesses or enjoy breakfast, the hotel's lobby boasts a bewildering array of flashing lights and garish displays. Elderly gamblers sit and feed quarters into the maw of the nearest slot machines. Occasionally—just often enough—the machines vomit coins.

Despite every effort to stimulate the senses, this is a tedious place, but the monotony is interrupted by a strange procession: a man, his face concealed with facial hair, mirror shades and a cowboy hat, strides across the lobby, pursued by admirers. Known to poker lovers as "Jesus," he is Chris Ferguson, one of the most successful poker players in the world. He's in Las Vegas to try reclaim his crown as World Poker Champion.

Ferguson is the best of a new generation of players trying to conquer poker with "game theory." It is a curious struggle, one that has pitted bespectacled geeks against hardened gamblers. Half a century of struggle by some of the world's smartest economists and mathematicians, backed by computers, has produced impossibly complicated poker strategy. All the while, thugs and hustlers have been bumbling along, playing the game the intuitive way. We'll discover that fifty years of formal brilliance have yet to provide more than the tiniest advantage over the experienced judgment of "ordinary" professional gamblers. It turns out that the slot machine junkies, too, are more rational than you would suppose.

This chapter traces the limits of rational choice theory as it bumps up against human fallibility. Economics is the study of how people react to incentives in their environment. Sometimes those incentives result not from background factors, but from the actions of identifiable people. These other people will try to anticipate one another's desires and strategies, trying to respond to them and perhaps thwart them. To understand the complexities of these interactions, we need a special branch of economics, called "game theory." Game theorists need to understand both rational behavior and human peculiarities.

The Las Vegas lobby with poker and slot machines is a visual metaphor for how game theory has matured—a story that can best be told by contrasting two of the most famous game theorists. Both were Cold War intellectuals, advising the US government at the highest levels and using game theory to understand the riskiest of all games, nuclear war. Game theory emerged from the sparkling mind of John von Neumann, a mathematical prodigy, when he decided to create a theory of poker. It was tempered by the earthier wisdom—usually expressed in witty prose rather than equations—of Thomas Schelling. Tormented by a tobacco addiction he could not kick, Schelling nudged game theory into a direction that now offers surprising insights into hapless slot machine addicts.

Late in the 1920s, the most ostentatiously brilliant man in the world decided to work out the correct way to play poker. John von Neumann, who helped develop both the computer and the atom bomb, was engaged with whether his beloved mathematics could uncover the secrets of poker, which seemed a quintessential human game of secrets and lies. Von Neumann believed if you wanted a theory—he called it "game theory"—that could explain life, you should start with a theory that could explain poker. His aim was to bring the rigor of mathematics to the social sciences, and that meant economics, because rational decisions of economics can be modeled using mathematics. Von Neumann thought he could develop a rational, mathematical explanation for much of life, and poker was the starting point. He told a colleague, "Real life consists of bluffing, of little tactics of deception, of asking yourself what is the other man going to think I mean to do. And that is what games are about in my theory."

Bluff, deception and mind reading were unpromising subjects for a mathematician, but if anyone could do it, it was Johnny von Neumann. His feats of calculation were notorious: after the war he helped design the fastest computer in the world, before challenging it to a calculation contest and demonstrating he was faster. Although there were those who delved deeper, nobody was as quick as Johnny. In the popular imagination von Neumann arguably outshone even his Princeton contemporary, Albert Einstein.

Nevertheless, to understand poker, von Neumann had to break new ground. Poker was not merely a game of chance, requiring probability, or a game of pure logic with neither random elements nor secrets, like chess. Poker is a far more subtle challenge. In poker players bet to earn the right to compare cards at the showdown, but most of the information in poker is private. Yet in many hands of poker, especially between skilled players, there is no showdown, because one player bets aggressively enough to scare away others. In short, there is no straightforward connection between what a player bets and the hand he holds.

Novices wrongly believe that bluffing is merely a way to win pots with bad cards. A player who never bluffs will never win a big pot. Then there's the reverse bluff: acting weak when you are strong. Trying to deceive your opponent seems like a matter of psychology, not mathematics. Could there really be a rational strategy behind these bluffs and reverse bluffs? Would pure mathematics nevertheless deliver those bluffing moves? Von Neumann thought so. His work on game theory culminated in a 1944 with *Theory of Games and Economic Behavior*, a book he wrote with Oskar Morgenstern that included a stylized model of poker in which two rational players faced each other in a highly simplified setting.

To understand von Neumann's approach, imagine playing a round of von Neumann poker. You and your opponent contribute a small ante to the pot, and then you go first. You pick up your hand. The simple rules give you two options: either check or make a big bet. In this simplified game, when you check, the hands are compared and the best hand wins the ante from the worst. (You're opponent doesn't get to make a decision at that point; like real poker, this is unfair, which is why players take turns.) If you bet, your opponent faces his own choice: he can fold, conceding you the ante, or he can call, matching your bet, which means a showdown for higher stakes.

What is your rational move and what is your opponent's rational response? You shouldn't decide without considering his response, and he cannot react to your bet without figuring out what strategy you have. The interrelatedness of both of your strategies is what makes this a problem requiring von Neumann's game theory. At first glance we have what seems to collapse into an endless chain of reasoning. If you bet even with terrible cards your opponent should always call the bet with any decent cards. Yet if you only bet with the best possible cards he should always fold when you bet. All we have is a thought process that runs, "If he thinks that I think that he thinks. . . ."

Von Neumann created a theory of perfect decision-making: he was looking for the moves that infallible players would make. Game theory finds those moves by looking for opposing strategies that are consistent, in the sense that neither of the infallible players wants to change once he hears about the other player's strategy. There are plenty of strategies that don't meet that standard. For instance, if your opponent is very cautious and often folds, you should bluff a lot. But if you bluff a lot, your opponent shouldn't be so cautious.

Instead, we need to consider both players' strategies in combination. Your opponent's strategy is the simpler. Because the simple game gives you no opportunity to fold it also gives him no chance to bluff. (He on the other hand, is allowed to fold, which means that you *can* try to bluff.) Since he can't bluff he should simply call you with his better hands, and fold with his worse hands.

What should you do? With an excellent hand, you should bet: you have nothing to lose if your opponent folds while giving yourself a good chance of winning a big pot if he calls. But with a middling hand, you should check and hope your hand wins the ante. What about a terrible hand? Should you bet or check? Checking would be unwise, because the hands will be compared and you will lose. It makes more sense to bet with these bad hands, because the only way you will win anything is if he drops out, and he might drop out if you make a bet. Perversely, you are better off betting with awful cards than with mediocre ones, the quintessential (and rational) bluff.

There's a second reason for you to bet with terrible cards rather than middling ones: your opponent will have to call you a little more often. Because he knows your bets are sometimes very weak, he can't afford to fold too often. That means that when you bet with a good hand, you are more likely to be called, and to win when you are called. "Of the two possible motives for bluffing," wrote von Neumann in *Theory of Games*, "the first is to give a (false) impression of strength in (real) weakness: the second is the desire to give a (false) impression of weakness in (real) strength."

Von Neumann had shown that bluffing, far from being some unfathomable human element to the game of poker, was governed by the rules of mathematics. His message was that there is a rational, mathematical foundation even to the apparently psychological game of poker, and if poker was a meaningful analogy for everyday problems, his success implied that it was just possible there was a rational foundation to life itself.

For many years after von Neumann's death in 1957, academics struggled to bend game theory to problems of economics, biology, and military strategy, but without living up to the expectations raised by *Theory of Games*. The problem was that von Neumann might have been regarded as a demigod, but for game theory to be successful, it needed to cope with the more limited brainpower of ordinary mortals.

Fundamental to von Neumann's approach was that both players were as clever as von Neumann himself. But in practice, there are two problems. The first is that a game may be so complex that not even the fastest computer could calculate the perfect strategy. The second is that game theory becomes less useful if your opponent is fallible. If player two is not an expert, player one should play to exploit his mistakes. The worse an opponent is, the less useful the theory is.

It's no surprise, then, that Princeton University Press put out a slightly sheepish advertisement in 1949 to celebrate five years of anemic sales of *Theory of Games and Economic Behavior*. It mentioned "a few copies bought by professional gamblers"—but there is little evidence that von Neumann's theories made any immediate impact on poker.

It's a safe bet that Walter Clyde Pearson was not a customer. "Puggy" Pearson was born in Kentucky in 1929, and his family was dirt-poor. But while von Neumann's publishers were defending *Theory of Games*, Pearson was stationed with the navy in Puerto Rico, cleaning up at poker and pool. Puggy was to invent the idea of tournament poker, and became world champion in 1973. And he did it all without a mathematical equation in sight.

Like many of the early gambling professionals, Puggy Pearson had a knack for getting himself into trouble. His close scrapes were hardly unusual. Puggy's rival, Amarillo Slim, was once robbed of fifty thousand dollars—the stakes on the table—by three armed men who broke into the house where he was playing. On another occasion he was rescued from a pressure negotiation with the Mafia by an army of heavies sent by poker impresario Benny Binion. "You never seen so many big hats and bulges in your life," Slim recalled.

These characters were a long way from Princeton and *Theory of Games*. Even if a cerebral university professor could have used game theory to clean up from the likes of Puggy and Slim, he might not fancy his chances of making it home with his wallet intact. But that is not why the professors stayed away from Vegas. For all of its sophistication, game theory could not offer any improvement on the lessons learned during a life as a road gambler.

It took a half-century, and two important developments, for this to change. The first development was social, as the casinos started to become places where anyone could feel that their physical safety was guaranteed, even if their wealth was not. The second was technological. The geeks found somewhere to practice that few people had heard of back in 1988: the Internet.

"IRC poker" was the craze among the deep geeks of the time, a simple program that used Internet relay chat, a precursor of today's online chat rooms. Thousands logged in to compete for bragging rights, as rising to the top of the IRC rankings meant beating the world's most obsessive geeks.

One of the leading players was a doctoral student at UCLA named Chris Ferguson. A computer science graduate, Ferguson was studying artificial intelligence and had been exposed to both poker and game theory, which his father taught at UCLA, from an early age. IRC poker, with its rapid play and the stream of electronic data it provided, was a much better laboratory than Las Vegas for someone who wanted to get inside the game and see what made it tick.

Just as von Neumann had had to simplify the game of poker before he could find the perfect strategy, Ferguson started on a simple version of the game: Asian stud, which is played with a deck of only thirty-six cards. Ferguson was using exactly the same game theory as von Neumann but, backed up by technology, he was able to work out strategies first for Asian stud and later the most popular form of poker, Texas Hold'em.

Using ever-faster computers to crunch numbers, Ferguson worked out probabilities of one hand improving enough to beat another. Then came game theory to explore which hands to bluff with, how often to bluff, trade-offs between raising a little with a promising hand, risking being overtaken by a lucky opponent, versus raising much and scaring people away. He memorized table after table of his results.

He began to produce some unexpected conclusions. For example, his game theory showed that the old-school poker professionals were raising too much with strong hands, believing you should force your opponents out and give them no chance to get lucky and overtake you. He found it was worth making small raises and encouraging your opponents to stay in. Sometimes your opponents would get lucky, but on the balance the strong hand would make more money with smaller raises.

Ferguson knew that game theory would give him an advantage, not because of his winnings at the table but because the best players were wrong. However, while the advantage was real, it was small. Ferguson was to discover there was a huge overlap between the rational approach and the intuitive game played by strong players.

By the late 1990s he was one of the most recognizable sights in poker, earning the nickname "Jesus" as he hid his face behind a long beard and hair that cascaded over his shoulders, buttressed by wrap-around shades and a big cowboy hat. He never spoke during play, trying to remove any sign of human emotion; he didn't pay attention to other players' nervous tics, either. He drew his information from the cards, like a computer—or like von Neumann himself.

The rational age of poker began at the 2000 World Series in Las Vegas. After outlasting five hundred rivals, the last two contestants faced each other. T. J. Cloutier, a sixty-year-old Texan road gambler regarded by many as the best player yet to win the World Series, was playing Jesus Ferguson. Cloutier was much more experienced, but Ferguson had destroyed the field and came to the table with ten times as many chips as his opponent.

Playing brilliantly and riding his luck, Cloutier ate into Ferguson's lead and was only slightly behind when he lured Jesus into serious trouble. With several million dollars at stake, Cloutier's raise of $175,000 seemed timid and convinced Ferguson that Cloutier was bluffing. Fergusson re-raised $600,000 and Cloutier pushed in roughly $2 million in the pot, going "all in."

Ferguson paused for more than five minutes, calculating the odds. He reckoned his chances at about a third—and that was better than if he folded and conceded all those chips to Cloutier. "I was getting the right odds from the pot," he now says. So Chris "Jesus" Ferguson removed his hat and shades, suddenly shrinking and exposing his human qualities: exhaustion, vulnerability. Then he called, and Cloutier revealed ace-queen to Ferguson's ace-nine.

Since there were no more chips to bet, the five communal cards were revealed at an agonizing pace. For Ferguson to win, one of the communal cards had to match his nine and none of them to match Cloutier's queen. But Johnny von Neumann's angel must have been watching over Ferguson. When the last card—a nine—hit the table, Ferguson realized what had happened before the hushed crowd did. His arms shot into the air and he leaped to embrace Cloutier.

Many poker fans remember Ferguson's luck, but he had arrived at the final table with more chips than the next five players put together. All told, Chris Ferguson has a respectable claim to be the most successful tournament player of the twenty-first century.

The fact it took over half a century for game theory to produce a world champion might seem like a severe criticism of von Neumann's approach. The exact opposite is true. The very fact that Chris Ferguson's struggle was so hard won and that the level of his play was not notably better than that of T. J. Cloutier is exactly what game theorists need to assume. Ferguson's struggle demonstrated experience could produce rational decisions, even if the decision-makers are not necessarily conscious of the rational basis for all their actions. Game theory often throws up such cases of unconscious rationality emerging from experience. Professional footballers have been shown to play perfect strategies when taking (or saving) penalty kicks, mixing up the placing of their shots in perfect accordance with the surprisingly complex prescriptions of game theory.

That's fine when we have time to practice and familiarize ourselves with a game. But that wasn't true of the most important "game" to which game theorists applied their thinking in the twentieth century—the game of world dominance played out by the US and the Soviet Union. The Cold War was a game that had to be played right the first time.

And the creator of game theory was right at the heart of it. Von Neumann was a leading mathematician on the Manhattan Project. If it had been up to von Neumann's purely intellectual reasoning alone, many of the bombs he helped create would have exploded on the Soviet Union. Thankfully, there was another thinker on hand whose deeper grasp of human foibles added a new dimension to game theory that, among other things, helped save the world from mutually assured destruction. Enter Thomas Schelling.

Camp David, Maryland, September 1961

Some of America's best foreign policy and military strategists were in the room: a young Henry Kissinger; McGeorge Bundy, President Kennedy's national security advisor; John McNaughton, the top arms control aid to Robert McNamara; and Colonel DeWitt Armstrong, the Pentagon's top authority on Berlin. They hadn't been sleeping much. The crisis in Berlin had been building for months, since Soviet leader Nikita Khrushchev had demanded that US troops withdraw from their bases in West Germany.

When the phone call arrived from the American base in Berlin, the news was bad. American forces had shot down Soviet planes, and riots were spreading across Eastern Europe. Terse communiqués over the next couple days made it clear matters were deteriorating: West German students started rioting, Soviet tanks encircled West Berlin and used the riots as a pretext for entering that sector of the city, breaking through barricades. US bombers responded, causing massive casualties. The Soviets had overwhelming local superiority, the Americans nuclear dominance: a nuclear exchange seemed inevitable. Would Kissinger and Bundy decide to press the button?

It wouldn't have mattered if they had, because those men at Camp David were playing a game. The phone calls weren't coming from Berlin, but from a Harvard professor, economist Thomas Schelling.

The real Berlin crisis had run out of steam a few weeks earlier without a shot being fired. Khrushchev had asserted Soviet authority over West Berlin and declared that US resistance would be an act of war. The young, inexperienced President Kennedy was being tested. He had turned to Schelling's strategic analysis of the plan before deciding—correctly—that Khrushchev was bluffing. Instead of invading, the Soviets began building the Berlin Wall in August, sat behind it, and glowered.

Thomas Schelling was one of many Cold War intellectuals at RAND, the Air Force's research arm, using game theory to dissect the possibilities of an event nobody had experienced: thermonuclear war. Applying a theory of poker to try to understand mutual annihilation may seem unhinged, but that is exactly what von Neumann and his disciples did. How else to develop nuclear strategy? Practicing was not an option, while history, fortunately, could provide no exact parallels.

Von Neumann demanded an aggressive approach. In the late 1940s, he favored a surprise nuclear assault on the Soviet Union, before it was able to develop the bomb itself. "If you say why not bomb them tomorrow, I say why not today?" he told *Life* magazine. Von Neumann, who spent the last months of his life in a wheel chair after being struck with bone cancer in his fifties, was an inspiration for the deranged and similarly wheelchair-bound film character Dr. Strangelove.

In game theory, von Neumann had crafted a tool that promised to analyze both poker and war. Yet rhetorically pleasing as the analogy is—and delighted as the RAND strategists were with game theory—analytically poker and war had very little in common. Poker is a zero-sum game: one player's loss is another's gain. It is also a game with well-defined rules. War is neither well defined, nor a zero-sum game. Compared to the likely alternative of mutually assured destruction, the Cold War is a win for both sides. Thomas Schelling's war games were part of his effort to bring about that mutual win.

Schelling realized that you could not take the human element out of war. While von Neumann was the consummate mathematician, Schelling, originally a trade negotiator, was more interested in concepts that eluded mathematical formalization—credible threats, deterrence and taboos—his ideas pushed the academic discipline of game theory away from the abstract and intellectual pursuits pioneered by von Neumann and further into the mainstream of everyday human experience.

Schelling argued that real human strategic interactions were governed not only by von Neumann's mathematics but by "focal points" that were invisible under mathematical formulation of the problem. Schelling did not believe that game theory was useless, merely that most human interactions were so shot through with ambiguity that these focal points could be the ultimate guide to what might or should happen. For example, a trade union leader might try to gain leverage in a negotiation over pay by publicly stating that his members won't accept less than a 10 per cent raise. Ten per cent is of no mathematical significance and von Neumann would have seen no basis for it. Yet Schelling knew that once the declaration is made, it becomes significant (and that it will be a round number such as 10 per cent, not 10.32 per cent or 9.65 per cent).

All this was still game theory, in that each player was acting rationally and trying to anticipate and respond to the strategy of the other player. But it was game theory of a simpler, more common sense sort than von Neumann had conceived. And for Schelling common sense was exactly the point, because the players of such games needed to understand one another.

With his emphasis on communication, it is not surprising that Schelling was the man who came up with the idea of the hotline to Moscow. He realized that a nuclear war could start easily as the result of some accident. If a crisis started, the leaders of the United States and Soviet Union could be looking at the wrong focal point, one in which there was a nuclear exchange. They would only be able to fix the situation if they could reach each other quickly, and talk. Yet no hotline existed, so Schelling proposed one to both sides in 1958. In retrospect the idea was obvious, but it took Schelling to realize how important quick, reliable communication might become.

Schelling also applied his focal point idea to strengthen the taboo against nuclear weapons. In the 1950s, while von Neumann still lived, the US government was desperate to avoid the sense that such weapons were beyond the pale. Dwight Eisenhower's secretary of state, John Foster Dulles, argued that inhibitions in the use of nuclear weapons were based on a "false distinction" between nuclear and conventional weapons that needed breaking down and President Eisenhower appeared to agree.

Schelling did not agree. His argument was that "bright lines, slippery slopes and well-defined boundaries" were everything in this debate. To avoid a full-blown nuclear exchange only one focal point should be emphasized: that nuclear weapons could never be used. There was no such thing as a "minor" use of nuclear weapons any more than one could become slightly pregnant. The taboo was purely psychological, invisible to a mathematician like von Neumann, but very real and very useful. He put forward this view, as part of a broad theory of deterrence and arms control, in a series of seminars that he organized at Harvard University and the Massachusetts Institute of Technology in 1960.

Schelling became the intellectual godfather of the Kennedy and Johnson administrations. By the time he broke off his connection with the government in 1970, that taboo was as strong as it has ever been.

Schelling compared the "minor" use of nuclear weapons to "one little drink" for an alcoholic. The analogy hit close to home: Schelling was fighting his own battle with cigarette addiction. Despite our obvious fallibilities, Schelling believed that addiction could be analyzed using rational choice perspective offered by game theory. In the 1970s he was asked to join the National Academy of Sciences committee on substance abuse and addictive behavior. It was the belief of the other committee members that addicts were irrational and helpless. Their reasoning was that since smoking or taking heroin is addictive and can have horrible effects, people who choose to take up the habits must be irrational. Economists Kevin Murphy and Gary Becker were putting an opposite view forward. Addiction, they said, was entirely rational. People who consume addictive products—cigarettes, alcohol, and slot machines—calculate that the pleasure of the habit will outweigh the pain.

Schelling thought neither view was true. For him, addiction was neither purely irrational nor purely rational. It was a battle for self-control that an addict could win, if only he had the right tactics. This was a simple contest between two decision-makers, one patient and the other eager for a quick hit—but both decision-makers were in the same body. He had to rely on introspection to develop what he called "egonomics," the view of addiction as a kind of mental civil war.

Now a bold new group of researchers armed with both brain scanners and rational choice theory, calling themselves "neuroeconomists," are starting to develop a view of the brain that provides some startling evidence for Schelling's split-personality model of decision-making. The impatient part of the brain is called the dopamine system. The system seems to be designed to make instant forecasts of pleasure as a way to make quick decisions about what to do. Addictive chemicals can cause the dopamine system to misfire, and some researchers think non-chemical addictions such as playing slot machines can do the same thing.

The other side in the mental civil war is the cognitive system. Better able to guide longer-term choices in certain environments, it can be slow to operate. Humans combine information from both and *voila*: Thomas Schelling's "egonomics," reborn as "neuroeconomics."

Schelling was not the first person to point out these tensions or to describe addiction as a battle for control of the self. But he was the first to think explicitly of the problem as a strategic one. He made a woeful strategic error in his own battle. He quit smoking in 1955, but in 1958, while sitting in a restaurant in London, he bought a cigar. He thought he was immune, but spent many years "tormented," trying to quit.

Schelling's days as a strategist gave him a book of tricks and tactics to recover from that initial stumble. He realized he didn't have the strength of will to simply quit smoking, but he also knew that a vague promise to himself to cut down would easily be dodged by his impatient, cigarette-craving side. So he decided to create a "bright line." He told himself that he would not smoke until after the evening meal. He obeyed that rule for years, but unfortunately Schelling's weaker half was also an expert strategist, and the hapless professor found himself hunting for sandwiches at around 5:30 p.m. so that he could have a smoke without having violated the letter of his self-imposed law.

No economist has come up with a convincing explanation for why these taboos and focal points work. But work they do, albeit imperfectly. Why else would people try to quit smoking on 1 January rather than on 24 February?

An addict, like a negotiator, may be able to gain an advantage by making binding decisions in advance. An everyday example is the dieter who shops for food over the Internet, only after a good meal, so that the sight of cakes and chips does not tempt him. The forward-thinking person outwits the impatient or weak-willed person who inhabits the same body.

In real negotiations, too, a negotiator can strengthen his position by tying his hands. This is what any shop assistant does when they tell you they're not authorized to offer you a discount. But such tactics can backfire. In the film, *Dr. Strangelove*, the Russians build a doomsday device, a computer that will launch every Soviet warhead if it detects any sign of an American attack. Such a device is obviously risky, but by making retaliation certain it should make surprise attack far less likely. This is the reasoning that Dr Strangelove, the fictional von Neumann, explains. Needless to say, predictable human error intervenes and things do not go quite according to plan. (Whom did the director Stanley Kubrick consult while scripting the movie? None other than Thomas Schelling.)

Suddenly it is not so hard to see how an alcoholic's rational side can successfully decide to quit after reading about an increase in liquor taxes in the newspaper—but that the very same person could kill herself drinking if she got hold of another bottle. While addicts can make the wrong choices, contradict themselves and be tormented by their frailties, as Schelling was, they can also weigh costs and benefits, anticipate temptations, and take steps to put those temptations out of reach.

Schelling himself won his personal civil war after a fifteen-year struggle. When I met him in 2005, he had gone three decades without smoking. At the age of eighty-four, he was the picture of health.

Thinking back to Las Vegas, it is clear that Ferguson's triumph at the 2000 World Series of Poker was a landmark in the history of game theory. Ferguson's approach was directly descended from von Neumann's pure mathematical brilliance, but while modern economics still drips with mathematics, much of the most successful game theory is of the Schelling variety: simpler in theory, and more aware of the messy details of real situations.

Just three weeks before Ferguson's victory, for example, the British government had scored a little win of its own, raising twenty-two billion pounds in an auction for mobile phone licenses that was designed by game theorists—arguably the most high-profile success of game theory in recent years. And while Ferguson's grasp of advanced game theory continues to make him one of the most feared faces at the poker table, more humble Schelling-style battles for self-control are being fought out at the doors of the Rio. Some gambling addicts cannot reach the slot machines because the casino manager and his security guards will intercept them. These men and women have been barred from the Rio and all the other casinos owned by the world's largest operator, Harrah's, by their own forward-looking better halves. Anyone who suffers from a gambling addiction—a misfiring of the dopamine system when the slot machines are in sight—can call Harrah's or log on to the website and volunteer to be banned. The rational decision-maker outwits the shortsighted addict with the help of Harrah's, their image recognition software and a couple of friendly bouncers. If you can't win the battle with yourself, you can recruit allies.

Game theory shows us the hidden logic behind poker, war and even addiction. It is inevitably a way to view the world through the lens of rationality, but most effective when it uncovers simple, common sense rationality in unexpected places. Von Neumann would have fully expected his beloved game theory to be achieving triumphs at Las Vegas. He might have been more surprised to learn that modern game theory has as much to do with the internal dilemmas of the slot machine junkies as with the brilliance of Chris "Jesus" Ferguson on the other side of the lobby.

(Included with permission from Tim Harford.[6])

Notes

1. John von Neumann and Oskar Morgenstern, *Theory of Games and Economic Behavior* (Princeton, NJ: Princeton University Press, 1944).
2. Robert Aumann, "Game Theory," in *The New Palgrave: Game Theory*, ed. John Eatwell, Murray Milgate, and Peter Newman (New York: Macmillan, 1989).
3. Ibid.
4. Thomas C. Schelling, *Micromotives and Macrobehavior* (New York: Norton, 1978), 26.
5. For an overview of available game theory books and levels for which they are designed, plus related material and games, see Gametheory.net, http://www.gametheory.net/.
6. Tim Harford, e-mail to Robert Dodge, July 3, 2009.

CHAPTER 5

The Two-by-Two Matrix

The most common game theory tool is the two-by-two matrix. This uncompli-cated rectangle illustrates the simplest of games, involving two players, each having a single choice between two options. It is a basic tool that Schelling has frequently used in his strategic work. He has protested that his use of the matrix does not make him a game theorist, arguing, "That's like saying because I use an equal sign, I'm a mathematician,"[1] but the Nobel committee and the academic world has thought otherwise. This simple way of illustrating a game has been central to game theory since the subject's formal inception and it remains a surprisingly versatile device for strategic decision making. This is a grid with one player's choices represented running north–south and the other's running east–west. The possible outcomes of their combined deci-sions appear in the intersecting cells of the grid. The matrix shows four cells that represent the four possible intersecting outcomes of the player's choices (Table 5.1).

Table 5.1

		Player A	
		Decision 1	Decision 2
Player B	Decision 1	A	B
	Decision 2	C	D

The two-by-two, or 2X2, matrix is illustrated and a number of basic game theory elements are presented with the "banknote game," developed by Robert Sugden in *The Economics of Rights, Cooperation, and Welfare*.[2] In this exercise Players A and B are in different rooms and the organizer says, "I have donated a $10 bill and a $5 bill for this game to be played. You say which bill you claim. If you both claim the same bill, you both get nothing, but if you claim different bills, you each get the bill you claim."

The players have an interest in cooperating, though they would not agree on which was the best choice. Each player has two strategies from which to choose. Player A can claim $5, which may be called strategy A1, or $10, labeled strategy A2. Player B can also claim $5, his strategy B1, or $10, his B2. For every possible combination of strategies there is a clearly defined outcome, and having such a list of outcomes is known technically as game form.

In this game, with the players in different rooms it is impossible for them to cooperate on choices of strategies, which is often true in decision-making. However, in game-like situations, deals between players are often both possible and mutually beneficial. Games like the banknote game with no cooperation are in the category of "simultaneous choice," meaning the players make their decisions at the same time and/or without knowledge of the other's decision.

Sugden says, "The idea that a game can be described in terms of strategies, and that players choose their strategies independently and simultaneously is a theoretical one. It represents a way of thinking about interactions between people, and not a particular and narrowly defined type of interaction."[3]

The banknote game can be depicted on a 2X2 matrix that shows both players' choices and the results of the different possible combinations of those choices in the following fashion (Table 5.2):

Table 5.2

	Your Opponent's Strategy	
	Choose S1 ($5)	Choose S2 ($10)
Choose S1 ($5)	You win nothing Your oponent wins nothing	You win $5 Your oponent wins $10
Your Strategy		
S2 ($10)	You win $10 Your opponent wins $5	You win nothing Your oponent wins nothing

The fundamental assumption of the theory of games is that players are concerned only with outcomes. Strategies have no values in themselves other than as a means to an end. In this case we assume the players are seeking the highest payoff possible, but that need not be the case. The assumption is the individual is seeking to maximize his own payoff, but that does not specify what the person values. In game theory it does not matter why an outcome is wanted. It is not necessarily greed or self-interest, since unselfish aims may come into conflict as much as selfish ones. Sugden's example of this is a married couple where one wants to give money to charity while the other wants money to support aged parents. As well, not all games are about conflict. Some are about coordination and involve players whose interests are not in conflict.

It is assumed each player can attach a subjective value to every outcome and that he chooses his strategy to do the best he can on the scale of value. The value a person attaches to an outcome is measured on a utility rating. The utility of an outcome to a player is a measure of how badly the player wants that outcome to come about.

Ranking Possible Outcomes

The payoff a person receives is presented on a matrix in one of two ways. In a case like the banknote game the numbers are cardinal, representing actual units of dollars or, in similar matrices, amounts of a product or time. In many cases when players rank the utility of the four possible outcomes the numbers are ordinal. Ordinal numbers are rankings, as in first, second, third, and so forth. If the "game" you are playing had four possible outcomes, like a 2X2 matrix, your numbers would be 4, 3, 2, 1, with 4 the outcome you would most desire, 3 your second choice, then 2 and 1 the least appealing. Maximizing your own utility number remains your goal. When two players have ranked their preferences for the four possible outcomes of the 2X2 matrix, it should not be assumed that their preferences are the same because the number of their ranking is equal. Both a rich man and a poor man would be likely to rank winning $10 to the other player's $5 as his highest utility ranking, number 4, but the rich man would be likely to be less concerned about the results.

Much analysis is done by keeping this as simple as possible, using ordinal numbers with payoff values based on order of preference. This allows for a surprisingly wide range of different situations to be portrayed by the simple four-cell matrix. There are just two players with two choices, so it would appear the options would be limited. But player A might want his first choice, his utility value of 4, in any of the four different cells, and the same is true of his second choice, his utility value of three. It is also true for his values of 2 and 1, and he might not want his 4 to the right of his 2, or his 3 below his 1. There are many ways for him to arrange his preferences. Thinking of arranging three pictures in a row on a wall it might help with this idea. There is not just one way of putting them up. They can actually be ordered in six different ways. That is determined by factorials. Factorials show how many different ways some set of things can be arranged and are written with the number followed by the symbol "!". For the pictures, the result is 3!, which is calculated 3 x 2 x 1. Determining the number of different possibilities for arranging utility priorities in a 2X2 matrix with four cells gives a player 4! options (4 x 3 x 2 x 1) for arranging them, which makes 24.

Both players have 4 possible arrangements of preference, so 4! different ways of arranging their decisions. This means the simple 2X2 matrix depicts 24X24, or

576 possible outcomes, though many have no meaningful difference from others. They may represent reversals of the left and right hand cells or the top and bottom cells. Still, with the single choice and two players there are 78 distinct matrices representing different games and strategies.[4] These can illustrate a great deal, and in them exists a powerful decision-making tool.

Many decisions involve more than one choice between two options and these can be represented on larger matrices. Analysis of business organization, such as oligopoly, can be depicted on a larger matrix using cardinal numbers, and equilibrium points where agreement might take place can be located. There is good reason to attempt to break decisions down to many smaller choices when using matrix analysis, as the possibilities involved with larger matrices expand rapidly. By adding one choice each to Player A and Player B, from two options to three, and keeping their choices ordinal, the possible number of outcomes has increased by an astonishing amount (Table 5.3).

Table 5.3

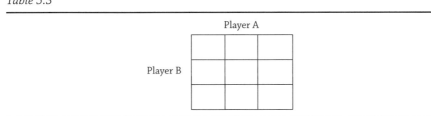

Such an increase appears simple and results in a 3X3 matrix with nine payoff cells. This change from a 2X2 to 3X3 matrix results in a difference of from four to nine possible outcomes. Each player would then have nine factorial, or 9! different ways of arranging his priorities which totals 362,880 variations. Since both players have this many possible choices, the number must be squared to determine the possible results that exist for a simple game of two players each facing the three interactive choices. That changes things from 576 for two choices each to 132,408,654,400 for three choices each, or more than 20 for every man, woman and child on the face of the earth.

Game theory looks at larger matrices, and many in the field are undaunted by the mathematics involved in the increasing complexity. There are "n" person games that involve more complex solutions for numbers of players that can be large. World chess champion Gary Kasparov made the point about how complex a matrix can become in a 1997 interview before his rematch against the IBM computer Deep Blue, which could calculate 200 million options per second. A chessboard is an 8X8 matrix (64! for each player) where each player has sixteen pieces with a variety of options available to each piece. Kasparov said, "There are more— vastly more—possibilities in a game of chess than there are atoms in the universe. So chess will never be 'worked out.'"[5]

It is apparent why much effort has continued to be put into the 2X2 matrix. It can represent a wide range of situations, and larger formats can become unwieldy. A common way of writing the payoff values that apply to each cell is to list two numbers, separated by a comma, as follows (Table 5.4):

Table 5.4

(2,4)	(1,2)
(4,1)	(3,3)

Schelling employs a different method that he believes is more easily read and understood. He made that point when commenting on an article assigned in his course that presented payoffs in the above fashion, saying, "Unfortunately, by printing payoffs on the same line separated by commas, they make the matrices a little harder to read than in the staggered form that I prefer."[6]

Schelling's staggered payoffs are easier to read, and strategic choices become less elusive. In his method the payoff values of the player named on the top, known generically as "Column," are written in the upper right corner of each cell. The values of the player named on the left side, who is generically labeled "Row," are written in the lower left of each cell. Column's payoff options are read as running north–south and side-by-side, while Row's run east–west and one above the other. A Schelling matrix with payoff values may appear confusing at first, but soon is easily read. An example to start with is a heads-tails choice (Table 5.5):

Table 5.5

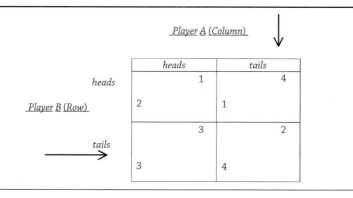

To read this matrix correctly, consider the following: Both players choose tails, and one wants to determine the payoff for Player A, Column. The "tails-tails"

intersection is the lower right quadrant, where Player A's payoff is 2 and Player B's payoff is 4. If B, Row, chooses heads and A chooses tails, the utility payoff value each would receive is the upper right quadrant, where A receives a payoff of 4 and B receives a payoff of 1.

When the payoffs are read correctly, this matrix makes it immediately apparent that the outcome of this game should be in the lower left cell. Player A will choose heads and Player B will choose tails. For Player B, choosing tails provides a higher payoff regardless of what Player A does. Player A realizes that Player B will make this decision, so he must choose between the options of choosing heads and getting a payoff of 3, or tails and receiving a payoff of 2. Since both are out to maximize their payoffs, he will select heads.

These payoff values are written as cardinal numbers. Cardinal numbers are important in many economic applications and transfer strategies, where the payoff is a number, such as dollars or units of a product that is measurable.

Simultaneous Play

This introduction to matrices begins with *simultaneous play* games such as the banknote game. That is, neither player, when making a choice, is aware of the choice made by the other player, whether or not the choices actually are made simultaneously. There also are *sequential play* games, in which one player makes a decision, or move, in advance of the other player, and the second player is aware of the move that was made. Simultaneous and sequential play games often involve different strategies, and it is important to be aware of which sort of game one is analyzing. This is exhibited the following matrix (Table 5.6):

Table 5.6

		PLAYER A	
		Column 1	Column 2
PLAYER B	Row 1	2 3	1 1
	Row 2	3 4	4 2

In this matrix if the game is simultaneous play, the outcome is the lower right quadrant, with Column receiving a payoff of 4 and Row a payoff of 2. If the game is sequential play and Row moves first, it is a different game. Row will choose Row 1, leaving Column with choices between payoffs of 2 for Column 1 and 1 for Column 2, so the outcome will be the upper left quadrant and the payoffs, 3 for Row and 2 for Column.

With this background, consider the following matrix (Table 5.7):

Table 5.7

		PLAYER A	
		Column 1	Column 2
	Row 1	1	4
PLAYER B		1	3
	Row 2	2	3
		2	4

If Player B chooses Row 1, and Player A chooses Column 1, Player B receives a payoff of 1. What is the payoff for Player A, if he chooses Column 2, and Player B chooses Row 2? If you see that it is 3, you are ready to move on.

Assume both participants are aware of the previous matrix, both participants want to secure the highest possible payoffs for themselves, and this is a simultaneous choice game. They must make their choices at the same time without conferring. What choice should Column make, left or right? What choice should Row make, up or down? What will be the payoff for Column? What will be the payoff for Row? If your answers put you in the lower right quadrant, you have solved a game, and applied a strategy that would have simplified the answers to several of the questions on the questionnaire in the earlier chapter, where strategy was necessary to determine the wisest choice.

Dominance and Natural Outcomes

In looking to see whether a player has a clear strategy to follow in a 2X2 situation, it is necessary to understand the concept of *dominance*. A player in a 2X2 situation has a choice between two options. If one choice is clearly better than the other, that choice is the player's *dominant strategy*. More specifically, a player has a dominant strategy if his choice leads to payoffs that are at least as high or higher than his other option, regardless of what strategy the other player uses (Table 5.8).

Table 5.8

	Player A, Column	
	Column 1	Column 2
Row 1	1 3	3 4
Row 2	2 1	4 2

Player B, Row

Is Column's strategy left or right? Is Row's strategy up or down? Clearly, Column has no choice, because his utility payoffs in Column 2 are higher, regardless of the choice Row makes. The same is true for Row about Column's choices. These are dominant strategies. This game has a determined outcome. Try another (Table 5.9):

Table 5.9

	Player A, Column	
	Column 1	Column 2
Row 1	3 1	3 2
Row 2	2 3	1 4

Player B, Row

Is Column's strategy left or right? Is Row's strategy up or down? As can be quickly seen, Column cannot err by choosing left, and Row is certain to choose down. Again both have dominant strategies.

What can often be seen as a logical solution to a 2X2 game is called its *natural outcome*. A game has a natural outcome under a number of different conditions, depending on whether or not dominating strategies are present. *When both players have dominant strategies*, the natural outcome of the game will be the intersection of their dominant strategies. A second condition that has a natural outcome exists *when only one player has a dominant strategy*. In that case, the person with the dominant strategy will choose it, and the other player will choose the strategy that gives him the best available payoff. Games with natural outcomes are easy to recognize when illustrated by staggered payoffs (Table 5.10).

Table 5.10

	Column 1	Column 2
Row 1	1 3	3 4
Row 2	2 2	4 1

In this case, Column has a dominant strategy of right, or Column 2. Row has a dominant strategy of up, or Row 1. The natural outcome of this game would be that intersection. Note that Column will be unable to achieve the solution that contains his highest payoff value in this particular game. This hints at the value of being able to illustrate interactive decisions on a matrix, as far as determining realistic hopes for negotiated settlements. And another case (Table 5.11):

Table 5.11

	Column 1	Column 2
Row 1	4 2	2 3
Row 2	3 4	1 1

In this matrix, Column has a dominant strategy, which is left, or Column 1. Row does not have a dominant strategy. Row knows Column will choose left, and his option is to choose up or down. Row chooses down, as his payoff is 4 for down, but only 2 for up. It is worth noting that while this is not necessarily the ordinary case, Row ended up with the higher payoff, even though it was Column that had the dominant strategy.

Games without Dominant Strategies

If *neither player has a dominant strategy*, the natural outcome tends to be that both will select the strategy that avoids their minimum outcomes. There are special cases, such as focal points, sometimes called "Schelling points," where one choice is prominent and obvious to both players (Table 5.12).

Table 5.12

	Column 1	Column 2
Row 1	2	3
	1	3
Row 2	4	1
	4	2

Here neither player has a dominant strategy but it should be apparent to both rational players that Column 1, Row 2, the lower left cell, is the outcome both would desire. The cell is prominent, and both can see it is to their advantage to select it.

Many games without dominant strategies in 2X2, those categorized as "zero sum" that involve pure competition, can have strategies determined by the introduction of randomization. This was begun with von Neumann's minimax theorem of 1928, which provided intellectual foundation for the development of the theory of games. While randomization is dealt with in more detail later in Chapter 20, the concept can be understood by a return to the banknote game. If a game like the bank note game is played repeatedly, the general tendency is that players will gravitate toward successful strategies. The bank note game could be in equilibrium in several ways. If all A players choose the $10 and all B players choose the $5 it is equilibrium, just as, vice versa, if all B players choose the $10 and all A players choose the $5. Where players always make the same choice when they have an option they are said to have adopted "pure strategies."

Experience shows and game theory teaches that other players will adopt "mixed strategies" where they will choose the $10 a certain percent of the time and $5 the remainder, and the choice will be random. Returning to the game, consider that the game has been played repeatedly and a player joins after it has been in progress for a considerable length of time. If he believes his opponent will choose the $5, his best strategy is to choose the $10 bill, but the same is true for his opponent. He realizes his opponent faces the same problem and rounds of circular reasoning follow. The new player must select some strategy and chooses the $10, then finds his opponent made the same choice, and he has won zero. He plays $10 again the next game and as he accumulates experience, he also chooses the $5 bill, and mixes his choices. Others playing the game are doing the same.

Later another person joins the banknote game who has observed the claims made by both the pure strategists and by those who are mixing strategies. He has learned from his observations of those who have been playing that the probability, p, of an opponent claiming the $5 bill is 30 percent, while it is 70 percent that the claim will be the $10, making p equal to 0.3.

In the bank note game, the player's outcomes were utilities of zero if he won nothing, 1 if he won $5, or 2 if he won $10. If a player claims the $5, the probability is p (.3) that he will receive zero, since his opponent might make the same claim. There is a $1-p$ probability that he will win $5, since his opponent would claim the $10 bill. The expected utility, or probable expected value from claiming the $5 then, is $1-p$, or .7. If a player claims the $10, there is a probability of $1-p$ he will receive nothing, so the expected utility from claiming $10 is $2-p$ or .6.

Players learn from experience and should gravitate to whatever strategy generates the larger expected utility. In the banknote game, if the game carries on long enough, the eventual outcome can be determined with some confidence by game theory. Claiming the $5 will decrease until it is just as successful as claiming the $10 note and if it goes too far, it will increase to where they are equal. That point is reached at $p = 1/3$, so in the long run, the value from claiming the $5 bill randomly 1/3 of the time is equal to the value to claiming the $10 bill randomly 2/3 of the time. They are equal, as $1-p$ (1/3) = 2/3 and $2-p$ (2 times 1/3) = 2/3. It is a self-perpetuating condition, a stable equilibrium.

The equilibrium of a repeated game may not be a condition anyone would choose. It is simply the unintended outcome of the independent choices of many individuals seeking to promote their own goals. The mathematics of randomization will not be introduced in this book.

With this introduction, we will return to one of the questions in Chapter 3 Questionnaire to see whether or not a 2X2 matrix helps in making a choice (Table 5.13).

8. A and B are to choose heads and tails. If both choose heads, both get $2. If both choose tails, both get $1. If A chooses tails and B heads, A gets $3, and B gets nothing. If A chooses heads and B tails, neither gets anything.

Table 5.13

		Player A	
		heads	tails
Player B	heads	2 2	3 0
	tails	0 0	1 1

As Player A, you can see that you have a dominant strategy to choose tails. Player B would know this and would also choose tails, gaining a payoff of 1, rather than the 0 he would get by choosing heads. You might ask, why not both choose heads, and both get 2? This seems more rational. That might appear to be a focal point solution, one that is prominent and attracts both players, but recall that it is basic in game theory that each individual will attempt to maximize his utility payoff. If Player B thought you were going to choose heads to avoid the 1, he still would be wisest to pick tails and get a payoff of 3.

Efficiency

Evaluating the outcome of a game can be done by determining its efficiency, called Pareto efficiency, after Italian mathematician Vilfredo Pareto. An outcome of a game is Pareto efficient if there is no other outcome that makes both players at least as well off and at least one player better off. In the following matrix the upper right cell is Pareto efficient (Table 5.14).

Table 5.14

	Column 1	Column 2
Row 1	1 / 3	3 / 4
Row 2	2 / 2	4 / 1

In the next matrix the natural lower right cell outcome is inefficient, nonoptimal (Table 5.15).

Table 5.15

	Column 1	Column 2
Row 1	2 / 2	3 / 0
Row 2	0 / 0	1 / 1

Learning how to create a 2X2 matrix to illustrate a situation and find an outcome is not a complicated process. The challenge is correctly assigning numerical values to individual utility and determining the values individuals or players are attempting to maximize. Learning by attempting several problems simplifies the process.

Constructing a Matrix to Evaluate a Situation

Suppose there are a boy and girl who are interested in each other, but not actually dating yet. It is a Friday, and each of them is trying to figure out what to do that night. There is a basketball game at school, and a dance in another part of town. The dance is far away, and it is going to end early, so attending both is not possible. The boy is a big basketball fan. The girl, who hates basketball, never misses a dance. They would like to end up together, except it's the biggest basketball game of the year. The boy really wants to be there more than anywhere else, and all his friends are going. The girl couldn't care less about basketball, and all of her friends are going to the dance. She knows that if she goes to the dance and he isn't there, she'll still have fun. The possible outcomes are:

a) both at basketball game
b) both at dance
c) girl at basketball game, boy at dance
d) boy at basketball game, girl at dance

The girl's preferences would be: b > d > a > c
The boy's preferences would be: a > d > b > c
To construct a matrix that illustrates these preferences we convert them into ordinal numbers, with 4 as highest priority and then 3, 2, 1 the least desired, and insert them in the appropriate intersection points. That leaves us with the following (Table 5.16):

Table 5.16

		Girl	
		basketball game	dance
Boy	basketball game	2 4	3 3
	dance	1 1	4 2

There are two dominant strategies in this matrix, so it is clear that although they are interested in each other, something will have to be done about that at some other time. On this Friday they are going their own directions.

Now assume it is 6:30 p.m., and you are in high school and are supposed to meet your friend at 7:00 p.m. at a restaurant. Neither of you can remember whether it was the Hard Rock Cafe or the McDonald's near the school, and there is no way for you to contact each other. You want to eat together, but your friend's preference is the Hard Rock Cafe, while your preference is McDonald's. Your friend has an image he wants to keep up, and the worst, most embarrassing outcome for him would be to show up at Hard Rock Cafe and have to sit alone and eat. Lots of people eat alone at McDonald's, so if it happens to him there, he will not be nearly as upset. You have no image to maintain, and it makes absolutely no difference to you whether you eat alone at McDonald's or the Hard Rock. You both need to anticipate the other's preferences and make a decision about what to do.

The possible outcomes are the following:

1) Both at Hard Rock
2) Both at McDonald's
3) You at Hard Rock, friend at McDonald's
4) You at McDonald's, friend at Hard Rock

Your preferences would be: b > a > d > c. Your friend's preference would be: a > b > c > d. This creates a matrix that can determine where you will be headed (Table 5.17).

Table 5.17

		YOU	
		Hard Rock	McDonald's
FRIEND	Hard Rock	3 4	2 1
	McDonald's	1 2	4 3

This is a more complex matrix with no dominant strategy, and the simple rule at this stage is that players will avoid their minimum payoff. That means you avoid the number one that is in the left column and choose right, or McDonald's, and your friend avoids his number one, which is in the top row and chooses down, which is also McDonald's. Since you know the time, you would make the right choice and meet at McDonald's at 7 p.m.

These may not have been difficult strategic problems requiring game theory analysis, but now apply the development of matrices to real world problems.

In 1969 a hockey player for the Boston Bruins was permanently brain damaged when he was hit in the head by a hockey stick. This raised the issue at of why hockey players didn't wear helmets to protect themselves. Although many players had differing opinions, the most common view was that wearing a helmet would put them at a disadvantage, unless all others were also wearing helmets. Most agreed that if everyone wore a helmet, they would all be better off. Many felt they would be risking their chances of staying in professional hockey by wearing helmets, when nonhelmeted players might have some slight advantage. Illustrating this in a 2X2 matrix suggests a policy requirement. First we must define the two players in the game. One way would be to have Player A be an individual and Player B the others in the league. A second difficulty is prioritizing utility rankings, and there is room for debate. Let's allow for disagreement and see what the matrix results tell us. The options are:

a) all wear helmets;
b) nobody wears helmets;
c) wear helmet while others don't wear one;
d) don't wear helmet while others do

Since we are told most agree they would all be better off if all wore them and that players felt there might be a disadvantage to be wearing one, there is room for disagreement on ranking. Probable ranking for an individual, concerned with remaining in the league, would be: d > a > b > c. That could apply to the players in general, giving both parties the same priorities. A second possibility could be that while some individuals might feel this way, the consensus of the league had a priority of safety first, making the players' priorities more accurately reflected in the following manner: a > c > b > d.

We get two different matrices (Tables 5.18 and 5.19), and what happens?

Table 5.18

| | | All other players | |
		Wear helment	Don't wear helmet
Player	Wear helment	3 / 3	4 / 1
	Don't wear helmet	1 / 4	2 / 2

Table 5.19

	All other players	
	Wear helmet	Don't wear helmet
Player — Wear helmet	4 4	3 1
Player — Don't wear helmet	1 3	2 2

The first matrix more accurately represents the situation, but in either case the players on their own were not going to achieve the goal to which they claimed to aspire: the increased safety of playing the game with helmets. Outside intervention was required. Beginning in 1979 all new National Hockey League players were required to wear helmets, though veterans could continue to play without. It wasn't until Craig MacTavish of the Edmonton Oilers retired in 1997 that all heads in the league had some protection.

The Arms Race

And now to develop a matrix that will be discussed at length, is of considerable significance, and involves Schelling directly. Throughout the Cold War era, enormous resources of the United States and the Soviet Union were devoted to the arms race. Weapons systems of unimaginable destructive power were developed at staggering costs, only to be made obsolete by even more destructive and expensive weapons systems. Both sides were aware that they could have made more beneficial use of their resources. However, the threat of world war was real enough that a "balance of terror" seemed to be the only way to prevent it. Neither side could allow the other to get a permanent upper hand in weapons technology and deployment. Over and over what happened and continues to happen in similar situations was the following: both sides develop the technology for a new, expensive, and superior, weapons system. Each side has to decide whether or not to go to the expense of deploying the new system.

This situation presents the following options:

a) Both expend the resources to deploy.
b) Neither deploys.
c) Soviets deploy; United States saves and does not deploy
d) United States deploys; Soviets save and not deploy

The priorities for the United States are: d > b > a > c
The priorities for the Soviet Union are: c > b > a > d
The matrix these priorities create looks like this (Table 5.20):

Table 5.20

	Soviet Union	
	Deploy new weapons	Don't deploy
United States Deploy new weapons	2 / 2	1 / 4
Don't deploy	4 / 1	3 / 3

As the matrix shows, the natural outcome is the upper left hand cell, since both players have dominant strategies. It will later be described as a stable, inefficient outcome. One of Schelling's greatest achievements will be convincing key personnel that the lower right quadrant is the efficient outcome and can be successfully monitored. Arms control became a reality with SALT I and with the ABM agreements.

Supplement: And Now for a Completely Different View

If the Schelling approach to strategic decision analysis seems at all daunting, the alternative offered here should provide relief. Another view on "strategic tactics" for achieving your desired outcome in situations involving conflicting views is presented by Dave Barry, described by the *New York Times* as "the funniest man in America." The Pulitzer Prize–winning columnist's website biography says that he was born "in 1947 and has been steadily growing older ever since without ever actually reaching maturity." Barry joined the *Miami Herald* in 1983, and the column he wrote for twenty-five years was carried by over five hundred papers in the United States and internationally. He also has written thirty books. The following column was published in the *Daily Local News*, West Chester, Pennsylvania, and republished in the *Miami Herald* on April 21, 2004.

How to Win Arguments

I argue very well. Ask any of my remaining friends. I can win an argument on any topic, against any opponent. People know this, and steer clear of me at parties. Often, as a sign of their great respect, they don't even invite me. You too can win arguments. Simply follow these rules:

Drink liquor

Suppose you're at a party and some hotshot intellectual is expounding on the economy of Peru, a subject you know nothing about. If you're drinking some health-fanatic drink like grapefruit juice, you'll hang back, afraid to display your ignorance, while the hotshot enthralls your date. But if you drink several large martinis, you'll discover you have strong views about the Peruvian economy. You'll be a wealth of information. You'll argue forcefully, offering searing insights and possibly upsetting furniture. People will be impressed. Some may leave the room.

Make things up

Suppose, in the Peruvian economy argument, you are trying to prove Peruvians are underpaid, a position you base solely on the fact that you are underpaid, and you're damned if you're going to let a bunch of Peruvians be better off. Don't say: "I think Peruvians are underpaid." Say: "The average Peruvian's salary in 1981 dollars adjusted for the revised tax base is $1,452.81 per annum, which is $836.07 below the gross poverty level." *NOTE:* Always make up exact figures. If an opponent asks you where you got your information, make that up too. Say: "This information comes from Dr. Hovel T. Moon's study for the Buford Commission published May 9, 1982. Didn't you read it? Say this in the same tone of voice you would use to say "You left your soiled underwear in my bathroom."

Use meaningless but weighty-sounding words and phrases

Memorize this list:

> Let me put it this way
> In terms of
> Vis-à-vis
> Per se
> As it were
> Qua
> So to speak

You should also memorize some Latin abbreviations such as "Q.E.D.," "e.g." and "i.e." These are all short for "I speak Latin, and you do not."

Here's how to use these words and phrases:

Suppose you want to say: "Peruvians would like to order appetizers more often, but they don't have enough money." You never win arguments talking like that. But you WILL win if you say: "Let me put it this way. In terms of appetizers vis-à-vis Peruvians qua Peruvians, they would like to order them more often, so to speak, but they do not have enough money per se, as it were. Q.E.D."

Only a fool would challenge that statement.

Use snappy and relevant comebacks

You need an arsenal of all-purpose irrelevant phrases to fire back at your opponents when they make valid points. The best are:

You're begging the question;

You're being defensive;

Don't compare apples and oranges;

What are your parameters?

This last one is especially valuable. Nobody, other than mathematicians, has the vaguest idea what "parameters" means.

You say: "As Abraham Lincoln said in 1873..."

Your opponent says: "Lincoln died in 1865."

You say: "You're begging the question."

OR

You say: "Liberians, like most Asians..."

Your opponent says: "Liberia is in Africa."

You say: "You're being defensive."

Compare your opponent to Adolf Hitler

This is your heavy artillery, for when your opponent is obviously right and you are spectacularly wrong. Bring Hitler up subtly. Say: "That sounds suspiciously like something Adolph Hitler might say," or "You certainly remind me of Adolf Hitler."

So that's it: you now how to out-argue anybody. Do not try to pull any of this on people who generally carry weapons.[7]

Notes

1. Thomas Schelling, interviewed by Robert Dodge, June 27, 2002.
2. Robert Sugden, *The Economics of Rights, Cooperation, and Welfare* (Oxford: Blackwell, 1986).
3. Ibid., 11.
4. Anatol Rapoport and Melvin Guyer, "A Taxonomy of 2 X 2 Games," *General Systems*, vol. 12 (1966), 204. Schelling wrote of this article, "Their classification scheme is not the only one: other people have divided them up differently. Believe it or not, these are the first people to take the trouble to print the exhaustive list in an available journal." Schelling, 1994 Course Syllabus, Conflict, Cooperation, and Strategy, 47.
5. "An Interview with Garry Kasparov," IBM Research Online, http://www.research.ibm.com/deepblue/meet/html/d.1.6.html, 1997.
6. Schelling, 1994 Course Syllabus, 47.
7. E-mail from Dave Barry's assistant to Robert Dodge on July 14, 2009. This column is used with Dave Barry's permission. ©2004 Dave Barry. Published by the *Miami Herald*. U.S. copyright laws prohibits any copying, redistributing, retransmitting or repurposing of any copyright-protected material.

STRATEGIES AND TACTICS

CHAPTER 6

Strategies Defined and Illustrated

When strategies were being introduced in Schelling's course on rational decisions, the following was included in the original homework.

The Three-Way Duel

Anderson, Barnes, and Cooper are to fight a gun duel. They will stand close to one another, so that each can kill one of the others or deliberately miss. The first to fire will be chosen at random, and they will rotate in the order Anderson, Barnes, and Cooper, each firing one shot at a time.

If there is more than one survivor after a number of rounds, one of the contenders will be chosen at random and required to shoot one of the others, and this will be repeated if there is still more than one alive.

Before the duel starts, Anderson may make any statement, followed by a statement from Barnes, and finally one from Cramer. They will adhere to the following rules:

1. A contender may not break any commitment he makes in his statement.
2. He will act in his own best interest when it does not conflict with Rule One.
3. He will act randomly when it does not conflict with Rules One and Two.

There are referees to ensure that the rules are followed. If a contender commits himself to a choice of action on a statistical basis (for example, if Anderson commits himself to miss with a probability of 1/3), the choice will be determined objectively (by tossing dice, etc.).

What is Anderson's best strategy and his probability of surviving? That is, what is the most effective commitment Anderson can make?

(A) Anderson's probability of surviving, if he adopts his best strategy, is:
(B) Anderson's statement, with explanation:

If you wish to challenge yourself and attempt this on your own before seeing an answer, read no further at this point.

A course based on Schelling's ideas was taught to high school students at the Singapore American School from 1991 to 2006. The following answer to the problem of the three-way duel is from a student who was in the course in the fall semester of the 2006–2007 school year, thirteen-year-old senior Eng Seng Ng:

> What A should say is: "If B does not commit to unconditionally shooting C, I will shoot him."
>
> Now B has two choices: he can commit to shooting C, or he can do something else. If he commits to shooting C, he has a 1/6 chance of survival (if C goes first and decides to take out A instead of B, since it doesn't matter which one he takes out, he is doomed anyway).
>
> If he does not commit, he has a 0% chance of survival—if A goes first, he will shoot B; if B goes first, no matter who he shoots the other will shoot him; and if C goes first he will let A shoot B. Since he has no influence over A's decision (to shoot him), the only thing he can say that will get him anywhere would be to somehow pressure C into shooting A. However, since C will be shot if he shoots A, there is no reason for him to do it and therefore B cannot influence C's decision. So if B does not commit, he is doomed. Therefore B will say, "I will shoot C."
>
> C now has a 0% chance of survival—if he goes first, no matter whom he shoots the other will shoot him; if B goes first he will be shot; and if A goes first he will let B shoot C and then shoot B. There is nothing C can do to increase his chances of survival from 0 (poor guy), because in order to do so, either A or B would have to shoot the other, so that C could shoot him. Given that B is already committed to shooting C, A would have to shoot B if C is to survive. Since this is a rather moronic thing to do, and A has not committed to doing any such moronic thing, we can assume that A will not shoot B and C is doomed.
>
> So what is A's chance of survival? If A goes first, he will wait and B will shoot C, after which he can shoot B at his leisure. (A wins.) If B goes first, he will shoot C and get shot for his trouble. (A wins.) If C goes first, he can either shoot A or B since it doesn't make a difference, after which the other person will shoot C for his trouble. (50% chance A wins.)
>
> Therefore A has a very decent 5/6 (84%) chance of survival using this strategy.

Eng Seng's answer is a good strategic answer, but not *the* answer, as there are other possibilities. Professor Schelling offered a solution that guarantees Anderson near certainty of survival, by including probabilities in his shots. In this solution Anderson commits to shoot with a small probability of missing at whoever has killed the other, but if Cramer fails to kill Barnes, to kill Cramer. He must include something to prevent any unilateral commitments either Barnes of Cramer could make to top his, so he would add that if either of them makes a commitment other than to accept his, he will kill that person in his turn or shoot in the air if the person is dead. If both make unilateral commitments, Anderson guarantees to kill Cramer or if Cramer is already dead, shoot in the air (rules of duel will be enforced). Schelling's answer:

Anderson has to forestall a commitment by Barnes that gives Cramer a better chance of surviving, which he could do by saying, "If you do not accept my proposal I shall kill you at my turn. If you accept it, I guarantee you a two-thirds chance of living, as follows: If Anderson is committed to kill me upon your accepting my proposal, then I promise to kill Anderson if you promise to kill Anderson. If Anderson is uncommitted as to whom he shoots once you have accepted my offer, there is a 50–50 chance he will shoot me. If you are the one to kill him, I will shoot at you with a 50% chance of killing you. Finally if Anderson is committed to kill each of us with specific probabilities such as .8 he will shoot you and .2 he will shoot me if we both commit, then I will shoot at you with a probability of .2 of killing you after you have killed Anderson."

If Anderson does not make as good an offer to Cramer, Barnes' offer will be accepted and Anderson will surely be dead. If Anderson makes the equivalent offer to Cramer, Cramer has a 2/3 chance of surviving or accepts Barnes' offer. If he accepts Barnes' offer there is a 1/3 chance Anderson will kill him, otherwise he lives because he kills Anderson if Barnes is killed first. If he does not accept Barnes' offer Barnes will kill him if he gets the chance, otherwise Anderson will kill Barnes. Since Cramer's chances are the same whether or not he accepts Barnes offer, rule three says he decides at random, so Barnes has a 50–50 chance of achieving a 1/3 chance of living if he accepts this.

If Anderson cannot top Barnes's 1/6 chance of living that would come with equal proposals he cannot forestall the commitment, which leaves him with the same probability. He must do better for Barnes to keep his mouth shut.So. Anderson's statement: "If Barnes makes an offer and Cramer accepts it, I will kill Cramer in my turn or shoot in the air if Cramer is already dead. If Barnes makes an offer and Cramer does not accept it I will kill Barnes in my turn or shoot in the air if he is already dead. If anyone makes a unilateral commitment not depending on a response, I will kill the last one to do that, or shoot in the air if he is already dead. Otherwise, if Cramer fails to kill Barnes at his first opportunity, Barnes being still alive, I shall kill him. If Cramer kills Barnes I will shoot at him with a 1% probability of missing. If Barnes kills Cramer I shall shoot at him with a 27% likelihood of missing."

If Barnes and Cramer keep their mouths shut there is a 2/3 chance of their firing first. If Anderson is first he will shoot in the air and Barnes will kill Cramer and have a 27% possibility of surviving. If Cramer is first Barnes is dead, so Barnes probability of survival is 2/3 of 27% or 18%. Cramer keeps quiet and has a 1% chance of surviving if he is first to shoot, and .33% chance overall. That leaves Anderson with 71.67% chance of surviving.

Schelling concludes that by giving Cramer an even smaller likelihood than 1% and Barnes an increment on top of 1/6 Anderson can make his own chances as near to 5/6, or 84%, as he wishes.

So Schelling's solution and Eng Seng's arrive at the same point, though the route was a bit more direct for the younger man. The key element of strategic thought involved is looking forward and reasoning backward—looking at the result and considering what has to be true to achieve that final step, and once that is understood, what must be done to reach the step that puts you in position to reach the step that reaches the final step, and so on.

This problem speaks mainly of one specific strategy, a commitment. The vocabulary for strategies is often used loosely, but not so poorly as once was the case. Schelling entered the world of strategic studies in June of 1956, when his "Essay on Bargaining" was published in the *American Economic Review*.[1] The well-received essay established a vocabulary for the emerging discipline, where various words were, and often continue to be, used interchangeably, but the tactics the words imply differ. Bargaining theory was Schelling's specialty as a Yale professor at the time he wrote the essay and it contributed to his receiving an invitation to the leading military think tank, labeled by Pravda as America's "Institute of death and destruction," the RAND Corporation in Santa Monica, California.

In his essay he spoke of bargaining power as the power to bind oneself, to burn bridges, and remove options. He generically referred to tactics as "commitments," but the essay dealt with irrevocable commitments, warnings, promises, and threats.

Put yourself in the position of a student. A teacher might "threaten" your class with how important that big test coming up next Friday is going to be and make it clear you should be studying. Perhaps that teacher will "warn" you about the importance of the event. That same teacher might "promise" that if you don't pay attention in class and study at home, you are in for serious trouble when the Friday test is handed out. He might make a "commitment" to your class to make the course more interesting in the future, especially if you will study more and all pass the Friday's test or at least try to look interested, but he might also "commit" to making things even more boring if you do not study. Whatever words the teacher might use, his goal is clear. He is attempting to motivate you and your classmates to improve your preparation for his upcoming test.

In everyday usage "threats" and "warnings" are often interchangeable and promises are offers of something. In conflict resolution and game theory these terms are labels for different specific strategic activities. Schelling added clarity to the distinctions the terms define, which contributed to an emerging field of study, deterrence, in which he was a pioneer. While these different terms continue to be used as synonyms at times, understanding their different meanings presents varied strategic approaches and deeper understanding.

Consider the following scenario, continuing your student role: Suppose you are seriously considering dropping out of school. You also *really* want your own car. Your parents really want you to stay in school, and are trying to convince you to change your ideas about quitting. They are short on cash, but if it will keep you in school, they might make some sacrifices to "buy you off" by giving you your own car. Your options are a) stay in school, or b) quit school. Your parents' options are a) buy you a car, or b) do not buy you a car. This creates a two-by-two game with four possible outcomes.

Your order of preference would be:

1. Quit school and have parents buy you a car.
2. Stay in school and get a car.
3. Quit school and not have a car.
4. Stay in school and not get a car.

Your parents' order of preference would be:

1. You stay in school, and they do not buy you a car.
2. You stay in school, and they buy you a car.
3. You quit school, and they do not buy you a car.
4. You quit school, and they buy you a car.

With a matrix this situation could be illustrated to present the views as in Table 6.1.

Table 6.1

		YOU	
		Stay in school	Quit school
PARENTS	Buy car	3 / 3	4 / 1
	Do not buy car	1 / 4	2 / 2

Given this matrix, both you and your parents have dominant strategies that lead to the lower right quadrant in the absence of any bargaining tactics. That is the third choice for both you and your parents. In a simultaneous play game, you would end up out of school with no car.

Your parents might try to alter this outcome. Suppose they say, "If you stay in high school, we'll buy you a car." In strategic studies terminology, this statement is a **promise**. This is so for two reasons.

1) When you make a promise, you are announcing that you will make a decision in the perceived interests of the other player.
2) When you make a promise, the choice you make is usually expensive to you when it succeeds.

As can be seen in the matrix, if quitting school were not an issue, your parents would prefer not to buy you a car (the lower left quadrant, where your parents' payoff is 4, represents this point of view). So the choice they are promising to make is in your perceived interest, not theirs. It is also clear that if the promise succeeds, they have the expense of buying you the car. The payoff of a successful promise for your parents is only an increase in utility ranking of 1.

Now imagine your family is finally in a financial position to take that great vacation your parents have always talked about and hoped for. Two weeks in Hawaii during the grey days of winter sounds like the perfect trip for everyone, including you. However, you are still thinking about quitting school. Your parents say, "If you quit school, then our trip to Hawaii is off." Or perhaps they say, "We promise you that if you quit school, our trip to Hawaii is off." Have they made a promise?

According to the way a strategic promise was defined, they have not.

The first characteristic of a promise was that it was the announcement of an intention to make a choice in the perceived interest of the other player. You want to go to Hawaii, and they have said they will cancel the trip. The announcement your parents have made is not in your perceived interest. The second characteristic of a promise was that they are usually expensive when they succeed. However, you all want to take the vacation, so their "promise" is expensive when it fails, in terms of personal utility.

This sort of statement is called a **threat**. You are making a threat when:

1) You announce your willingness to make a choice you would prefer not to make.
2) Your statement of a threat is expensive to you when it fails (there are exceptions to this).

We can see that these qualities apply to the situation just described. Your parents want to go to Hawaii, but they have announced their willingness to sacrifice their enjoyment. If their threat succeeds, their payoff is high, but if it fails, the threat was expensive—they lost out on their trip without having gained anything.

In wider applications a threat can be decomposed into a series of smaller threats to provide an opportunity to demonstrate on the first transgression that it will be carried out.

Back to the story. The following matrix illustrates this situation (Table 6.2):

Table 6.2

		You	
		Stay in school	Quit school
Parents	Go on trip	3 4	4 2
	Stay home	1 3	2 1

The natural outcome of this matrix, if it were simultaneous play, would be the upper right quadrant. However, by the threat your parents have made, they have left you with only two quadrants—lower right, and upper left. In this case it would be a successful threat. Your payoff value in your remaining "stay in school" quadrant is higher than your payoff in your remaining "quit school" option.

Two generalizations about threats should be included:

1) To be effective, they must often be accompanied by promises. (It would not be enough to say "If you quit school, then our trip to Hawaii is off," without a stated or understood promise of "If you stay in high school, we will take you to Hawaii")
2) To be effective, the person making them must not be moving first in a sequential game.

So, by now you are driving around in your own car, showing off your Hawaiian tan, and thinking your "I want to quit school" line is pretty effective. You wonder what else you might be able to get out of it. Maybe a new laptop would keep you convinced that school is worthwhile.

You tell your parents about a great laptop a friend of yours was given by his parents. Shortly after that, you mention you are still thinking about quitting school. You might reconsider staying in school longer if you were happier, which you would be if your parents would buy you a new laptop.

By this time, however, your parents have heard it enough. They make the following statement: "You know that we hope you stay in school, but whether you do or do not, we are not going to buy you a new laptop."

Their statement is a third form of strategic communication. It is an irrevocable **commitment**. In this form of commitment, *one party announces that it is making a certain choice regardless of what the other party chooses*. This can be a powerful tactic to adopt. It is the "burning bridges" idea Schelling advocates as a successful means of gaining the upper hand in bargaining situations. It creates situations that can put opponents in positions where they may have to consider the order of their priorities, or play strategically to achieve a payoff of lower value than would have otherwise satisfied them. We can illustrate this situation as follows (Table 6.3):

Table 6.3

		YOU	
		Stay in school	Quit school
	Buy laptop	3	4
PARENTS		3	1
	Don't buy laptop	1	2
		4	2

While your parents' utility scale shows they value you staying in school, you can see that your parents' statement of commitment, by announcing their decision as final and the lower row, reduces the possible outcomes of this matrix to the bottom right and bottom left quadrants. Your ability to influence their decision in your favor no longer exists.

A tactic that is often spoken of interchangeably with "threat," but that has a different strategic definition, can be illustrated by continuing the story. Suppose your parents inform you that your grandparents have left a sizable inheritance for you, on the condition that you finish school. If you do not finish school, the money goes to your parents' favorite charity. The will cannot be altered. You parents' informing you of this is classified as a ***warning***. In a warning, *one party makes the other party aware of a condition that exists, or in the case of these examples, the matrix that illustrates the condition.*

The matrix for this case could look like this (Table 6.4):

Table 6.4

		YOU	
		Stay in school	Quit school
	encourage you to finish school	4	2
PARENTS		4	1
	support a charity	X	1
		X	2

This is a case where a matrix that uses ordinal, or ranked payoff values rather than cardinal numbers representing real amounts of dollars may not be the best indicators of rational choice. Here, the lower left cell is not possible; if you stay in school, you receive the inheritance and supporting a charity with that money cannot happen, so no values can be assigned to it. The above matrix assumes both you and your parents assign some value to money going to a charity of your parents' choosing. The upper right cell is also nearly meaningless, but your parents probably value encouraging you to complete school, whether or not you do, and you may value quitting for that very reason, so assigning some value is not unreasonable. The warning is an apparently successful strategy in this case.

In summary, four similar strategies have been introduced. They are:

1) Warning—you make the other party aware of the situation and outcomes. You would make the same decision, whether or not the warning had been issued.
2) Commitment—you announce you will make a certain choice, regardless of the choice made by the other party.
3) Threat—you are willing to make the choice that you would prefer not making.
4) Promise—you will make a choice that is in the perceived interest of the other party.

To apply a strategy, consider the following problem. The following matrix (Table 6.5) is for a sequential play game, where Player A makes his decision before Player B. Before Player A makes his choice, Player B gets to announce his use of one of the strategies to try to improve his outcome. What strategy could he make use of, and what would be different?

Table 6.5

| | | PLAYER A | |
		column 1	column 2
PLAYER B	row 1	2 4	1 1
	row 2	2 4	3 2

Player A does not have a dominant strategy but can see Player B has a dominant strategy of Row 2, giving this a natural outcome of the lower right quadrant, where Row's payoff is 2 and Column's payoff is 3.

Since Row has a strategy available, he could make a commitment to choosing Row 1. That would change the game, since if Player A went ahead with his decision to choose Column 2, his payoff would then be 1, the same as Player B's. He would do better by choosing Column 1, where he could receive a payoff of 2. It is a disappointment from the natural outcome of 3 if it had been simultaneous play, but the commitment strategy would increase Player B's payoff from 2 to 4, and his own outcome is his only concern.

A Quick Review

To check your understanding of these terms, name the strategy being employed in each of the following (answers immediately following):

1) "I'll destroy my property if you approach it."
2) You fail to complete a major research paper for one of your classes by the end of the marking period. You receive an "Incomplete" on your report card. Your teacher keeps you after class and says, "Incompletes are changed to Fs two weeks from the day your report card was sent, unless the teacher says the work has been finished."
3) "I will not fight for my property, so you don't have to kill me to get it."
4) "If a predator spots us, it will prefer me to you."
5) A man robs a bank, but during the robbery a clerk pushes a button that alerts the police of the situation. As the man is about to leave, he sees that a crowd has gathered, and the bank is surrounded. He takes out a hand grenade, and pulls out the pin (it will automatically explode within seconds of the time he releases his grip on it). He walks out the bank's door.
6) Parents to child: "If you are not good, Santa Claus isn't going to bring you what you want for Christmas."
   a) From the child's point of view—
   b) From the parents' point of view—
7) You are driving on a road that has two lanes of traffic moving in the same direction. There is a car next to you on your left. As you look ahead, you see that one of the lanes is closed for construction, and a quick glance to your left tells you that the other driver has also just noticed it. He is looking directly at you, waiting to see your reaction. You accelerate.
8) A man is attacked by a mugger. He says, "I'm harmless. Here is my wallet. I won't call the police.
9) "I attack anyone who comes near me."
10) (To cannibal) "I do not taste good."

Answers to "A Quick Review"

1) "I'll destroy my property if you approach it." This is a threat. You are announcing that you are willing to make a choice you would prefer not making, and it is expensive to you if your strategy fails.

2) You fail to complete a major research paper for one of your classes by the end of the marking period. You receive an "Incomplete" on your report card. Your teacher keeps you after class and says, "Incompletes are changed to Fs two from the day your report card was sent, unless the teacher says the work has been finished." This is a warning, making you aware of existing conditions.

3) "I will not fight for my property, so you don't have to kill me to get it." This is a promise, since the choice announced is in the other's interest and is expensive, involving loss of one's property.

4) "If a predator spots us, it will prefer me to you." This sounds like a promise, if it is intended to draw another into an area where predators for some reason are present for some reason, since it could be expensive, if it succeeds. If it is a statement where they are in an area of predators, it is a warning, making existing conditions known.

5) A man robs a bank, but during the robbery a clerk pushes a button that alerts the police of the situation. As the man is about to leave, he sees that a crowd has gathered, and the bank is surrounded. He takes out a hand grenade, and pulls out the pin (it will automatically explode within seconds of the time he releases his grip on it). He walks out the bank's door. This is a unilateral commitment, as the man has made his decision and it is final. The others must react to his choice.

6) Parents to child: "If you are not good, Santa Clause isn't going to bring you what you want for Christmas."
    a) From the child's point of view—this is a warning, a statement of existing conditions.
    b) From the parents' point of view—it is a threat, since if it fails they will make a choice they would prefer not to make, assuming parents want to see their children receive gifts on Christmas morning.

7) You are driving on a road that has two lanes of traffic moving in the same direction. There is a car next to you on your left. As you look ahead, you see that one of the lanes is closed for construction, and a quick glance to your left tells you that the other driver has also just noticed it. He is looking directly at you, waiting to see your reaction. You accelerate. Such an action is a commitment, since you have made a decision and the other driver must respond to that choice.

8) A man is attacked by a mugger. He says, "I'm harmless. Here is my wallet. I won't call the police." This is a promise, since if it succeeds, it is expensive because the man loses his wallet, and his pronouncement is in the mugger's interest.

9) "I attack anyone who comes near me." Such a statement is a threat, since the speaker would prefer not to take this action.

10) (to cannibal) "I do not taste good." Though this sounds like a promise, it is a warning, making a condition known. If it succeeds it is not expensive to the issuer of the statement, which is one part of the promise definition.

Supplement

The Chicken Dilemma

The article that begins this supplement centers on a strategy that was employed at an extremely dangerous moment in history. It is excerpted from a review of the Tom Schelling's biography, *The Strategist*,[2] that appeared in the *Singapore Straits Times Sunday Times* on January 7, 2007, written by Janandas Devan. Devan is an associate editor of the *Straits Times* and serves as director of the Institute of Policy Studies in the Lee Kuan Yew School of Public Policy at the National University of Singapore. His review describes a strategic commitment, and the impact Schelling's advice had on a situation that had all the ingredients for nuclear holocaust during the Berlin crisis of 1961.

Who will chicken out?

The "chicken dilemma" comes "from the teenage dueling practice depicted in 1950s movies, in which two teenagers drive their cars at each other, the one who turns away being the 'chicken'. There are four possible outcomes in this game. The best outcome is you drive straight and the other fellow blinks: You win; he is humiliated. The next best is both blink: Both are 'chicken'; neither is humiliated. The next-to-worst outcome is you blink, but the other fellow drives straight: You are humiliated, but live; he lives and gets to gloat. And the worst is both drive straight: Both avoid humiliation; both die. At first glance, since it is better to be alive than dead, it might seem that the logical thing to do would be to blink and trust the other fellow would too. But it is not so simple.

If you know the other player knows that turning away is the logical outcome, why not drive straight? But the other person is probably thinking the same thing. He might think he could drive straight without consequence. But since the other person is probably thinking the same thing, he would know you're thinking the same thing, too, so he wouldn't do it—o it would be safe for you to do it, after all. . . ." And so on and so on forth, a logical mouse chasing its logical tail.

Prof Schelling proposed a simple solution. Shorn of its complexity, it came down to Janandas Devan's description: Jam your foot on the accelerator; drive straight; rip off the steering wheel; wave it out the window; and scream: "Hey buddy, this car can't turn!" That was the strategy that Prof Schelling proposed the United States adopt during the 1961 Berlin crisis.

Tension was mounting as a stream of East Germans escaped to West Germany. A blustering Nikita Khrushchev, the Soviet leader, had threatened war.

Prof Schelling wrote a paper arguing that the role of nuclear weapons "should not be to win a grand nuclear campaign, but to pose a higher level of risk to the enemy. The important thing in limited nuclear war is to impress the Soviet leadership with the risk of general war—a war that may occur whether we or they intend it or not".

Prof Schelling was suggesting the US should make a clear commitment— "hey buddy, this car can't turn"— so the Soviets would know that an attack on West Berlin would trigger an escalation.

President John F. Kennedy read his paper and decided to adopt his strategy. "We have given our word that an attack upon (West Berlin) will be regarded as an attack upon us all," Kennedy announced. "The choice of peace or war is largely (the Soviet's), not ours."

Khrushchev got the message. He didn't attack West Berlin. Instead, he built a wall around it. The wall was odious, but it was better than nuclear Armageddon.

The Sunday Times © Singapore Press Holdings, Ltd. Permission required for reproduction.

Used with the author's permission.[3]

On a matrix the chicken dilemma game appears as follows (Table 6.6):

Table 6.6

		PLAYER A	
		Turn away	Drive straight
PLAYER B	Turn away	3 3	4 2
	Drive straight	2 4	1 1

It is rational to want the opposite of whatever the other player is going to do in this game, and the game does not have a natural outcome. If both players follow the rational choice method of avoiding their minimum payoffs, they will avoid the lower right cell and the game would end in the upper left with both turning away. But the circular reasoning in vicarious thinking is that if Player A knows that Player B is rational and concludes Player B will turn away, he could achieve his highest payoff by driving straight safely. However, Player B also knows that Player A is rational and has considered the same thing, so that is no longer so, and both would be driving straight. Player A would realize that he should turn away, as would Player B, which makes it all right for Player A to go ahead and drive straight again. Or does it?

That is why, if it is possible to make a credible irrevocable commitment that one will "drive straight" as Kennedy succeeded in doing with his speech on Berlin, the other player, if rational, will do the opposite, which Khrushchev did, in spite of all predictions and indications to the contrary.

Notes

1. Thomas Schelling, "An Essay on Bargaining," *American Economic Review* Vol. 46, No.3 (June 1956), 281–306).
2. R. Dodge, *The Strategist* (Hollis, NH: Hollis and Singapore: Marshall Cavendish, 2006).
3. Janandas Devan, e-mail to Robert Dodge, July 16, 2009.

CHAPTER 7

Tactics

A strategic move is one that influences another's choice in a way favorable to one-self by affecting the other's expectations about how you will behave. Strategies are plans that require implementation. The strategies of commitments, threats, promises, and warnings need to be executed in ways that make them useful. This chapter looks at tactics used for making strategies effective, both personal strategies and those Schelling advocated during the Cold War that remain politically relevant.

Effective tactics often involve a voluntary but irreversible sacrifice of freedom of choice. It is a paradox, Schelling points out, that a person's ability to constrain or control his adversary may depend on the power to bind oneself. Weakness may be strength. Burning bridges may undo an opponent. The essential point is that a person's or player's ability to remove all of his options in a situation gives him the upper hand in certain encounters. When Xenophon backed his army against a gully to fight the massive army of ancient Persians, he removed all options for his forces other than to fight to victory. This was a tactic to create a credible commitment.

Influencing Another's Expectations

A story from the Battle of Waterloo offers an excellent example of influencing other's expectations of one's own future behavior and thus influencing others' choices, that is, using tactics to make an effective strategic move. Schelling wrote, "Bargaining power has also been described as the power to fool and bluff."[1] Online notes from the Yale School of Management tell a story of such manipulation of others' choices by fooling and bluff being successfully used as follows:

> The greatest investor of all at exploiting market over-reaction was Nathan Rothschild, the London banker. He was known to have the most sophisticated information network in Europe, and everyone knew he would have the latest news about the outcome of the battle of Waterloo. Would he buy or sell Bank of England securities? One day Rothschild came out and quietly sold. Suddenly, astute investors got wind of this,

and reacted with a flurry, dumping everything they owned. Rothschild then quietly bought in the panic. He made a killing! By the 18th century, financial news traveled fast—in Rothschild's case, it may have even traveled by carrier pigeon. Studies of the efficiency of stock prices in this era indicate that when prices moved on the Amsterdam Stock Exchange on Monday, by Thursday they would move on the London Exchange—this is about the time it took for a fast messenger to travel the distance from city to city, crossing the English Channel. The Rothschilds were said to have used carrier pigeons and were first to receive the word that the British had won at Waterloo. They immediately proceeded to sell English bonds publicly and the price tumbled, at which point they secretly bought many more back at much lower price. When word of the great British victory arrived they were far wealthier. The London stock market had not been aware of the tactical bluffing and the strategic move by the Rothschilds had affected them as intended.[2]

It is worth noting that during this war the Rothschilds made a fortune by shipping gold across the Channel to supply the British forces, while at the same time they were loaning money to Napoleon to build his army. The manipulation of the stock market after Waterloo has been challenged as myth by some,[3] and the story is included as an example of tactical manipulation of others' expectations for the purpose of them making choices that would prove favorable to the manipulator.

In more generally applicable two-player situations, one player constrains the other's choice by constraining his own behavior. By constraining one's self it is possible to be left with a simple maximization problem that has a solution that is optimal for oneself, but destroys the possibility that your opponent could achieve the same thing. By eliminating your ability to choose you have no option but the one you already have chosen, but your opponent must make a decision. A Schelling example of this kind of self-constraint follows the chapter.

Credibility

Threats are hard to make believable, as parents know from saying, "one more chance," and not always following through with stated consequences. It is the same at many levels. It might be necessary to get oneself into a position where it is not possible to leave one's threat an empty statement, or where one is obligated by some overwhelming cost of not reacting in the manner that had been threatened.

For tactics that are implementing strategic moves to have an effect on one's opponents, it is important to establish your credibility. Having credibility enables you to carrying out unconditional moves, keep promises, and make good on threats. Threats and commitments may be tested, and credibility must be earned by following through. If commitments are just oral, there may be doubt about whether they will be carried out, especially if they do not appear to be in the maker's best interest. Credibility requires finding a way to prevent going back on one's commitments.

Like Xenophon, armies have achieved credibly committed status by denying themselves an opportunity to retreat. In 1066, William the Conqueror's army burned the ships that carried it over the Channel to attack England. Cortez followed a similar tactic in Mexico. The advantages in these cases were that the soldiers became more united, and they knew the influence this commitment had on their opposition. For Cortez and his army, their option was to succeed or perish, but their enemies had the choice of retreating to the hinterland.

Avinash Dixit and Barry Nalebuff in their book *Thinking Strategically*[4] discuss establishing credibility and exploiting it and set out an eightfold path to doing so. To make strategic moves credible one may need supporting or collateral action. Three underlying ideas are involved in making a credible commitment: first, change the payoffs of the game; second, make it in your interest to follow through on your commitment; finally, turn a threat into a warning, a promise into an assurance. Dixit and Nalebuff's eightfold path[5] is:

1) Establish and use a reputation.
2) Write contracts.

Both of these tactics can make it more costly to break a commitment than to keep it. They change the game to limit your ability to back out.

3) Cut off communication.
4) Burn bridges behind you.
   In using these tactics, the most radical of those listed, you deny yourself any possibility of backing down.
5) Leave the outcomes to chance.
6) Move in small steps.

Randomization is a way of dealing with decisions when unpredictability is the most rational approach. And a big commitment can be broken down into many smaller ones. The gain from breaking a smaller commitment may be offset by loss of remaining contact.

7) Develop credibility through teamwork. A team may achieve credibility more easily than an individual.
8) Employ mandated negotiating agents. [6]

In the Berlin crisis of 1961, John Kennedy, the young, untested president, made a strategic move that helped build a reputation when he said the United States would meet its commitments to Berlin. His reputation was being established.

Another example of a clearly established reputation is Israel's long-standing policy of not negotiating with terrorists—a policy also articulated by the United States. Giving in to terrorist demands makes future terrorism more likely. Maintaining a reputation for not negotiating is intended to deter terrorist acts but it presents difficulty when it fails to deter—if a plane is hijacked, ignoring the hijackers presents difficulty for the country seeking to maintain that reputation. The United States has frequently gotten around its no negotiating policy by calling in third parties like Japan or Switzerland and "going through channels" or making semantic distinctions between "talking" and "negotiating." This nonnegotiation stance is part of an Israeli or U.S. tactic of cultivating a reputation for "keeping one's word," and has offered a strategic advantage in certain circumstances. In more recent days the approach of the United States has been toward opening dialogue, but with hope of a different international reputation being established or with a different credibility.

Last Clear Chance

To be certain you can employ your strategy, it is often necessary to maneuver into a position where there is no longer much choice in what you do. This is one example of the burning bridges approach. Often it depends on getting into position where the initiative is up to the enemy, as is true with many interactions that involve sequential play. Like the chicken dilemma, it is the other who has to make the awful decision to proceed to the action that leads to mutual disaster (recall that a threat can be expensive to you if it fails and the opponent proceeds). This is the doctrine of "last clear chance." Words are rarely adequate, but some form of "trip wire" or "plate glass window" may suffice. During the 1961 Berlin Crisis, that plate glass window was the twelve thousand Allied troops stationed in Berlin. For the Soviets to take the city they would have to capture or kill those troops. The United States had burned its bridges by leaving its troops in Berlin since the loss of those troops would have guaranteed the start of a war. The Russians were aware of the costs involved of moving on the city and wisely chose not to.

In addition to getting yourself in a position where you cannot retreat, your commitment can assume credibility and validity in several ways: by incurring political or social involvement; putting your honor at stake, whether it is family, school, or country involved; incurring obligations; or putting your reputation at stake by your response.

Irrationality

A reputation for being crazy can sometimes make for successful threats. Irrationality can be strategically rational. Schelling called this the "mad man theory" and he wrote about it but never advocated it. The United States adopted it in the late stages of its bombing campaign in the Vietnam War [7] Dixit and Nalebuff say that if you have a child who is too irrational to be deterred by your threats of punishment, then the child is a better game theory player than you.

A straightforward way to make commitment credible is to agree to a punishment if you fail to fulfill it. A contracting approach is better suited to business dealings, but it is possible to write contracts with neutral parties as enforcers.

There are paradoxes with credibility and rationality. Threatening to hurt someone if he misbehaves need not involve a significant difference in how much it would also hurt you, if you can make him believe your threat. It does not always help to be believed to be fully rational. On the opposite side, a threat will not work when the object of the threat does not understand it. It is like having a little puppy and threatening to beat it if it pees on the floor again. It does not comprehend, and the threat will not keep the floor dry.

Sometimes one can get a reputation for not having everything under control and being impulsive, unreliable, and unpredictable. Teaming up with an impulsive ally or friend might accomplish the same thing. Soviet Premier Khrushchev said to Averill Harriman in 1959, "Your generals talk of maintaining your position in Berlin with force. That is bluff. If you send in tanks, they will burn and make no mistake about it. If you want war, you can have it, but remember it will be your war. Our rockets fly automatically." [8] It was the same defiant Khrushchev who attended the UN in the fall of 1960 and shouted interruptions during Prime Minister McMillan of Britain's speech on the Belgian Congo and in the following week, when a delegate from the Philippines spoke of Soviet imperialism in Eastern Europe, took off his shoe and began banging it on the desk before him. While it had comic overtones, it was the most dangerous time in the history of the world, and this bizarre behavior may well have provided a shortcut to deterrent strategy, as such displays of unpredictability can be effective.

Moving in Steps

A tactic that can sometimes improve a strategy's chance of success is moving in steps. When the stakes are high and a large-scale commitment is to be made, the dangers of putting everything on the line at once may be reduced to a smaller scale. Homeowners and contractors are often mutually suspicious. Homeowners fear paying for jobs upfront, since they then may receive careless, shoddy work. Contractors are concerned that if they are not paid ahead, when they finish their work they will not be paid. A common solution to these concerns is to pay on the basis of progress made on a daily or weekly basis—moving in steps.

Reason Forward, Look Back

This fear of being cheated can involve a key point in strategic thinking: *reason forward, look back*. Look at the endgame and reason backward, sometimes called backward induction, to see the decision points that will take you there. Decision trees will be presented in the voting chapter, where backward induction can be graphed by looking at all points where decisions take place and the results of following different paths. This need not be formal, but should be automatic. Having the result in mind and looking at the step needed to achieve if, then considering what is needed to get to the point to have success at the penultimate step. From there it is the step before and so on, back to where you are now. As a caution, if you expect to be cheated at the end of negotiations, you might break off negotiations a round early. But if you are going to break off negotiations a round early, that then becomes the final round, so it really is not a solution. To avoid a complete unraveling of trust there should be no clear final round, because, as long as there is a chance of business continuing, the incentive to cheat is not strong. Be on guard if someone you suspect may be untrustworthy tells you that the deal you are making will be the final one.

Teamwork

Teamwork can be useful for achieving credible commitments. Peer pressure and setting up social conditions that put pride and self-respect on the line can help ensure that commitments go unbroken. At the U.S. Army academy, West Point, exams are not monitored, as their honor code is that cheating is dealt with by expulsion. Failure to report a violation also results in expulsion. It is a military sense of duty and honor that harkens back to ancient Rome, where falling back during an attack was a capital offense. A soldier who saw someone near him retreating was to immediately kill the person, and failure to do so was also a capital offense.

Having a mandated negotiator deal for a person or a group has tactical advantages. The strength here is that your negotiator may not be granted the authority to make any concessions without going back to you or the organization being represented, so he may seek concessions but do so without the authority to bargain away anything.

Eliminating Options

Sometimes cutting off communication can succeed as a credible commitment device. By eliminating your ability to receive messages you can make a change of your position impossible, since you are unable to respond to counterproposals or demands. Although cutting off contact is an effective tactic, its weakness is that without communication, it may be difficult or impossible to be sure that a rival has acted according to your wishes. However, if you are better off not receiving messages that might put you in a position to be forced to accept a poorer arrangement than you presently have, failures in communication can occur. Your transmitter could be too weak, or if you are communicating with someone and using a translator, it could be someone who speaks the sender's language poorly. Your e-mail server could always be down for a time if you sent yourself monstrous files beyond your limit.

Leaving the outcome beyond your control to ensure credibility was dramatized with black humor and terror in the movie on which Schelling advised Stanley Kubrick, *Dr. Strangelove*. The great fear at the time of the 1964 movie for both the United States and the Soviet Union was surprise attack, and as long as the Soviet premier had a choice to make about whether to respond, Americans might risk an attack. The Soviet Union's Doomsday device was an effective deterrent, or should have been, because it was triggered automatically, and massive retaliation would be launched without the premier's orders, nor could he prevent it, and all life on earth would be exterminated. Schelling worked with Kubrick and Peter George, author of *Red Alert*, [9] the book on which the film was based, to try to figure a way to get the story told without depicting an Air Force officer as demented, but could find no alternative. When a paranoid Air Force officer at the Strategic Air Command decided the communists were contaminating America's precious bodily fluids as part of their plan to take over the world, he launched a wing of nuclear bombers against the Soviet Union. The result was a "comedy" that ends with all life on earth coming to an end, as one bomber manages to make it through and the doomsday device is set off. The message of leaving events beyond one's control was powerfully brought home, but Schelling admired the film's efforts to show cooperative attempts between the Soviet premier and the U.S. president to avert the disaster during a time when such close direct cooperation was not standard. [10]

Salami Tactics

Getting around an adversary's commitments involves another fundamental skill in strategic thinking: *salami tactics*, violations in very piecemeal fashion like salami slices, so nothing is ever enough to provoke a confrontation. Salami tactics were no doubt the invention of a child. Imagine you are at a lake and supervising a little boy. It's a nice, sunny day, and you tell the boy he is not to go in the water. He sits on the bank and puts his feet in, but "he" is not in the water. No big deal. Soon he's standing, but it really seems to be just his feet in the water. You look away for a minute and when you check again he is wading, but it is not like really being in the water, is it? While you are asking yourself that one, he has waded out so the water is above his waist, and you tell him not to go any deeper.

He tries bobbing up and down, but it turns out the water is up to his neck. You are wondering how this happens when he starts swimming out into the lake. At first you start to shout, "Get back here," but somehow it comes out, "Don't swim out of sight."

Most commitments are ultimately ambiguous in detail, as in the preceding paragraph, when you were to "supervise a little boy." The approach to dealing with them is like the little boy's, by probing in a noncommittal way, with a seemingly inadvertent trespass. If there is no challenge to your move, then your operation continues. One can make an intrusion on a scale too small to provoke a reaction and increase it by imperceptible degrees, never presenting a sudden, dramatic challenge to invoke a committed response. An article discussing China's continuing increase on claims over the many outcroppings that constitute the Paracels and the Spratly Islands, which are claimed by a number of countries said, "China may be practicing Cold War 'salami tactics,' absorbing the South China Sea in small bits so as to avoid a violent response from potential adversaries."[11]

Salami tactics do not always work, and one can risk getting a reputation for not honoring commitments because they are nibbling at details that are ambiguous. The ambiguity can be seen as certainty in hindsight from different perspectives, again creating difficulties on whether commitments are being honored when one side makes piecemeal steps in a new direction. The long debate over the U.S. obligations to Iraq and Afghanistan illustrate the dangers to both parties of ambiguous terms.

Rocking the Boat

Competition in risk-taking can result when players have made mutual threats. A player can approach this situation with a tactic that may carry some risk of disaster he does not intend. He can initiate a process that does not guarantee certain catastrophe, but has a certain risk of mutual disaster if other party fails to comply within a short enough time to keep their cumulative risk within reason. "Rocking the boat" is a metaphor for this tactic. It would be ineffective to say to the other player, "Row or I'll tip boat over and kill us both," because the statement would not be believed. If you start rocking the boat so that it might tip because you do not completely have control over it, it becomes a war of nerves, and your opponent may willingly choose to row.

An example of this tactic came in March of 2008, when competition between threatening strategies was evident. Prime Minister Nouri Maliki of Iraq vowed to "re-impose law" in the city of Basra, as radical Shia cleric, Mogtada Sadr, threatened "general civil disobedience" with the support of the Mehdi Army.[12] Basra had been under the control of United Kingdom forces but, with the Iraqi government taking responsibility for its own security, it had been turned over to Iraq's police control three months earlier. It is of critical importance to Iraq's economy, since most of the country's oil exports pass through the city. The militias had taken over much of the city, and law and order did not exist. The prime minister's personal involvement in the campaign was ineffective, and government forces suffered losses, but the Mehdi Army was losing popular support, as it became involved in looting and criminal exploitation while it spouted antiforeign rhetoric. An indefinite nighttime curfew was imposed, and local chieftains aided the government in establishing order, plus the British provided reconnaissance. No extreme demands were made, but conditions improved.

Five months after the conflict began, British Prime Minister Gordon Brown cited a "marked improvement" in Basra's security conditions, adding, "The most important development is that the improvements we have seen have been increasingly Iraqi-led."[13] Maliki had made a strategic commitment that threatened Sadr and he was ill prepared to enforce it on his own, but he had risked prestige and reputation by issuing his statement, which helped lend it credibility. He and Sadr were in the same boat together and he was rocking it with the message that Iraq could maintain order without outside occupying forces, and Basra was a test the new country needed to pass. While it was a very modest achievement, the crisis passed.

Brinkmanship

Brinkmanship was a Cold War option that can be applied to nonwar situations, and has had some success as a method of deterring undesirable actions of an adversary. In the Cold War it meant going to the brink of war, which was really more of a slippery slope than a drop-off, and involved exposing the enemy to a shared risk to show that if he made a contrary move, you would be forced over the edge and he would be dragged along. It involves being so close to the edge that in spite of one's own best efforts at self-preservation, slipping over the edge is possible. It is a game Schelling says little children understand very well. Players can influence the course of events by creating a genuine risk for their adversaries, and brinkmanship creates that situation. It is a risky tactic that involves true commitment, and a player risks going down in the same tumble as his adversaries.

Brinkmanship and its dangers were exhibited in 1994, when the Major League Baseball owners decided to put a salary cap on teams and force them to spread their pay to players with more balance. The owners announced their decision early in the season. The salary cap idea did not sit well with the players, and in July they officially rejected it. Strike talk among players began in June, and the owners responded by withholding millions from scheduled payments to the player's pension fund. Both sides grew more entrenched and edged toward the brink as the season carried on through July and into August. The players announced a strike date but did not walk out. Federal mediators failed to solve things and when September came, unacceptable proposals and counterproposals were made.

On September 14 the remaining season was canceled, as the players went on strike, making it the first time in ninety years that the World Series had been called off. Following the season five bills were introduced in congress addressing baseball's collapse, and President Clinton ordered the owners and players to resume negotiating, all to no avail. When spring training time arrived, strike-breaking "replacement players" were being found by owners to have teams ready to take the field for the opening game.

In mid-March the players association announced that the strike would continue if replacement players were used. They took their case to federal court, alleging unfair labor practices on the part of the owners in bringing in the non–Major League replacement players. On March 30, 1995, two hundred and thirty days of a strike in "America's pastime" came to an end when Judge Sonia Sotomayor issued an injunction against the owners' use of the replacement players. Two days later, the Second Circuit Court of Appeals upheld Sotomayor's decision upon appeal, and the following day, a new season of baseball began.

It had been costly to both sides. The brinkmanship had dragged them down together. To the public it appeared that greed mattered more than sport. As well, this came at a time when baseball's popularity was declining in comparison to the other major televised sports: football and basketball. Gallup polls indicated the public's displeasure. During the strike 68 percent favored limiting players' salaries, while 29 percent opposed. As far as who the fans felt was more concerned with them, 53 percent responded neither, as 21 percent sided with the players and 18 percent felt it was the owners.[14]

So brinkmanship could be a very successful tactic, as it was for Kennedy in Berlin, but the risk is real that there will be outcomes such as when the players in the Major Leagues went to the brink over the salary cap and the obstinate owners held their hands as they all tumbled down together.

War and Terrorism

Much of Schelling's famous work dealt with strategy as it related to war, and while the height of his influence was during the Cold War, his ideas on deterrence and terrorism have relevance in the present, as similar issues confront society. His view of war is unlike what first comes to mind. He wrote, "War appears to be, or threatens to be, not so much a contest of strength as one of endurance, nerve, obstinacy, and pain. It appears to be, threatens to be, not so much a contest of military strength as a bargaining process—dirty, extortionate, and often quite reluctant bargaining on one side or both—nevertheless a bargaining process."[15] He sees war as a violent exchange of threats, promises, commitments, and warnings carried out as those strategies are in other circumstances, but with more devastating outcomes.

Violence, pain, and destruction can threaten, deter, blackmail, or cause any number of outcomes. Total war is not a modern invention, as in ancient wars, the losing side had its women taken and sold into slavery, while the men were put to death and the young boys castrated. Cattle were slaughtered and buildings torn down, in notions of justice, revenge, custom, and personal gain. This violence is most successful when it is threatened but not used, as has often been the case in the relations between unequal powers, as Thucydides noted, "The strong do what they can, the weak suffer as they must."[16]

Terrorism now immediately conjures up suicide bombers, but terrorism can be any form of violence that is intended to coerce rather than weaken militarily. World War II saw devastating terrorist attacks by the Germans when they launched the vengeance weapons against Britain, first in 1944 the V-1, known as the "buzz bomb." The following year came the V-2, the world's first ballistic missile, developed by Dr. Wernher von Braun, the future head of NASA. The greatest terrorist attacks in history came in 1945, when the atom bombs were dropped on the Japanese. These were weapons of terror and shock. The real targets of these bombs were not the dead of Hiroshima and Nagasaki or factories where they worked, but the survivors in the government in Tokyo. It is said that since the development of atomic weapons man for the first time has military power to eliminate the human species from earth. Schelling says it was not nuclear weapons that turned this corner. He contends that Japan could have been eliminated without nuclear weapons, as, "Against defenseless people there is not much that nuclear weapons can do that cannot be done with an ice pick. And it wouldn't have strained our Gross National Product to do it with ice picks."[17]

Nuclear weapons can make it happen quickly, and depending on the nuclear powers involved, it could be the end of everything. There is an illusory perception of the United States as the sole superpower since the end of the Cold War, but nuclear weapons held by Russia remain equal to those held by the United States under the terms of START I. China, France, and the United Kingdom are all nuclear powers and signers of the Nuclear Non-Proliferation Treaty, while India, Pakistan, and Israel possess substantial arsenals but have not signed the treaty and North Korea has a nuclear device while several other countries have worked to develop one.[18]

We are now in an era of dirty war; the science of military victory no longer dominates. Instead, our wars are fought with the tools of coercion, intimidation, and deterrence. Deterrence is about influencing an enemy's intentions. What is difficult is clearly communicating your own intentions so that a threat does not sound like a bluff and thus is credible.

Deterrence and Compellence

Related but different uses of the threat strategy are seen in deterrence and compellence. Deterrence involves a threat that undesirable consequences will follow if the other party acts in a way one wishes to prevent. A threat that compels rather than deters often requires that punishment be administered *until* the other acts, rather than *if* he acts. The prisoner interrogation techniques employed in counterterrorism have at times employed compellent threats. Compellence usually involves initiating an action that can cease when an opponent responds as desired. Deterrence tends to be indefinite in timing, such as MAD. Compellence must be specific in stating what must be done.

Coercive threats require corresponding assurances. The object of the threat is to give the other player a choice. Deterrence may be implicit, as in your parents' "If you quit school, then our trip to Hawaii is off" in the previous chapter, where the unstated implication is that if you stay in school the trip is on. For a compellent threat to be successful it must involve an action that can be brought to successful closure. The payoff for prisoners being tortured came if they gave up some information, as did disaster, such as further water-boarding, if the threat failed. The bombing of North Vietnam was an example of Schelling's view of war as a violent exchange of tactics. It was a compellent threat to stop North Vietnam from supplying equipment and forces to aid the Viet Cong, the communists in South Vietnam. The compellent threat failed to achieve its objective.

Deterrence between nuclear powers rests on the threat of pain and extinction, not just on military defeat. Extinction has again become the possibility of a successful surprise attack on both the Asian subcontinent and in the Middle East, as Iran and Syria have shown interest in developing nuclear weapons at some time.[19] Overcoming the fear is achieved by guaranteeing the capability to retaliate if attacked. The metaphor Schelling used to explain this was written at a time when cowboy shows were popular on black and white television. He wrote of the "six-shooter" in the old West that made it possible for either man in a duel to kill the other. The fact that both had guns did not assure that both would survive or both would be killed. The advantage of shooting first aggravated the incentive to shoot. In a tense situation, such as the current international encounters, the perverted reasoning could be, "He was about to kill me, so I had to kill him in self-defense." It might go, "He, thinking I was about to kill him in self-defense, was about to kill me in self-defense, so I had to kill him in self-defense."[20] But if both gunslingers were assured of living long enough to shoot back with unimpaired aim, there would be no advantage in jumping the gun and also little reason to fear that the other would jump the gun on him. So attacking an enemy's retaliation forces has been the first priority in a modern war, not attacking the urban centers.

There is deterrence and compellence on the personal level with such threats as "you will receive no allowance for a month if you fail any classes this term," being deterrent, and "you are grounded and are not going out of the house on weekends until we get a report that says your grades have improved," as compellent.

At times a deterrent threat cannot be made credible in advance. It may require some overt act by the party doing the threatening to begin the deterrence. This is where defense and deterrence may merge. If the object is to make enemy realize he cannot succeed even if he tries, it is pure defense. If the object is to make an adversary not proceed by making his actions painful or costly, it is coercive or a deterrent. Israel's September 2007 attack on a nuclear site being developed in Syria had elements of deterrence and defense. The Israelis launched the secret raid without warning as an act to strengthen their deterrent stance and also as an indirect warning to Syria's ally, Iran, where nuclear development had reached a more advanced stage.[21] A defensive action may even be undertaken with no serious hope of stopping the enemy's opposition, as Syria is likely to remain in opposition to Israel as long as the Israelis occupy the Golan Heights, territory seized from Syria in the Six-Day War of 1967.

The ideas Schelling speaks of on how to use tactics to make strategies effective can be applied, as he did, to grand ideas of thermonuclear strategy. The same ideas also have application to personal and group interaction. In the final chapter, when the Cuban missile crisis is discussed, there will be a look at how some were applied in what was the most serious threat to existence the world has faced.

Supplement: Cutting off Communication a la Schelling

One tactic listed on Dixit and Nalebuff's eightfold path and discussed often by Schelling is cutting off communication. Siddharth Mohandas is a former student at Singapore American School and is now a Harvard PhD candidate in government. Mohandas did his degree at Harvard in government and postgraduate degree at Cambridge in the U.K. in international relations before taking his first full-time job, as associate editor of *Foreign Affairs*. In that role he was assigned an article submitted for publication by Thomas Schelling, and learned firsthand the effectiveness of the tactic Schelling has often described. The following is his report of the situation.

> As an editor at *Foreign Affairs*, I had my own experience with Tom Schelling's mastery of strategy. He had submitted a piece to the magazine on handling global climate change and I was assigned to edit it. Like many of the draft articles *Foreign Affairs* receives, Schelling's article was filled with interesting insights but was somewhat technical in its expression of them. Accordingly, I edited the piece to excise it of jargon and to render the prose as accessible as possible to a general audience, without compromising the arguments it contained. I sent the piece back to Schelling explaining that this was standard practice at the magazine and that I would be happy to discuss any of the edits with him. I also mentioned that we were on a fairly tight production schedule and so I needed to hear from him in the next few days.
>
> Three days passed and I heard nothing. So I called and left a message at his office explaining that we were going to press in a week and that

I needed to discuss the article with him. Two more days passed without a response, so I called and left another message. Another two days passed and, growing increasingly panicked, I called his home number and left a message with his wife. Finally, the next day I received a phone call from Schelling in which he flatly informed me, "I didn't like your changes." Moreover, he explained that we could pretty much take the article in its original form or withdraw it. With only a few days left to our press deadline, we were in no position to sub in another article. In the end, Schelling's article was published with only minor revisions.

What made the situation hilarious in retrospect was that it dawned on me that Schelling had employed a gambit straight out of *The Strategy of Conflict*: cutting off communication to prevent further bargaining. ("An asymmetry in communications may well favor the one who is unavailable for the receipt of messages, for he cannot be deterred from his own commitment by the receipt of the other's," p. 26.) Schelling had played me like a violin. All in all, the episode only increased my respect for the man: he practices what he preaches!"

Used with Mr. Mohandas's permission.[22]

Notes

1. Thomas Schelling, "An Essay on Bargaining," *American Economic Review*, Vol. 46, No.3 (June 1956), 282.
2. William N. Goetzmann, "ChVIII: Information and the Efficiency of the Capital Markets," Yale School of Management, http://viking.som.yale.edu/will/finman540/classnotes/class8.html.
3. Among those who consider the story of the market manipulation a myth is Rothschild biographer, Niall Ferguson, *The House of Rothschild: Money's Prophets* (New York: Penguin, 1999).
4. Avinash Dixit and Barry Nalebuff, *Thinking Strategically* (New York: Norton, 1991).
5. *Ibid.*, 144–161.
6. Permission to summarize from Barry Nalebuff, e-mail to Robert Dodge, September 11, 2008, and Avinash Dixit, e-mail to Robert Dodge, September 13, 2008.
7. "Pentagon Study: 'Irrational' Nuclear Policy a Deterrent," *CNN News Online*, March 1, 1998, available at http://www2.owen.vanderbilt. edu/mike.shor/courses/game-theory/docs/lecture07/irrational.html.
8. "My Alarming Interview with Khrushchev," *Life*, July 13, 1959, 33.
9. Peter George, *Red Alert* (New York: Rosetta Books, 1958).
10. R. Dodge, *The Strategist* (Hollis, NH: Hollis Publishing; and Singapore: Marshall Cavendish, 2006), 83.
11. Michael G. Gallagher, "China's Illusory Threat to the South China Sea," *International Security* Vol. 19, No.1 (summer 1994), 172.
12. "Iraq Forces Battle Basra Militias," *BBC News* online, Wednesday, March 26, 2008.
13. "UK Troops to Start Withdrawal by Early 2009," CNN.com/world, July 22, 2008.
14. George Gallup Jr., *The Gallup Poll: Public Opinion, 2002* (Wilmington, DE: SR Books, 2003).
15. Thomas C. Schelling, *Arms and Influence* (New Haven, CT: Yale University Press, 1966), 7.
16. Thucydides, Richard Crawley translation "The Melian Dialogue," in *The Peloponnesian War* (London: Dent, 1914), book 5, chapter 17.

17. Schelling, *Arms and Influence*, 19.
18. "Nuclear Weapons: Who Has What at a Glance," Arms Control Association, Strategic Arms Control and Policy Fact Sheet, October 2007, http://www.armscontrol.org/factsheets/ Nuclearweaponswhohaswhat.
19. *Ibid.*
20. Thomas C. Schelling, *The Strategy of Conflict* (Cambridge MA: Harvard University Press, 1960), 232.
21. Leonard S. Spector and Avner Cohen, "Israel's Airstrike on Syria's Reactor: Implications for the Nonproliferation Regime," *Arms Control Today*, July–August 2008, http://www.arms control.org/act/2008_07–08/SpectorCohen.
22. Siddharth Mohandas, e-mail to Robert Dodge, May 2006.

CHAPTER 8

Self-Command

Individual decisions can form the basis of a two-player game that also can be effectively employed by a person playing the game alone. A valuable reason for doing such a thing is to achieve what Schelling labeled "self-command." Self-command is the structured attempt to constrain oneself from committing undesired behavior or to compel oneself to engage in desired behavior. It is based on the concept of the divided self.

Schelling explained:

> Many of us have little tricks we play on ourselves to do the things we ought to do or to keep us from the things we ought to foreswear. Sometimes we put things out of reach for the moment of temptation, sometimes we promise ourselves small rewards, and sometimes we surrender authority to a trustworthy friend who will police our calories or cigarettes. People who are chronically late set their watches a few minutes ahead to deceive themselves. I have heard of a corporate dining room in which lunch orders are placed by telephone at 9:30 or 10:00 in the morning: no food or liquor is then served to anyone except what was ordered at that time, not long after breakfast, when food was least tempting and resolve was highest. A grimmer example is people who have had their jaws wired shut. Less dramatically, some smokers carry no cigarettes of their own, so they pay the "higher" price of bumming free cigarettes.
>
> In these examples, everybody behaves like two people, one who wants clean lungs and a long life and another who adores tobacco, or one who wants a lean body and another who wants dessert. The two are in a continual contest for control: the "straight" one in command most of the time, but the wayward one needing only to get occasional control to spoil the other's best laid plan.[1]

It is this rational "straight" you of the present that plays a game with a less rational future you. How to best approach such a game? Says Schelling, "Often the ways people try to constrain their own future behavior are like the ways they would try to constrain someone else's behavior; they appear to be treating their 'future self' as if it were another individual."[2] The same tactics that apply to two player games are effective when used in the game with the divided self.

Self-command tactics vary and they range from mild to extreme; some require outside help and many are successfully employed without assistance. Some successful tactics that involve outside help center on breaking difficult habits. They put people in the position of being extorted if they fail and their future self lets them down. A dedicated Republican can write a sizable check to the Democratic National Committee or a devoted Democrat write one to the Republican National Committee and put the check in some trustworthy person's hands. If the individual who wrote the check is ever seen smoking, for example, the check goes in the mail.

A more extreme example is found at a cocaine addiction center in Denver, Colorado, where some patients write a self-incriminating letter that presumably confesses to their addiction. The letter is kept on deposit with the clinic, where random tests for cocaine use are conducted. If the patient tests positive, the clinic sends the patient's letter. In one case, a doctor's letter confessed to cocaine use and was addressed to the State Board of Medical Examiners, with the request that his license be revoked for violating Colorado law. Such a letter beyond the patient's control, promising the end of his career and social standing, was a powerful deterrent threat that would tend to ward off an impulsive decision.[3]

Such a threat on a two-by-two matrix would appear as follows (Table 8.1):

Table 8.1

		Future You	
		abstain	indulge
Withhold letter		3 / 4	4 / 2
Release letter		1 / 1	2 / 3

You of the present

The future "you" has a dominant strategy to indulge, which is why he is in for treatment. The next priority for the future you is to abstain.

The natural outcome of this matrix, if it were simultaneous play, would be the lower right quadrant. However, by the threat that the you of the present has arranged by submitting an incriminating letter that will be released, the likely outcome is changed. Your payoff value for abstaining is higher than your payoff for indulging. And, as is true of threats, this would be expensive to you if it fails, given the damage to your reputation and career that would ensue from release of the letter.

Some methods and tactics that involve cooperation from others may be less dramatic. Denial, intervention, relinquishing authority, or restructuring incentives are such methods. You might ask someone to deny you a cigarette, a second drink, the keys to your car if you have been drinking, or a loan of money. You might instruct someone to not let you go back to sleep, to interrupt you if you get into an argument, to blow the fuse if you are caught watching television. Relinquishing authority, you might let someone hold your car keys. Restructuring of incentives might include making wagers on who can lose the most weight, train the most hours, study the most for final exams or whatever is the desired goal. When you have work to do and do not trust yourself to stay busy at it, you might incarcerate yourself—have someone drop you off at a cheap motel without a telephone or television and call for you after eight hours.

There are tactics an individual can adopt without the aid of others that may be helpful. One such approach might be called "commit or contract." Ordering your lunch when you aren't terribly hungry rather than waiting until lunchtime is one example. If you anticipate being unable to drive later in the evening, you might disable yourself by throwing your keys into the darkness. If you foresee the situation you are in leading to some temptation you will be unable to resist, you can remove yourself by making yourself sick, if that is required to make it possible for you to leave. Don't keep liquor or sleeping pills in the house if they are a problem for you. Give yourself rewards for behaving as you hoped to and punishments for failing. Some people reschedule their lives, for example doing their grocery shopping right after eating. It can be useful to identify and watch for precursors of undesired behavior. If having a cup of coffee or alcohol seems to go with a cigarette, some just avoid the food and drink and thus succeed in avoiding the cigarette.

In all such cases it is important that you set rules for yourself that are enforceable. Use bright lines and have clear definitions, with qualitative rather than quantitative limits, if possible. It may help to arrange ceremonial beginnings and to be successful, permit no exceptions.[4]

This concept has practical value but can also raise ethical questions concerning which "you" in the divided self is the real you when there is a dispute and other parties are the enforcers. For example, a woman might ask her obstetrician to withhold anesthesia during the delivery of her baby. The doctor proposes that a facemask be placed next to the woman with nitrous oxide in case she should decide she really needs it, but she refuses even this, knowing that if it is there, she will use it, and she is determined to experience this birth "naturally." The woman is of sound mind and body and has given birth previously, so she knows what she is in for, and knows she will be thankful to the doctor for withholding the anesthetic once the birth has occurred. She is seeking to be the rational person of the present who is frustrating her weaker self of the future. The doctor consents. But ethical and legal issues can arise in the delivery room when she asks for gas to ease her pain, and her husband and the physician disagree about what the woman really wants.[5]

For many people simple self-command procedures can be adopted that may curb unwanted behavior. Laying down one's fork between bites if one is a binge eater, or scheduling workout times with a partner to encourage regular attendance are examples. For people who scratch bites in the night or for children who wish to stop sucking their thumbs heavy mittens can be worn, while those whose snoring comes from sleeping on their backs can but a bulky pillow under their backs so that they will sleep on their side rather than bearing the discomfort of turning onto their backs. Oversleepers can set their alarms a distance from their beds so they must get up to turn them off, and if that is not sufficient they can arrange to have someone call them in the morning to see they are awake. There are many ways creative people devise for their rational present selves to cope with their less trustworthy future selves, but with many addictions and conditions the challenge can be great.[6]

Notes

1. Thomas C. Schelling, "Egonomics, or the Art of Self-Management," *American Economic Review* Vol. 68, No. 2 (May 1978), 290.
2. Thomas C. Schelling, "Coping Rationally with Lapses from Rationality," *Eastern Economic Journal* Vol. 22, No. 3 (summer 1996), 251.
3. George Loewenstein and Jon Elster, *Choice over Time* (New York: Russell Sage Foundation, 1992), 167.
4. Thomas C. Schelling, "Self-Command in Practice, in Policy, and in a Theory of Rational Choice," *American Economic Review* Vol. 74, No.2 (May 1984), 6–7.
5. Ibid., 1.
6. Schelling has written extensively on this topic, and a reader interested in reading more on his views can access online such articles as "Self-Command in Practice, in Policy, and in a Theory of Rational Choice" "Enforcing Rules on Oneself," *Journal of Law, Economics, and Organization* Vol. 1, No. 2 (autumn 1985), 357–374; "The Intimate Contest for Self-Command," *National Affairs*, No. 60, (summer 1980), reprinted by *International Library of Critical Writings in Economics* Vol. 83, No.1 (1997), 446–470; "Strategy and Self-Command," November, 1985, http://www.rand.org/content/dam/ramd/pubs/papers/2006/P7200.pdf.

MODELS AS METAPHORS FOR WHAT DECISIONS DO

CHAPTER 9

Interaction Models

Social interaction involving groups is sometimes easy to understand when all the participants behave as if they were a collective individual, as at sports events where fans are cheering for one team or the other, or at political rallies where all are exhibiting a common candidate preference. But often individuals make decisions in response to the environment they perceive or anticipate, and in doing so alter that environment, for example when different racial groups enter previously segregated neighborhoods, or when people in poor health join insurance groups that had covered people without known health risks. In these cases individual choices might influence choices made by other individuals and alter the group status. It is useful to understand the group dynamics of such cases.

To explain how individual decisions operate in the aggregate, when they are combined with the decisions of others making related decisions, Schelling wrote a book entitled *Micromotives and Macrobehavior*.[1] Micromotives are the individual's decisions, and the macrobehavior is the resulting conduct of the many decisions in the aggregate. Schelling's book features easily understood models, or social studies constructs, that demonstrate the underlying features of many such situations.

Models simplify situations by embodying the relationships involved in some transparent manner and make the phenomenon that is taking place more easily recognized. They may help make aggregate behavior easier to predict and to encourage good outcomes or prevent negative ones. The outcomes of aggregate decisions may not always reflect individual preferences, though policy planners sometimes assume that they do. Is the fact that segregated neighborhoods continue to exist proof that people are prejudiced or desire to live in segregated neighborhoods? It would be jumping to an unsubstantiated conclusion to make such an assumption based on the result of existing segregation alone, as a Schelling model presented in Chapter 18 will demonstrate.

Models in social science are often "first approximations" presenting a simple underlying structure for a situation that can be elaborated on to represent more accurately what one hopes to understand. A block of wood sliding across the floor could be a first approximation model for an automobile. The first approximation model of a national economy might be presented as a formula that illustrates the interaction of consumption, government spending, investment, and net exports. This basic national economy model can be elaborated on to include more and more factors, such as nonmarket activities, environmental costs of activities, the value of leisure time, and much more, so that the model more accurately approaches a description of reality. If we were to start off with the many components of an automobile or the description of reality in the economic system, it may well be beyond our understanding. So we begin with the first approximation, a simple understanding on which we can elaborate until we achieve comprehension of the more complex reality.

A second type of social studies model is the "starting set" model. This type of model is not to be elaborated on, but represents the kind of analysis necessary to understand a situation and identifies questions to ask and concerns to be aware of in certain situations. These models are often metaphors that offer insight into behavior that might not otherwise be apparent. This insight can be useful for decision making, as it helps make clear what decisions do. These are the models Schelling presented in his work, and they appear in this and following chapters. The first model presented was Schelling's creation.

Thermostats

The thermostat is an easily understood mechanism that illustrates the starting set model concept. It represents ideas and brings up questions of what should be done at what stage in a situation that involves cyclical behavior patterns. A typical thermostat can make two decisions: it can turn a furnace on, and it can turn a furnace off. You set your thermostat for a certain temperature. When the air falls below that temperature, the thermostat turns the furnace on. The furnace then heats water, which takes time. The hot water circulates in radiators that heat air, which also takes time. Eventually the room temperature rises. When it reaches the temperature at which the thermostat is set, the thermostat turns the furnace off. At this time, however, the radiators are at peak temperature, so they continue to heat the air and the temperature continues to rise, overshooting the thermostat setting. As the radiators cool, the temperature begins to drop, until it reaches the thermostat setting, when the furnace is turned back on. The furnace then heats water (taking time), which heats air (taking more time), while the temperature continues to drop below the thermostat setting. This cycle continues on indefinitely. The temperature is always overshooting then undershooting the desired temperature. Better thermostats may reduce the range, but they do not eliminate it. The result is cyclical behavior. This cyclical behavior is evident in a wide range of situations.

The thermostat model demonstrates two interacting qualities that prevent the achievement of a target or goal: time lag and accumulated inventory. There is a lag in the time between when the thermostat turns the furnace on until the radiators warm the air to the thermostat setting. Once it reaches the thermostat setting and turns off, there is an accumulated inventory of hot water that raises the temperature beyond the intended level.

While this book generally steers clear of mathematics, it is possible to substitute algebraic abbreviation for the behavior demonstrated and to create a mathematical description that is independent of the original model. Such an abstraction allows prediction of the outcome of behavior in a wide range of physical, mechanical, and social situations. On an individual level the phenomenon is familiar as when children eat Halloween candy or others sweets until they feel they have had enough or when adults consume alcohol until they reach that same feeling. Both these moments of satiation typically occur at a point where the amount consumed has been too much; the stomach functions much like the radiator.[2]

On a broader level there are many examples. One is the changing demand for careers in the job market. In 1982 Dan Dorfman warned young people of the challenges they faced if they hoped to enter certain professions, as job opportunities were limited. He used a joke to introduce his point, that went: There was a small plane that had four passengers, the president of the United States, the pope, the world's smartest man, and a hippie. When the plane was airborne, a fire suddenly broke out, and there were only three parachutes. Disaster was imminent. The president said, "I owe it to the American people to finish my term," and grabbed one and jumped out. The smartest man in the world declared he was an irreplaceable asset to humanity, and took another and hopped out next. The pontiff and the hippie remained looking at each other, and then the pope spoke, saying, "My son, I'm in God's hand now. I want you to have the parachute." The hippie replied, "Hey man, that's really cool, really religious. But there's no problem, there's a parachute for each of us. The smartest man jumped out of the plane with my backpack." Dorfman's point was that being intelligent and educated was not any assurance of a secure future in 1982, as he reported that graduates in law, medicine, and architecture, as well as some engineers and those with MBAs would be hard pressed to find jobs. There were too many graduates for too few new positions, and not enough who had jobs were eager to leave them.[3] The thermostat had switched to off on the careers he mentioned, and there was an accumulated inventory of occupants in the available positions.

By 1990 the situation had changed as CNN's Money report listed the 15 "hottest jobs in the next decade"[4] Two of the fifteen were law specialties and one was a doctor, while two others were health care workers, two were engineering jobs, and two of the remaining hot jobs advised an MBA as the proper training. By the summer of 2009 the President's Council of Economic Advisors was anticipating that job growth would be "in industries such as health care, education, transportation, and construction. There will also be strong growth in employment in industries devoted to the production and distribution of clean energy. In general, the U.S. economy appears to be shifting towards jobs that require workers with greater analytical and interactive skills."[5] Dorfman would not be telling the joke about the smartest man at this time, as the thermostat had switched on for careers that required academic training, but there would be lag time required for those people to get through the system to meet the demand.

The thermostat also can be useful in analyzing matters of personal health. A recent example is the Centers for Disease Control's concern with the return of measles as a significant health problem. The CDC reports that in the decade before the measles vaccine was introduced in the United States in 1963, between three and four million people were infected each year, with many becoming seriously ill and some suffering permanent disability.[6] The vaccinations virtually eliminated the disease, but it has reappeared, as vaccinations have been neglected or refused. Unfounded rumors of a connection between the vaccine and autism led to some parents' refusal to have their children inoculated, as have philosophical and religious objections to vaccination.[7]

The thermostat turns on and off, resulting in changes that can be of importance in people's lives. Anticipating the changes in these and similar patterns in advance offers insight into developing personal and public plans for coping with them. There will be lag time and accumulated inventory to notice, and effective planning and decision making requires being in accordance with them.

Self-Fulfilling Prophecy

The self-fulfilling prophecy is a dynamic that is familiar in social sciences and applies to rational choice. That is, sometimes expectations induce behavior that causes the expectation to be fulfilled. Examples abound in history and other social sciences.

In the United States in 1933, the word spread that bank deposits might not be safe. Many people headed for their banks to withdraw their money. The expectation that deposits might not be safe proved to be true—the banks had nowhere near enough money to refund all deposits. The increasingly panicky run on the banks led President Roosevelt to declare a "bank holiday" and to close all banks. Many eventually reopened, but many others did not, and people who had their deposits in those banks never saw their money again. It is true that the procedures followed by many banks at that time were unwise. But if everyone were to head to the bank today to withdraw all of their money, the banks would be equally incapable of making the payments. The 1933 crisis was created not because a crisis existed but because people expected one.

In 1923 the German government tried to assist its country's striking workers who were making a stand against the French occupation of the Ruhr Valley. In order to support these workers, the government printed paper money to pay their salaries. Many workers, lacking confidence in the government and not expecting the paper money it issued to be of full value, demanded more pay when they were being paid in the new currency. This led to a self-reinforcing process that quickly created a spectacular spiral of people continually expecting paper money to be less and less valuable. The government inflated the numerical value of the money it was printing in an attempt to keep up with the people's declining expectations. The result was the worst inflation in all history.

Imagine that the richest man in the world had converted all his money into German marks in paper currency at the outbreak of World War I and stored it in some safe place before heading for a secluded island away from the world's problems. Ten years later in 1924 he returned to Germany and withdrew all of his money. He would not have had enough money to buy a piece of gum. The German government could only regain control of the runaway inflation by issuing new money backed by real government assets. The old currency could be turned in and redeemed for new currency at a rate of one trillion old marks for one new mark.

Another less dramatic, but equally illustrative example of self-fulfilling prophecy is an education experiment done in the early 1970s, called the Pygmalion Effect. "Pygmalion" is a George Bernard Shaw story, the basis for *My Fair Lady* on the stage and screen. In it a poor, Cockney London flower girl is taken off the streets, and transformed into an elegant lady by a language expert who teaches her to speak "upper class" English. In this experiment, teachers in a public elementary school met with Harvard psychologist Robert Rosenthal before the beginning of the school year. They were told that results from the Harvard Test of Inflected Acquisition had identified certain students who were going to be "spurters." These special children did not learn by making steady progress, but in sudden large steps. There was actually no such thing as the Harvard Test of Inflicted Acquisition and the children named as "spurters" had actually been chosen at random.

At the end of the school year, objective testing revealed a high correlation between the students who were predicted to make great progress that year, and the students who actually did. In other words, it was not merely a matter of teachers just thinking the randomly selected "spurters" had learned more, they actually had. [8] The common explanation for this is that teachers had been expecting great progress from these students, and behaved in ways that encouraged the achievement of that progress. It may have been that the identified students ended up receiving extra help, or extra encouragement in some way that teachers were not aware they were providing.

The negative-outcome self-fulfilling prophesy shows up in everyday life frequently, whether it is expecting to be unsuccessful in getting a date, not doing well in an interview because you expect things will go poorly, or failing to remember what you studied so hard last night for today's test because it's "just what you do." In sports it is thought to be behind the phenomena called "choking" as in missing an important free-throw because you are worried that you will let everyone down. The athlete, anticipating missing the shot, will cause himself to miss it by getting tense. In lists of the greatest "chokers" of recent times compiled by both *The Observer*[9] in London and by the sports network ESPN,[10] the same man was listed first, "The Great White Shark," Greg Norman. Norman was considered the best golfer in the mid-1990s, but when the major championships were played, his game abandoned him. The prime example described in both sources is the 1996 Masters, where Norman had shot a course record 63 on the opening round. Going into the final round he had a six-stroke lead, the largest in Master's history. A good round by Nick Faldo was matched by Norman's disastrous 78, and his six-stroke lead turned into a five-stroke loss. While this is extreme, such cases of failure to perform at a time when there is pressure are common occurrences in sports competition at every level, and the self-fulfilling prophecy is often a factor.

There are those who have success in turning prophecy of how they will perform into a positive thing and can see what is going to happen the way it should and believe it, gaining assurance and confidence to act accordingly. But, it is the possibility of bringing about undesired outcomes that one must be aware of in strategic analysis, not only in oneself, but also in social and policy analysis, as the 1930s banking example indicates.

Schelling adds variations to this model, including "self-displacing prophecy," where everyone has some desire to behave just a bit above or to a greater degree than others, to shift or displace their own behavior, but believes others hold that same desire. Some examples of this include wanting to tip just a bit higher than others, or professors wanting to give grades that average just a bit higher than other professors' grades. In the case of tipping the limiting factor is people's inability to tip any higher, but with grades it can mean grade escalation that will only be limited by the A+.

Another variation is the "self-negating prophesy." If everyone believes an event will be overcrowded and decides to avoid attending, the event will not be overcrowded. Or if a radio traffic station, or television traffic announcement predicts terrible overcrowding on certain streets following a snowstorm, people will avoid those streets and there will be no overcrowding. In an example from politics, when states are called for one candidate early in presidential elections on the East Coast and pundits discuss election projections based on those calls, there is real concern that voters in the West will not go to the voting booths, thinking the election has been decided, even though their votes might be decisive.

Lemons

A model with wide commercial application came from 2001 Nobel Prize winner in Economics, George Akerlof, in his 1970 essay "The Market for Lemons."[11] The Nobel committee called the essay "the single most important study in the literature on economics of information."[12] The "lemons" on which this model is based are not fruit but poor quality used cars. When someone sells a used car, it is likely that he knows whether or not it is a lemon. The buyer, however, more likely only knows the average value of that year's model of car. The key aspect of the lemons interaction mechanism is this "asymmetrical information" that exists between the parties involved, or the players in the market.

The average price for used cars is based on the overall distribution of "lemons," average cars, and better-than-average cars. Therefore, the average price for a used car is a high price for a "lemon," but a low price for a good used car. Owners of better quality used cars are reluctant to sell them at a cost based on an average price; so better cars appear less frequently on the market, but those who know they have lemons are more eager to find buyers.

The result of this is that the percentage of lemons on the market increases. Cars that had been the average cars at first become better-than-average cars in a later market with increased lemons. That secondary market will be based on the average frequency of "lemons" in a market that no longer includes as many of the best quality used cars as had been on the earlier market. Now, cars that earlier had been average cars will begin to vanish from the market, since the next new average price undervalues them and further undervalues the original good used cars.

This process is continuous, and, if left unchecked, can completely destroy a market. The asymmetry of information applies to many areas. It explains why third world countries have paid higher rates to borrow from established lenders. Akerlof said, "Credit markets in underdeveloped countries often strongly reflect the operation of the Lemons Principle."[13] His 1970 essay discusses India, where industrial enterprise was dominated by "managing agencies" that relied on reputation, positive information, and local money lenders charged extortionate rates because of lack of information. He also mentions Iran, where in the cotton ginning trade, companies engaged in loaning money for the coming season, but in the first years of operation they anticipated large losses from unpaid debts due to asymmetrical information. The borrowers knew their circumstances, but the lenders had a poor knowledge of the local scene.

Life insurance is another area where one can find examples of asymmetry of information. An insurance company has a great deal of general statistical information to use when it sets its rates for an individual's policy. This information is derived from experience and study of life expectancy. The individual, however, may well know things that make the company statistics inaccurate. The company bases its rates on the premise that some people are going to die soon and their beneficiaries will collect more than the insured contributed, but others are going to live long enough to pay in more than the company will pay out. For those who are not likely to survive to the company's break-even point, the insurance is a good deal. Some people may know where they fit into this statistical array. Perhaps all their ancestors died young from heart disease, or perhaps they are contemplating suicide in some easily disguisable form.

On the other hand, there are likely to be some people with a high probability of surviving well beyond normal life expectancy. People in this category may find themselves unwilling to pay an insurance premium based on a range of life expectancies from short to long. If they decide not to "subsidize the poorer insurance risks" and quit buying insurance, then the life expectancy of the remaining customers will go down. When the life expectancy goes down, the insurance rates go up. As the rates go up, another group of people is put into the position of subsidizing the remaining group. They may then drop out of the insurance schemes, leaving a group with an even shorter life expectancy, forcing the insurance company to raise rates even higher. The market in this scenario is doomed to collapse, as it moves in the direction of only retaining the worst insurance risks, and charging rates that could only be afforded by those who have no need for insurance.

At the time Akerlof was named Nobel Laureate, there had been a stark example of his model's implication going unheeded. A new economic sector had entered the market, the IT startups, or dotcoms. To uninformed outside observers they were like used cars, identical in many ways. To insiders with better information about potential future profitability of the many startup companies there were clear differences. Firms with below average profitability were overvalued because of investor's lack of information. These firms were more inclined to finance new projects by issuing their own shares than were highly profitable undervalued companies. The share issuing caused the less-likely-to-succeed dotcoms to grow rapidly and "lemons" eventually dominated the market. When uninformed investors eventually discovered their mistake, share prices fell and the IT bubble burst.[14]

Asymmetrical information is not always seen as a negative. The right to possess control over information asymmetrically is embedded in the U.S. Constitution. The Patent Copyright Clause, Article 1, Section 8, which says "The Congress shall have Power To . . . promote the Progress of Science and useful Arts, by securing for limited Times to Authors and Inventors the exclusive Right to their respective Writings and Discoveries." This provision has allowed individuals to profit from their ideas and discoveries but also includes a limit on the time they may do so, after which beneficial ideas are made available to a wider public. Such a policy leads to eventual copying of branded goods and industrial ideas, and after time to generic medicines, for example, that are often available at considerably lower costs to the consumer.

This protection of asymmetrical information is seen as controversial by some who consider it to create government-sponsored monopolies; a method of promoting economic inefficiency that suppresses progress in developing countries. *Reason* magazine, describing how much popular culture is a matter of copying bits and pieces, voiced another concern: "There is an inherent conflict between intellectual property rights and freedom of speech."[15] Disney spearheaded a drive to have the corporate copyright extended by two decades just when Mickey Mouse was about to enter the public domain, that is, to no longer be Disney's private property. Disney was joined by Fox, Lucas Films, and Bob Dylan among others. The author says "the irony was rich" when Disney became so involved, after drawing on public domain characters for the studio's own productions, like *Aladdin*, *The Little Mermaid*, and *Mulan*, and concluded that copyrights are often restraints that turned intellectual property laws into "protectionism for the culture industry."

The major concern and relationship of the Lemons model to the patent and copyright laws is the proliferation of counterfeit products, especially common in East Asia. Akerlof addressed this issue in his famous essay, writing, "The Lemons model can be used to make some comments on the costs of dishonesty. Consider a market in which goods are sold honestly or dishonestly; quality may be represented or it may be misrepresented. The purchaser's problem, of course, is to identify quality. The presence of people in the market who are willing to offer inferior goods tend to drive the market out of existence—as in the case of our automobile Lemons. It is this possibility that represents the major costs of dishonesty—for dishonest dealings tend to drive honest dealings out of the market. There may be potential buyers of good quality products and there may be potential sellers of such products in the appropriate price range; however the presence of people who wish to pawn bad wares as good wares tends to drive out legitimate business. The cost of dishonesty, therefore, lies not only in the amount by which the purchaser was cheated; the loss must also include the cost incurred from driving legitimate business out of existence."[16]

Dishonesty and how legitimate businesses feel threatened was captured in a March 1, 2009, *New York Times* article, "Facing Counterfeiting Crackdown, Beijing Vendors Fight Back."[17] The article concerns the struggle that companies face trying to protect the legitimacy of their brand name products and the views of those who deal in copying them. The story focuses on twenty-nine stalls in Beijing's Silk Street Market being shut down over selling counterfeit goods. The outraged vendors launched protests against the Beijing legal firm that represents five foreign luxury-brand manufacturers. The vendors marched on the legal firm's offices, referring to the employees as "bourgeois puppets of foreigners," and Chinese characters were written on the walls of the office's building that said, "We want to eat!" A thirty-seven-year-old vendor with a fake Dolce & Gabbana handbag on her arm said, "They don't have any proof," and when asked about the bag she was carrying, replied, "We don't read English. We don't know what the letters mean. We just think it is pretty."

This showdown had originated when Burberry, Gucci, Chanel, Louis Vuitton, and Prada had employed the Chinese firm two years earlier to take action against the Silk Street's market operator, and now the quality goods producers were faced off against generally uneducated merchants who didn't intend to yield. Protestors stormed the law office building, and as police mediation failed, the senior partner fled and spent three nights in a hotel because he feared going home.

There was a court-mediated settlement, and the law firm brought in twelve armed guards, but the protest continued, as shop owners chanted slogans and waved signs. A defiant vendor said, "We want to be compensated for our losses. And we want a public apology."

This Silk Street Market protest is a small skirmish in the copyright and patent difficulties that exist between the United States and China. *The Times* of London wrote in January 2009 that, "The FBI conservatively reckons that international intellectual property theft cost America $250 billion last year, and perhaps 750,000 American jobs. The lion's share of that piracy is believed to have taken place in China."[18]

Dr. Susan Schwab is especially familiar with this aspect of the Lemons model. Dr. Schwab served as U.S. Ambassador of Trade from June 2006 through January 2009. Prior to that she was Dean of the School of Public Policy at the University of Maryland, College Park, from 1995 to 2006, and has returned to the department as a professor. Before her academic career Dr. Schwab was legislative director for Senator John Danforth, served in the Department of State as a foreign service officer, the Department of Commerce as Director-General of the Foreign and Commercial Service, and the U.S. Embassy in Tokyo as Trade Party Officer. She was a strong advocate for free trade during her tenure as ambassador of trade, negotiating bilateral trade agreements with a number of countries. She also was devoted to protecting intellectual property rights. Her thoughts on intellectual property:

> Why attempt to protect intellectual property? Because it's the right thing to do (yes, there is a sense of moral righteousness involved). History/ constitutional considerations are involved re: personal property and ownership. Another reason is respect for innovative entrepreneurial/ creative endeavors and accomplishments; enabling the entrepreneurs, inventors, innovators, artists to gain (including making a living in some cases) from their efforts and creativity.
>
> A very important reason, it's the law, including on the international trade side, Special 301, from trade legislation in the mid/late 1980s, TRIPS agreement (Agreement on Trade Related Aspects of Intellectual Property Rights) in the WTO, Section 337 of the trade act of 1930 (I believe it originated in the Smoot Hawley tariff act!), etc.
>
> How to protect intellectual property? That is done through negotiations ACTA (Anti Counterfeiting Trade Agreement, launched 2007, under negotiation with various countries to set a higher plurilateral bar based on cooperation across borders and best practices), IP provisions of bilateral and regional Free Trade Agreements negotiated by the U.S., TRIPS agreement in the original WTO, WTO accession negotiations, e.g. with Russia in bilateral deal of 2006).
>
> Protection also is done through enforcement activities/leverage, e.g. through Special 301, filing cases under WTO (e.g. two cases filed against China under my watch).[19]

Allowing enterprising or creative people to profit from their endeavors is the law, and in many cases it is a daunting struggle to slow down copying and imitating intellectual property and branded goods. There are those who feel the copyright laws promote inefficiency by granting monopolies to overpriced products, while manufacturers who invested in development and advertising feel exploited when their patents or copyrights are violated.

So asymmetrical information cuts two ways. In the case of creative works, one-sided information requires protection because it can encourage the development of new ideas and technology. Innovation may be discouraged when the investment of time and money required to create something provides little return to the innovator. This would be the case when what the innovator knows and can produce becomes public property immediately. As a model for decision-making it is especially important to watch for what Akerlof pointed out: asymmetrical information can destroy markets unless steps are taken or policies implemented to prevent that natural, logical outcome.

The models presented in this chapter can be modified or tailored to help discover questions to ask, and they offer general modes of analysis for attempting to better understand human interaction. They provide metaphors for many situations that can be observed around us and help us anticipate outcomes that might not otherwise be apparent. Additional models will follow that warrant entire chapters.

Supplement: The Lemons Concept, Illustrated

A homework assignment called, "Concepts Illustrated" was given when a course on Schelling's ideas was first offered as a high school social studies elective at Singapore American School in the 1991–1992 school year. After discussing various social models in class, the students were to find or imagine examples and write them up for the following class. The following is one of several turned in by Russell Leidich, his Lemons example. It is followed by an e-mail Leidich sent eighteen years later, recalling the assignment.

> *Concepts Illustrated*, Russell Leidich, Singapore American School, homework assignment, 1991:
>
> Ed runs a lemon grove in California, just outside L.A. Due to his proximity to the city, his lemons are contaminated with industrial pollutants such as lead and mercury, which really makes them lemons. Ed believes that people will realize this, and therefore sells his fruit at the appropriate price of $10^{\wedge}(-45)$ cents per ton.*
>
> Mark's lemons are not lemons, however. Grown in a largely undeveloped area of Florida, his quality fruit is virtually free of toxins. He believes that people will see this, and therefore sells his fruit at the exorbitant price of 3 cents per ton.
>
> Unfortunately, neither Ed nor Mark was correct in his reasoning: to the average consumer, a lemon that looks sufficiently yellow is a good lemon, regardless of where it is grown. Additionally, the Society for the Prevention of Cruelty to Lemon Consumers produces a set of average lemon prices in its journal, the *Puckerface Monthly*.
>
> In the same month that Ed and Mark were trying to sell their lemons at the prices given above, *Puckerface Monthly* put the average lemon price at 1.5 cents per ton—halfway between Ed's and Mark's prices. As a result, very few people bought Mark's lemons. The following month, *Puckerface Monthly* revealed that the average lemon price had fallen to

1 cent per ton, as high-end lemon prices had not attracted buyers, while low-end lemon prices had. This time, the same thing happened: lemons selling for more than 1 cent per ton were undersold by cheaper ones, again pushing the average lower.

Soon enough, Ed found himself the proud owner of a monopoly, despite the fact that he was selling lemons. He was quoted in *Pucker-face Monthly* as saying: "I know that my competitors may be sour about their rotting lemons, but consumers just don't know lemons from lemons, that's all!"

*[note: $10^{(-45)}$ = 10 to negative 45th power, or price near $ 0.0]

The Sequel

An e-mail from Russell Leidich, nineteen years later, March 6, 2009:

Did I say "lemons"? I meant "dragon fruit". Check out this textbook example, which is relevant to the international agriculture trade today—a topic increasingly important as the world tries to negotiate the tradeoffs in oil prices, currency fluctuations, pesticides, soil management, labor conditions, and food distribution—and does so in an oversimplified manner, by employing the crude and stupid Lemons Model to destroy the dragon fruit export industry.

I stumbled upon this article because I was lucky enough to meet the USDA guy in charge of dragon fruit irradiation in Vietnam on my recent trip. He explained that the required equipment was only just recently getting installed. I spoke to him just a few weeks before this was written. Moreover—the interesting part, for game theory—is that my Vietnamese friend insists that she can obtain dragon fruit in the countryside for 3 cents per kg! This is, ironically, the same "impossible" number that I used in the Lemons paper, but in this case, she's absolutely convinced that it's true. She indicated that other fruits and vegetables sold for at least 14X as much—26X in the case of rice! I could not understand how this could be possible as, if this were true, then poor people should be eating dragon fruit for 3 meals per day until the price rises.

I wanted to know the cause of this bizarre market inefficiency, so I started doing some research. It turns out, ironically, that the recent price collapse began with an attempt to export the fruit to the US at about $4/kg. But due to the Lemons Model, the price imploded, creating aftershocks even in the local market, which apparently resulted in the $0.03/kg figure that my friend gave me. (She just visited Binh

Thuan province a month ago, which is where most of them are grown in Vietnam. I asked her about 10 times if she was sure. She's a physics student with impeccable honestly, so I tend to think she's correct.)

Now, the export business is targeting China, at about $1/kg, which after transport costs might resolve to a profit in the neighborhood of the local price itself.

Notes

1. Thomas C. Schelling, *Micromotives and Macrobehavior* (New York: Norton, 1978).
2. Ibid., 86.
3. Dan Dorfman, "Prestige Professions Near the Saturation Point," *The Ledger*, Lakeland, FL, June 20, 1982.
4. Michele Morris and Lauren Sinai, "15 Fast-Track Careers: The Hottest Jobs in the Next Decade Will Fatten Your Bank Balance and Enrich Your Life," *CNN News Online*: Money, June 1, 1990, http://money.cnn.com.
5. Executive Office of the President Council of Economic Advisers, "Preparing the Workers of Today for the Jobs of Tomorrow," Washington, DC, July 2009.
6. Centers for Disease Control and Prevention, "Most U.S. Measles Cases Reported since 1996," August 21, 2008, http://www.cdc.gov.
7. Centers for Disease Control and Prevention, "Many Unvaccinated because of Philosophical Beliefs," August 22, 2008, http://www.cdc.gov.
8. Robert Rosenthal and Lenore Jacobson, "Pygmalion in the Classroom," *Urban Review*, Vol. 3, No. 1 (September 1968), 16–20.
9. Jon Henderson and Oliver Owen, "The 10 Greatest Chokes in the History of Sport," *The Observer: The Observer Sports Monthly*, February 2, 2002.
10. "Worst Choke Artists of All Time," *ESPN: Page2*, http://espn.go.com/page2/s/list/chokers.html.
11. George Akerlof, "The Market for Lemons," *Quarterly Journal of Economics*, Vol. 84, No.3 (August 1970), 488–500.
12. "Information for the Public," http://nobelprize.org/nobel_prizes/ecomonic/laureates/2001/public.html.
13. Akerlof, "The Market for Lemons," 497.
14. "The Dot-Com Bubble Bursts," *New York Times*, December 24, 2000, "Information for the Public," http//nobelprize.org/nobel _prizes/ecomonic/laureates/2001/public.html.
15. Jesse Walker, "Copy Catfight," *Reason* (March 2000).
16. Akerlof, "The Market for Lemons," 495.
17. Sharon LaFraniere, "Facing Counterfeiting Crackdown: Beijing Vendors Fight Back," *New York Times*, A6, March 2, 2009.
18. Leo Lewis, "China's Counterfeiters are the Biggest Pirates of Them All," *The Times* (London), January 28, 2009.
19. Susan Schwab, e-mail to Robert Dodge, February 9, 2009.

CHAPTER 1 0

The Dollar Auction

The dollar auction is a game that models two interrelated phenomena: escalation and sunk cost. It has transparent relevance in contemporary society and is a deceptively simple game that is generally remembered once it has been played. Its lesson is clear and offers a warning to be alert to certain specific considerations in a variety of situations.

A dollar is offered for auction to be sold to the highest bidder. One condition of the auction is that both the highest bidder and the second highest bidder must pay the amount of their final bids. For example, if the highest bid ended up being $.25, and the second highest bid was $.20, the highest bidder would pay the auctioneer $.25 and receive the dollar, and the second highest bidder would pay the auctioneer $.20 but receive nothing. A second condition is that no communication is allowed among bidders so no collusion is possible.

Generally, this innocuous game of selling a dollar for bids begins at five cents with bidding in the same small units. It usually seems comical when the bidding begins, but the humor fades as reality sets in. There is a serious trap in this. Typically, the dollar auction proceeds as follows: Someone makes the opening five cent bid, which is quickly raised by other bidders. At this stage the participants commonly are taking part in a spirit of fun or possibly hoping to get a cheap dollar from a foolish teacher, and are not seriously considering the consequences of their bidding. For illustrative purposes, say the opening bid is $.05 by bidder X. Bidder Y raises it to $.10, followed by a bid of $.15 by bidder Z. X ups it to $.20, Y to $.25, Z to $.30, and then X to bids $.35.

At this point things are often happening quickly and it may still appear to the bidders that the auctioneer was foolish to offer to sell the dollar, but the participants are beginning to realize they stand to lose money if they do not win in the bidding. Perhaps Y, being the low bidder at this point, will drop out, since it will cost him nothing. This leaves X bidding against Z. Z also could drop out at this point, but it would cost him $.30, while upping the bid only $.05 might get him the dollar. So Z raises the bid, thus putting X in the same situation at a more costly level (X would lose $.35 by dropping out). When one bidder reaches $.50, if the other raises the bid, the auctioneer is guaranteed a profit.

The trap in the Dollar Auction is that at each round a participant has more and more to lose by not raising the stakes. Bidding is usually reduced to two participants as the amount gets beyond $.50, but there is always the driving force of merely increasing the bid by five cents and having the possibility of winning the dollar and earning some profit or getting nothing for finishing second. Class interest is often intense when the bid reaches $.95, putting the remaining bidder in the awkward position of either giving away $.90 for no return or raising the bid to $1.00 to buy the dollar on auction. Uniformly, the bid goes to $1.00 and to the amusement to the remainder of the class who had not carried on in the bidding, the other remaining bidder finds himself in the awkward and embarrassing position of being forced to bid more than a dollar to avoid losing the $.95 he has bid so far, so $1.05 seems the reasonable option, since it could recover $1.00.

At this point the game has reached the stage where both remaining bidders are now bidding to minimize their losses. It has become a game in which both bidders are going to lose money, and the question has become how much. While results have varied widely over the years, at the Singapore American School the height was reached when one bidder finally dropped out after being overbid at $10.55 to $10.50 for the teacher's dollar. The $20.05 that was collected after paying out the dollar remained in the teacher's pocket, making it a lesson that was remembered by most observers and remembered well by the bidders.

A surprising thing about playing the game is that in all cases after students had bid on the dollar and ended up paying some combined sum to the teacher that was substantially beyond the value of the dollar, the auction was immediately repeated with the same rules. At first students were typically reluctant to bid, but taunts of, "No one is willing to pay me five cents for a dollar?" were enough to start things off. The repeat auction never failed to show a profit on the sale of the dollar.

Sunk Cost and Escalation

The Dollar Auction's significant characteristic is that it is based on the problem of how to deal with "sunk costs." A sunk cost is an investment that cannot be retrieved. In this game it is the money one has already bid if he or she is one of the final two bidders. One will either spend that money buying the dollar by being the highest bidder in the auction, or paying for nothing by staying in and finishing second.

This is a model of escalation that students long recall. They also remember the trap of becoming involved or incurring a sunk cost when there can be no retrieving invested assets and the outcome is uncertain.

Sunk costs and escalation examples are common in history. In the late nineteenth century in San Francisco there were still gentlemen who felt compelled to defend their honor by dueling if they were insulted. They also felt that civilization had moved beyond sword fighting or "pistols at twenty paces." To fight a duel, these gentlemen would stand side by side on a pier in San Francisco Bay, and take turns dropping gold coins into the harbor. The first to quit lost the duel. Their dropped coins were literally a "sunk cost" as they escalated the dropping.

On June 28, 1914, a Serbian nationalist assassinated Arch-Duke Francis Ferdinand of Austria. Austria wanted to halt nationalist movements in its polyglot empire. Before taking any action against Serbia, Austria consulted its powerful ally, Germany. Germany's response was to give Austria a "blank check" to do what ever it chose, with a guarantee of the German support. Russia began to mobilize its forces in support of its fellow Slav country, Serbia, and Germany ordered Russia to cease its mobilization. Austria issued an intolerable ultimatum to Serbia, which Serbia rejected. Austria invaded Serbia on July 28.

On August 1 Germany declared war on Russia. On August 3 Germany declared war on France. When the Germans marched into Belgium to attack France, England declared war on Germany. These countries had empires that were spread around the globe. What had been a response to an assassination at the end of June had become the First World War by the beginning of August.

These are two very different examples that are tied by a definition, escalation. Escalation is when two or more parties raise their level of commitment to achieve a goal by making a more and more costly and intense effort.

When geologists do a thorough analysis and conclude they have found an area where oil deposits appear likely to be underground, a form of dollar auction can occur. Though the game is unlike selling the dollar, the same key issue is involved of sunk cost and at what point continued investment is justified if the prize might return something from the otherwise irretrievable investment. Equipment and workers are brought in and a well is sunk where the oil is likely to be found. If no oil is extracted, it's a big investment for nothing. Or was it? Perhaps the oil wasn't at 4,000 feet as the calculations suggested. It would be a shame to miss a good return if the oil is just a little deeper. So why not go to 4,100 feet? Still no oil, but it could be at 4,200, so better try 4,200. No luck at 4,200, well perhaps it's inches away still. This is becoming a big investment to come up dry, so drill another 100 feet. Are those calculations really accurate or sort of general? Maybe they were accurate about the oil and general about the depth, so they had better try 4,400 feet. Nothing. Well we're not going away empty-handed. Go to 4,500 and see what turns up. What? No oil! What if it is just two more feet from where we are? When to decide it is a dry hole and sacrifice the sunk cost is a choice someone has to make.

On personal levels people face similar situations frequently. You might want to make a phone call at booth where there is a line, or to purchase a shirt and find a long cashier line, or approach a cash machine and find several people ahead of you. Once you get in a line you have sunk (invested) the cost of your time. When you get in the line expecting it to move along you wait and expect the investment of time to be valuable enough to justify your having made it. If you end up standing in line and not getting anywhere, you may reach a point where you will eventually give up, or you may think that if you had known it was going to take this long, you would have never entered the line. If that is your thought you are in a sort of dollar auction situation where your time in the line is a sunk cost that cannot be retrieved and the only value you can recover from it is achieving your initial purpose.

Marketing battles between Western companies to grab hold of newly opened markets in the developing world and Eastern Europe, teenagers running away from home after disputes with parents that began with parents determined to see their children perform some small task the teen refused to do, police forces and drug dealers arming themselves with increasingly powerful weapons—these are but a few of many everyday examples of escalation.

Among the most terrifying of all dollar auctions followed World War II, when the United States and the Soviet Union entered into an arms race to produce more sophisticated and destructive weapons. This will be discussed in game theory terms in the chapter on the Prisoner's Dilemma, but a central element was the sunk cost, the unrecoverable investment each side had. And like the dollar auction, it was seen by many as a competition in which one country would be the "winner," and the other would never recover its investment. The costs of developing new weapons, which were often quickly rendered obsolete, were astronomical. Both sides maintain weapons of unimaginable destructive power. In spite of this enormous expense, and the overhanging threat of war that could conceivably put an end to mankind, each side felt its only assurance of safety from attack by the other side was to maintain at least equality, or even better, superiority, in military might.

In 1954 the Vietnamese defeated the French at Dien Bien Phu, leading to France's withdrawal from its former colony. The country was divided at the seventeenth parallel by international agreement, until elections for a unified nation could be held. The North was governed by communist Ho Chi Minh, who had led the independence movement against the French. It was apparent he would win any nationwide elections, so noncommunist South Vietnam refused to participate. The United States supported both the South Vietnamese decision and the South Vietnamese government.

To many Vietnamese, the Americans appeared to be nothing more than another Western imperialist nation attempting to take up where the French had left off. The United States saw what was happening in Vietnam as part of a larger global struggle between the forces of the communist and the noncommunist world. Vietnam was a "domino" that could set off a chain reaction, turning all of Asia communist. Historic relations and attitudes among Asian nations were not part of the U.S.'s simple "communist = bad, noncommunist = good" formula.

In the civil war in Vietnam, the United States sought to aid the South, first with money, then by sending military advisors, and in 1961, by sending a small number of ground troops. By 1962 there were four thousand American troops, and the first American battle death occurred. At this time the Viet Cong (communists in South Vietnam) were fighting with primitive, homemade weapons and with weapons left over from the earlier struggle against the French. The four thousand U.S. troops didn't prove to be enough, and the American government felt greater involvement was called for. In addition to increasing troop commitments, the United States involved itself in a plot that led to the overthrow and death of the South Vietnamese leader, hoping his successor would prove less corrupt and more inspiring to his people.

At the same time, the quality of Viet Cong equipment and direct North Vietnamese involvement were increasing the size and efficiency of the communist forces. Each increase in the intensity of the war effort by either side was countered by the other. The naive and relatively casual initial step taken by the United States of sending a small ground force dragged America into a larger and larger commitment.

By 1965 there were 200,000 U.S. troops in Vietnam; by 1969, nearly 550,000, and there was bombing on a scale never previously seen in world history. Between 1965 and 1968 the United States dropped more explosives on the Vietnamese than were dropped on all the Axis nations (Germany, Japan, Italy) in World War II.

In spite of this, the communist forces were able to launch a coordinated attack throughout Vietnam (including an attack on the U.S. Embassy in Saigon) during the Lunar New Year of 1968. By this time the war was tearing the United States apart politically, and the United States eventually resorted to turning the fighting back over to the South Vietnamese.

In 1973, after a cost of more than 47,000 battle deaths and 58,000 total American deaths, direct U.S. involvement in the Vietnam War ended. In 1975, Saigon, the South Vietnamese capital, fell to the North, and was renamed Ho Chi Minh City. Vietnam was united under communist rule.

Vietnam is an especially poignant example of escalation that the dollar auction models well. The sunk costs made commitment to the cause more and more expensive to both sides. That cost had never been foreseen, at least on the part of the United States, but once so much had been invested, issues of credibility and pride that had not existed at the beginning arose as well.

More recent issues echo a familiar refrain. The invasion of Iraq to overthrow Saddam Hussein and eliminate his presumed weapons of mass destruction was launched on March 20, 2003. Anticipation of a short war with a happy ending was fueled by comments such as that Vice President Dick Cheney made during his September 9, 2002, appearance on CNN's *American Morning*, when he said, "I think that the people of Iraq would welcome the US force as liberators"[1]

Iraqis appeared happy with the ouster of Saddam, but not all were so pleased with the presence of the Americans. Optimism about a U.S. presence was still being voiced, however in the United States, as when John McCain made the following comment about the removal of Saddam and his Baathist Party on March 24, 2003: "There's no doubt in my mind that once these people are gone, that we will be welcomed as liberators."[2]

Control of Iraq continued to require more and more troops, and National Guard and Reserve units were activated to fill the void, while service personnel were being given extended tours and repeated tours to try to maintain stability in the splintered nation. As the war in neighboring Afghanistan regained virulence, the U.S. military intervention in the Middle East and nearby areas escalated at the cost of thousands of lives

As for the monetary cost of the Iraq War, the former secretary of defense Donald Rumsfeld had said "baloney" to the prewar estimate of former White House economic advisor, Lawrence Lindsey, that the total would run between $100 billion and $200 billion.[3] Administration officials put the probable cost at between $50 billion and $60 billion.[4] Escalation has taken a heavy toll on those figures, and a March 9, 2008, article in the *Washington Post* reported an updated estimate of the total costs of the war as being three trillion dollars.[5] This followed the release of a book by Nobel Laureate in Economics Joseph Stiglitz and Kennedy School lecturer Linda Bilmes entitled *The Three Trillion Dollar War.*[6] The authors counted many costs to society from the war including intelligence gathering, death benefits, and survivor care and benefits. They wrote in *The Times* of London that they felt their estimate had been cautions, saying, "A $3 trillion figure for the total cost strikes us as judicious, and probably errs on the low side. Needless to say, this number represents the cost only to the United States. It does not reflect the enormous cost to the rest of the world, or to Iraq."[7]

Escalation often involves a tremendous waste of potentially useful resources, and raises the significance of incidents or situations far beyond their original importance. Military escalation may result in situations that range from dangerous on a regional scale to potentially disastrous on a worldwide scale. This is easy to see in hindsight, yet that does not seem to make it easy to avoid. Why is this so?

The Dollar Auction effectively demonstrates how easily escalation can take situations beyond the original idea of participants as to what they are risking. It makes clear the importance of understanding situations before taking steps that result in a commitment to a specific outcome.

The Dollar Auction, however, is a game. It lacks the external pressures that may be critical or overriding in real world situations. It is also important, in determining the value of this game as a model for other types of escalation, to identify the characteristics of the game. If real world situations possess the same characteristics, the game can provide realistic insight.

The difficult question with sunk costs, as the Dollar Auction illustrates, is to know when to press forward and when to give up. Two common attitudes toward sunk costs are: "I have this much tied up in this already. I am not going to miss out on my chances for success by stopping now." versus "This has already cost me much too much. I am not throwing away any more effort or money on it." Economists generally conclude that, if possible, it is best to disregard sunk costs. They say you should just look at what the potential rewards are for future investment, that is, what will you gain versus what you will lose, regardless of how much you have already invested.

Several characteristics of the Dollar Auction game make it a bit unlike many cases of real-world escalation situations. The Dollar Auction involves a "winner take all" situation. This is not necessarily typical of every escalation situation, although it describes some. Another game quality is that a third party, the auctioneer, offers the prize. This is not usually the case in real-world escalation situations. Generally, the participants sustain the losses and gains, other than the incidental (but often significant) indirect affects the competition has on others. In the game both parties have full information of exactly what the prize is, and the degree to which an opponent has escalated (raised his bid). This is often not true in situations for which the game may appear to be a good analogy.

Other characteristics of the Dollar Auction include the restriction against cooperation or collusion, the absence of a termination rule, and the fact that the game is played by the principles, rather than their agents, so the element of personal ego is a factor. Obviously, not all situations involving escalation include all the characteristics of the game and analogies must be drawn carefully. Nonetheless, it provides a vivid, simple, and useful model. It demonstrates the ease with which rivalries or competitions can escalate out of control, and its message is important.

So, what is the best strategy for the Dollar Auction or similar situation? Martin Shubik notes that the auctioneer cannot prevent a loss of 95 cents if a coalition of two bidders is successful in controlling the bidding. Under the game rules this should not happen, but in reality it is often attempted. Bidders' concerns are with relative losses in the game as it progresses.[8] Howard Raiffa comments that in the game players tend to make it the object to "win" over the other as bidding advances. It sometimes becomes an ego contest where one is not going to allow the other to "beat" him in getting to pay too much for the dollar. Raiffa says that the catch is that if the wise thing to do for one player is not to play, then the wise thing for the other to do also is not to play. If that is so, it is no longer wise to avoid playing, but then the same is true for the other, so it is back to square one. In Raiffa's opinion, the best strategy is to bid aggressively to the maximum that is not a deficit, and then stop.[9]

Schelling's advice is that the wisest choice appears to be: "Don't Play." The trap of the increasing sunk costs, which decrease or eliminate possible rewards, seems to warn the rational participant to stay out altogether. Unfortunately, as is hinted in Raiffa's view, this strategy rewards the irrational participant who fails to foresee the dangers, and goes ahead and plays. If, for instance, you perceive the dangers involved in the Dollar Auction, but another bidder does not, you may decline to bid after an opening bid of $.05 by the other person. Paradoxically, his ignorance will have bought him a very cheap dollar. Does this mean you should join in the bidding?

Whatever you should do, the lesson of the Dollar Auction is that one should be aware of what he is getting into before committing a sunk cost of any amount that matters since, once in, there is no turning back. Whether it is your time, your money, your effort or a matter of public policy such as involvement in the affairs of other nations, beware of sunk cost and how you can be trapped into escalation and this model will have served you well. Sometimes that can be done by setting predetermined limits, such as when gambling on depths of drilling for oil, or waiting for your turn in line at a busy Starbucks.

To conclude this chapter, two problems are included for consideration.

Problems:

1. Assume you are playing the Dollar Auction game against one other person, with the same rules (high bid wins, both must pay what they bid, bids can be made in as small or large amounts as you choose). In this case, however, the item auctioned is not one dollar, but $1,000. You are unable to attend the auction, and you have an agent to do the bidding for you.

   How would you instruct your agent to bid?

2. Suppose the situation is the same as in problem one ($1,000 being auctioned, both bidders pay what they bid, entire prize goes to top bidder, you have an agent doing your bidding). This time, however, there is no auctioneer. In his place is a clock. When both your agent and the other bidder are seated, the clock begins. Bidding for both parties is automatically $1 per second, as long as they remain in the room.

   What would your instructions be to your agent?

There are no correct answers, but there are different strategies one could employ. The first reaction might be to follow the Schelling idea of "don't play," but the other person might be doing the same, as Raiffa suggests. It is probably reasonable to have your agent enter some minimum bid in this case in the hopes of escaping with a cheap $1000. What might also be a reasonable strategy is to consider the possibility that your opponent would have thought of the same idea, and since the bids have no specific amount set, you could instruct your agent to bid $1 more than your opponent if he overbids your opening bid. In this case you would be likely to want to set some maximum amount for your bidding, in case your opponent jumped in with a large amount. Bidding $1 more would put you at a level where if he outbid you, you would be required to pay a large amount for nothing by being the second highest bidder. You could think your opponent might give instructions to overcall your overcall, so perhaps you should outbid that by a small amount. But if you continue this procedure, you could end up trapped in the Dollar Auction.

With number two there is the temptation to avoid strategic considerations in favor of tricks, like shouting "fire." Again one could just not play, but it is probably worth giving the instruction to remain in the room initially, in case your opponent has been told not to play. Setting a maximum time for how long your agent will stay would be important so that you do not become trapped.

There are other, more aggressive ways to play and this can be attempted by writing strategies in pairs for agents and matching them to see what would result.[10]

Notes

1. "Events Leading Up to the 2003 Invasion of Iraq," History Commons, http://www.history commons.org/timelines.jsp.
2. "Special Comment: 'Not Too Important,'" thenewshole.msnbc.msn.com, Thursday, June 12, 2008, http://www.msnbc.msn.com.sharedcopy. com/id/25126582/4a0785958f6b4249d41 32b67f4b2a697.html.
3. Gordon Adams and Nigel Holmes, "Op-Chart: The Price of War," *New York Times*, June 28, 2004.
4. Elisabeth Bumiller, "White House Cuts Estimate of Cost of War with Iraq," *New York Times*, January 2, 2003.
5. Linda J. Bilmes and Joseph E. Stiglitz, "The Iraq War Will Cost Us $3 Trillion, and Much More," *Washington Post*, March 9, 2008, B01.
6. Linda J. Bilmes and Joseph E. Stiglitz, *The Three Trillion Dollar War: The True Cost of the Iraq Conflict* (New York: Norton, 2008).
7. Linda J. Bilmes and Joseph E. Stiglitz, "The Three Trillion Dollar War," *The Times* (London), February 23, 2008.
8. Martin Shubik, "The Dollar Auction Game: A Paradox in Non-Cooperative Behavior and Escalation,' *Journal of Conflict Resolution* Vol. 15, No. 1 (March 1971), 109–111.
9. Howard Raiffa, *The Art and Science of Negotiation* (Cambridge, MA: Harvard University Press, l982), ch. 6.
10. While it is not directly related to the game, Schelling assigned additional associated reading the reader might find valuable, as he felt it was important research on two-party interaction. That is Erving Goffman, *Interaction Ritual* (New York: Anchor Books, Doubleday, 1967). He recommended the whole book but required "On Face-Work," 5–31, and "Character Contests," 239–258. Goffman has since released a newer updated edition of this book available from New Brunswick, NJ: Transaction, 2005.

CHAPTER 11

Musical Chairs and Inescapable Mathematics

To improve strategic planning and make situations more understandable Schelling frequently uses the metaphor of musical chairs to clarify and analyze social interactions. The metaphor encompasses a broad range of observations and behaviors in which the same patterns emerge in the aggregate regardless of how the individuals who comprise the aggregate behave. Perhaps too general to be thought of as a behavior model, it is more accurately seen as a reference to situations that involve certain inescapable mathematical relationships. Understanding the sometimes simple and at times counterintuitive nature of musical chairs can enable one to foresee relationships and outcomes valuable for rational choice decisions.

Regardless of how well or aggressively it is played, the pattern in musical chairs is always the same—one person always loses when the music stops. That is what he means by saying the same patterns emerge in the aggregate regardless of how the individuals who comprise the aggregate behave. Similarly, a day on the stock market may be described by television analysts as being dominated by "heavy selling" or "heavy buying." However, a stock is only sold when someone buys it, so the amount of buying and selling is always equal, and the aggregate, or combined, pattern is like musical chairs. It is equal regardless of the behavior of individuals who are involved. Poker also illustrates this characteristic of aggregate outcomes being the same regardless of how well of poorly the individuals play. After all is said and done, when the game is over, the result is always the same; the total winnings and losses always add up to zero.

Paired Phenomena

This general "musical chairs" characteristic can be divided into a number of observations of frequently occurring behavior that may help provide new ways of analyzing problems. One of these observations is "paired phenomena." Like buying and selling on the stock market, many phenomena occur in pairs. At times this is obvious. In the aggregate, the number of telephone calls made is equal to the number of telephone calls received (presuming telephone calls are defined as something both made and answered). Although any single individual may make far more calls than he or she receives, or receive far more calls than he or she makes, the aggregate number of calls made and received is equal.

Awareness of this concept can be helpful. The existence of this pattern of phenomena occurring in pairs is sometimes obvious and at other times may be a bit more obscure, but equally useful. Consider its application in solving what might otherwise be a time-consuming problem. Suppose you are in charge of a large single-elimination tennis tournament, and you are about to buy the tennis balls. A total of 175 people have entered the tournament, and for each match played the contestants will be given three tennis balls to use. How many balls should you order? The following is a method tournament directors frequently use:

Map out the draw sheet, which would have to include 256 first round slots (single-elimination tournaments must be constructed on a format that begins with two to some exponential power, so they will eventually come down to a final match between two people). Insert 81 byes (automatic advances to the next round) in the first round, to occupy the spaces not taken by the 175 players (175 + 81 = 256). Count the number of actual matches that would be played in the first, second, third, fourth, fifth, sixth, seventh, and eighth rounds. Add up the total number of matches to be played, multiply by three. This is the number of balls needed for the tournament.

All of this can be greatly simplified by applying the observation that this involves behavior occurring in pairs. In a tennis match, one person wins and the other loses. Only one person wins the tournament, so 174 will have to lose. Each match that someone loses requires three balls, so you need to order (174X3) tennis balls.

This same understanding is applied in situations such as tollbooths on bridges and ski lifts. Recent reports say the Oakland Bay Bridge connecting San Francisco and Oakland carries 40 million toll-paying vehicles annually on five east-bound and five west-bound lanes of traffic.[1] Traffic is slowed to pay a toll only as it heads from Oakland to San Francisco, where drivers converge on a 20-booth toll plaza. Driving from San Francisco to Oakland is toll-free. The reasoning is paired phenomena: the vast majority of the bridge's users will cross the bridge twice—once coming and once going—and can be charged for both uses at the same time. Ski lifts are more foolproof. The resort provides one with two services, transportation up the mountain (ski lift), and also maintaining ski slopes on which to ski down the mountain. It is apparent that to ski down the mountain, one must go up the mountain. Therefore, the resort need only charge patrons one time (at the bottom) to have them pay for both of their services.

Paired phenomena can be removed farther from the obvious and may also be valuable in understanding social science at a more advanced level. Suppose you buy what you think is a pair of shoes you've really been wanting. They cost $150.

From your point of view, you lose $150 and gain one pair of shoes. From the store's point of view, they lose one pair of shoes and gain $150. Of that $150, perhaps $90 was the wholesale price of the shoes that the store paid, $40 went to the store's payment of rent, wages, electricity, and other expenses, and $20 was earnings.

That $90 wholesale price could be traced back to the manufacturer, where it went to wages, rent, electricity, and so forth. The amount spent on electricity at the store and at the manufacturer could be traced to the power plants, where it went to wages, fuel, interest on the generating plant, dividends, taxes, and so on.

When everything is traced to its ultimate conclusion, the earnings deriving from the $150 you originally spent on your shoes, inclusive of income and profits and payroll taxes, will add up to a total of $150. It is an accounting equality or identity, a paired phenomena result that cannot be avoided.

Examples such as the shoes are elementary paired relationships that exist in the area of macroeconomics called national income accounting. These relationships are that output = income = spending. $150 of spending must produce $150 of income. The numbers have to add up to the numbers that there are. This is "inescapable mathematics."

Paired phenomena can provide rational, quick answers for what might appear to be difficult or time-consuming problems in social decision-making. Consider the following question a social policy may want answered in anticipating future conditions. Assume the following approximations of U.S. society to be correct, as they once were, and the marriages are being defined as traditional monogamous male-female marriages:

a) Average life expectancies of women, 77; of men, 71.
b) Women begin to marry at age 17.
c) Men begin to marry at age 21.
d) One-fifth of men are unmarried.
d) Population is stable.

Given these conditions, what is the ratio of women to men who are eligible for marriage?

Married women are eligible to marry for an average of 60 years while men are eligible to marry for 50 years. That creates an eligible population with a ratio of women to men of 6:5. If one-fifth of the men are unmarried, four-fifths are married. In the 6:5 ratio, four of the men's five are married. By paired phenomenon this also means four of the women's six are married. So one in five of the men and two in six of the women are not. This gives the answer to the question of the ratio of unmarried women to unmarried men: 1/3 of the women to 1/5 of the men.

The counterintuitive nature of paired phenomenon is seen in the following problem: You have a glass of water and a glass of milk. You take a tablespoonful from the glass of milk and pour it into the glass of water and stir it. You then take a tablespoonful of the liquid in the second glass (water with some milk in it) and pour it in the first glass. Which now has the greater quantity, milk in the water glass or water in the milk glass?

It seems obvious at first thought and often after repeated consideration that by adding a tablespoon of pure milk to one glass then returning a diluted mixture of water and milk from the other, there can be no doubt that there is more milk in the water glass than water in the milk class. It is just common sense.

It appears to be common sense, but it is not the answer. The amounts are equal and once again it is a matter of paired phenomenon. It is not known exactly how the milk was stirred in to dilute the water and it does not matter. Whatever portion of the returned spoonful is water, the remainder is milk, and the milk left behind must occupy the same volume as the water returned. It could not be otherwise without changing the volumes of the two containers, which is not done by exchanging a tablespoon back and forth.

Either/Or

A related phenomenon is that certain things occur in situations with only two options. A flipped coin can only turn up heads or tails. It is as probable (unless the sides are weighted unequally) that a flip will come up heads as tails. The fact that you might flip a coin five times and it landed heads every time has no affect on the probability of what the result will be on the next toss. The probability is still 50–50. The notion that past results will influence future ones in this sort of situation is sometimes called the "gambler's fallacy."

Keeping in mind that previous results do not alter probability can sometimes simplify more complicated problems. In many Asian cultures importance is still placed on having a male child, and the male population in fact outnumbers the female population in every age group until the superior female life span comes into play. A seemingly reasonable explanation for this, given the nearly 50–50 probability involved, is the "stopping" rule.

According to this explanation, if a male child is first born, a couple stops, and has no more children. If a girl is first born, the couple has a second, hoping for a boy. This means that there will be many families with one child only—a boy, and many families with two children—a girl followed by a boy. Since there are many single sons, but few single daughters, and many families with one boy and one girl, boys will outnumber girls.

However reasonable this may appear, the unalterable fact is that the probability of having a boy or a girl remains equal at every round of childbirth. Therefore, it is meaningless whether a couple stops after having a firstborn son or not. Half the first round of babies will be of each sex. For those who have a second child, half of that group will be of each sex. For those who have a third child, half of that group will be of each sex, and so on. The explanation for male children outnumbering females must lie elsewhere.

This same sort of either-or logic is exploited in a stock market investment scam adapted from a description in John Paulos' *Innumeracy*.[2] Suppose you were an avid investor in the stock market and you received a glossy brochure from a company that claimed to have achieved a scientific breakthrough in determining the direction shares will go. They said they could name stocks and tell you whether to invest or sell with absolute certainty. The brochure had pictures of serious looking men and women in lab coats, and a bank of computers in the background and a prediction for the following week that a lesser-known stock will go up in value.

In fact, the prediction turned out to be correct. Your first reaction would likely be that this was nothing special. Perhaps it was just a lucky guess. The next week you received a second prediction for a stock that would go up. This turns out to be correct again. You are becoming mildly interested. You receive a third prediction the following week, which advised immediate sale of what they had tipped the first week, because it was going to drop in value by the end of the week. Once again they turned out to be right. You are definitely interested; as this is taking place during an unpredictable market and the shares you own have been inconsistent in their values recently. Prediction number four also is correct. This can no longer be luck. Prediction five comes with a suggested stock to buy, and you are ready to base an investment on it. It turns out to be a good decision, as it is right again. The sixth prediction is again correct—thank goodness you invested heavily.

The seventh letter from the company arrives, but this time it contains no prediction. It says that the company has obviously clearly demonstrated what it is capable of doing. It will be happy to provide you with the company's analysis of what a certain investment will go in the following week, but the predictions will now cost $500 apiece. That seems like a small price to pay for a "sure thing." You send in your money.

The scam is this: It is an either or situation. Stocks can go up or down in value. The average value of stocks, as indicated by the Dow-Jones average, also goes up or down. The probability of it remaining exactly unchanged is minute.

The "company" sends out 32,000 letters originally, half of which predict the value will go up, and the other half of which predict the value will go down. Of these, 16,000 will be correct, and 16,000 will be incorrect. The second week letters are sent to the 16,000 who received accurate predictions the first week, again with half of the letters predicting "up," and half predicting "down." Of these, 8,000 will be correct. This process is repeated six times, which will leave 500 people with continuously correct predictions, even though predictions have never actually been made. This may well be an impressive enough appearance to get 500 subscribers. Even then there will be 250 correct predictions for the following week, leading to 250 more payments for the upcoming prediction.

Positions in a Distribution

Another musical chairs observation concerns positions in distributions. Ten percent of the people are in the tallest 10 percent of the population. One-third of the seniors in high school are in the top one-third of their class, according to academic ranking. One-fourth of the members of a bowling league are the best 25 percent of the bowlers. These are all statements that hold true regardless of changes in the individuals who comprise the populations being discussed. If all those bowlers who were the best 25 percent of the bowlers in the league decided to quit, one-fourth of the bowlers in the league will still be the best 25 percent. The individuals who remained in the league will have their individual positions in the distribution elevated, but the statement about the league will be unchanged. You cannot eliminate the top 25 percent by eliminating the top 25 percent.

Humorist Garrison Keillor bases many of his stories in the fictional Minnesota town of Lake Woebegon, where "all the children are above average." And if one were to conduct a survey of adults, asking them whether or not they are better than average drivers, it would be likely there would be a similar result—most would probably say they are. But not all can be better than average. If there is a test in class, some students will do better than average and others will do worse, unless everyone receives the same score.

If all participants want to attain a certain position in a situation involving a distribution, it may end up unraveling the entire situation. Suppose a project is given in a class that will determine final grades for that course. The project is to be done by groups of three students, all of whom will receive the same grade. Everyone is assigned to a group of three, but not required to remain in that group. In this case, if all social pressures are eliminated, it is likely that nearly all of the class members would prefer to be in a group in which they rank in the lowest two-thirds. In other words, most people would like to have someone in their group who knows more than they do about the subject. This would also be true of those who were initially the top students in their groups. Everyone would be trying to avoid being the best student in his or her group, as the others might bring the group grade down. As in the prior examples, one-third of the students have to be in the top one-third. Everyone cannot end up in the bottom two thirds. The entire situation would be likely to eventually result with the top three students in one group, the next three in another, and so on.

When analyzing the changing positions of individual items on a distribution, it should be noted that certain seemingly independent phenomena are in fact unavoidable by-products of related phenomena. For example, consider this 1955 newspaper headline:

> "LUNG CANCER UP FROM FIFTH TO THIRD LEADING CAUSE OF DEATH IN PAST DECADE; RESEARCHERS SEEKING EXPLANATION FOR THE DISEASE'S ALARMING INCREASE."

This headline makes the seeming logical assumption that since lung cancer has changed positions dramatically on the distribution of causes of death; the incidence of the disease is increasing rapidly. However, if all that is know is that lung cancer has become the third leading cause of death, one does not know whether there has actually been any increase in the occurrence of the disease at all. All deaths (100%) have causes, so an increase in the percentage of deaths caused by one thing may merely be a reflection of a decline in the percentage of deaths caused by other things. If the incidence of fatal cases of cancer were to remain constant, but the incidence of other fatal ailments (polio, yellow fever, tuberculosis, typhoid, etc.) declined, the percent of the population dying from cancer would be increasing. Taking this one step farther, if the incidence of cancer were declining, but at a slower rate than the average of other causes of death, the very misleading result would be that cancer would appear to be on the increase, because it would account for an increasing percentage of deaths.

Acceleration Principle

Another mathematical certainty that holds true in the aggregate regardless of individual choices is the acceleration principle. The acceleration principle describes the relationship between independent activities when one is the source of the other's growth. It provides an insight into requirements needed to increase the rate of production that may not otherwise be obvious. More specifically, it analyzes the rate of increase of the rate of production, rather than just the increase in the rate of production alone. The faster the rate of change in the rate of producing something, the greater the proportional increases required in the changes of the factors of production.

Suppose the long Iraq-Afghanistan actions have ended and U.S. soldiers have all come home. It remains an uncertain world, and an army is maintained that has two million active duty soldiers who are enlisted for a period of two years. Assume that these enlistments are evenly spread out (each six months a batch of soldiers is discharged and an equal sized batch is added), and basic and advanced training takes a total of six months. That means there are .5 million in training and 1.5 million trained soldiers. Assume also that there are currently 45,000 troop trainers. These people are also in the army for a period of two years, but only spend two months being trained to teach a specialty. The turnover rate for this group is two thousand per month. In other words, two thousand of them are discharged each month, and two thousand more are taken in. Since their training requires two months, four thousand are being trained at any one time.

Suddenly a new and very threatening crisis breaks out that looks likely to require commitment of ground forces in large numbers. The future is very uncertain. A decision is made to double the size of the trained army within six months. To double the number of soldiers within six months, requires having to increase the number of new recruits by what multiple? How many new recruits are needed immediately?

Problems are immediate—what about the number of trainers that need to be taken into the army immediately? The two-month course for trainers is housed in facilities that are adequate for the current four thousand recruits it has been handling up to the present. How many trainers are now needed right away? What multiple is this of the current situation? Can you anticipate any major problems here (assume that the new recruits in the regular army can spend their first two months in general physical training)?

It would work out to needing four times the number of draftees or enlistees and four times the number of trainers, all of them immediately. Eight thousand trainers would be trained for two months while two million do basic physical training. At this starting point .5 million soldiers would have been discharged. After their own training the trainers then have the remaining four months with the new two million men inducted or volunteered into service to complete their advanced training, at which point, another .5 million would have completed their tours and would be discharged. There had been 1.5 million trained soldiers originally, but now in six months four million would have been taken in and one million released, so the army would have doubled to three million in size in six months.

The key variables in acceleration are the increase in the level of some stock or population, the speed at which that increase is to occur, and the rate of turnover to which that growth rate is added.

Schelling noted the complexities of acceleration as more variables are involved when he discussed the housing industry. He wrote, "Housing construction is important, and not only because it happens to replenish and add to the stock of housing. It is what a lot of people do for a living. It draws on industries like cement and lumber, paint and plumbing; and it is important to the people who sell automobiles and baseball tickets to the people who make a living by building houses. But housing is durable stuff. . . . For the stock of housing to grow by an extra 2½ percent per year, the construction industry must expand instantly by nearly 100 percent."[3]

Nelson Mandela's failed housing plans for South Africa illustrate the importance of awareness the relationship involved in the acceleration principal. Francisca Kellet reported, "He promised one million houses by 1999, but by the time he left office, Mandela's administration had built only 40,000 houses."[4] Schelling stated that to achieve a 2½ percent growth in housing stock requires an expansion in the construction industry of nearly 100 percent. It is unlikely this disproportionate change necessary in the rate of increase in production and total stock of product produced, and the interdependency involved in the growth of construction industry and growth of housing was clearly understood in South Africa, and Mandela was destined to disappoint his followers.

The behavior presented in this chapter differs from most of what is presented in the book, while still dealing with interactive behavior and its outcomes. Most chapters look at ways to attempt to predict the logical implications of behavior choices people make when those choices will affect the behavior choices made by others. In this chapter that has not been the case. The behavior patterns presented—paired behavior, either-or, positions in distributions, and acceleration—are fixed by inescapable mathematical certainty.

While "musical chairs" is a metaphor for situations determined by mathematical certainty, this chapter at times illustrates a Schelling approach to public policy over the years, which has been to view problems as puzzles. It was his love of puzzles and the relationship he could see between puzzles and economics that first drew him to the study of the discipline. When the greatest puzzle of all became survival in a nuclear age he became a nuclear strategist.

Supplement: Political Mathematical Puzzles

The following article is by John Allen Paulos, professor of mathematics at Temple University, and originally appeared in his ABC column. Dr. Paulos is best known as a writer and appears as a guest on radio and television frequently. Among his five books are *Innumeracy*, which was on the *New York Times* bestseller list for five months, and *A Mathematician Reads the Newspaper*, which reached number one on the Amazon.com order list and was adapted into a four-part series by the BBC. His many appearances on varied television programs, including *David Letterman*, *Larry King*, *McNeil Lehrer*, and the *Today Show*, have made him unusually well known for an academic, as has his monthly column, "Who's Counting," which he writes for ABC News.com.

The American Association for the Advancement of Science named Paulos recipient of the 2003 AAAS Award for Public Understanding of Science and Technology in recognition of his being "one of the greatest mathematical storytellers of all time."

Politicians, Liars, and Mathematical Puzzles

by John Allen Paulos

Many recent bestselling books have titles stating directly or indirectly that politicians and political partisans in general are flat-out liars; they fabricate, spin, deceive, and prevaricate.

On the left these books include Al Franken's *Lies and the Lying Liars Who Tell Them*, Joe Conason's *Big Lies: The Right-Wing Propaganda Machine and How It Distorts the Truth*, Eric Alterman's *What Liberal Media? The Truth about Bias and the News*. The latter do battle with Ann Coulter's *Slander: Liberal Lies About the American Right*, Dick Morris' *Off with Their Heads: Traitors, Crooks & Obstructionists in American Politics, Media & Business*, and Bernard Goldberg's *Bias: A CBS Insider Exposes How the Media Distort the News on the Right*.

These book scuffles bring to mind three tricky puzzles having to do with lies and lying, which, although not very realistic, lead to some important ideas in logic, probability, and number theory.

The Three Puzzles

1. The first sort of puzzle was made popular by the logician Raymond Smullyan and it concerns, if I may adapt it for my purposes here, a very unusual state, each of whose politicians either always tells the truth or always lies. One of these politicians is standing at a fork in the road and you wish to know which of the two roads leads to the state capital. The politician's public relations person will allow him to answer only one question, however. Not knowing which of the two types of politician he is, you try to phrase your question carefully to determine the correct road to take. What question should you ask him?

2. The politicians in a different state are a bit more nuanced. Each of them tells the truth 1/4th of the time, lying at random 3/4th of the time. Alice, one of these very dishonest politicians, makes a statement. The probability that it is true is, by assumption, 1/4. Then Bob, another very dishonest politician, backs her up, saying Alice's statement is true. Given that Bob supports it, what is the probability that Alice's statement is true now?

3. In a third unusual state, there is another type of politician. This type lies at times, but then becomes conscience-stricken and makes it a point never to tell two lies in succession. Note that there are 2 possible single statements such a politician can make. They may be denoted simply as T and F, "T" standing for a true statement and "F" for a false one. There are 3 possible sequences of 2 statements, no 2 consecutive ones of which are false—TT, TF, and FT—and there are 5 sequences in which to make 3 such statements—TTT, FTT, TFT, TTF, and FTF. How many different sequences of 10 statements, no 2 consecutive ones of which are false, may a politician in this state utter?

The Three Solutions

The following are more than hints, but less than full explanations. For full understanding, time and a quiet corner may be necessary.

1. You could ask him, "Is it the case that you are a truth-teller if and only if the left road leads to the capital?" Another question that would work is, "If I were to ask you if the left road leads to the capital, would you say Yes?" The virtue of these questions is that both truth-tellers and liars give the same true answer to them, albeit for different reasons.

2. First we ask how probable it is that Alice utters a true statement and Bob makes a true statement of support. Since they both tell the truth 1/4 of the time, these events will both turn out to be true 1/16 of the time (1/4 x 1/4). Now we ask how probable it is that Bob will make a statement of support. Since Bob will utter his support when either both he and Alice tell the truth or when they both lie, the probability of this is 10/16 (1/4 x 1/4 + 3/4 x 3/4). Thus the probability that Alice is telling the truth given that Bob supports her is 1/10 (the ratio of 1/16 to 10/16). The moral: Confirmation of a very dishonest person's unreliable statement by another very dishonest person makes the statement even less reliable.

3. Consider all possible sequences of 10 statements, no 2 consecutive ones of which are false. Some of these sequences end with a T and some with an F. There are exactly as many 10-element sequences ending in T as there are 9-element sequences of T's and F's, since any sequence of either of these types can be turned into one of the other type by adding or subtracting a T at the end. Furthermore, there are as many 10-element sequences ending in F as there are 8-element sequences of T's and F's, since any sequence of either of these types can be turned into one of the other type by adding or subtracting a TF at the end.

Putting these two facts together shows us that there are just as many 10-element sequences of T's and F's as there are 8-element sequences and 9-element sequences put together. In particular, there are as many 3-element sequences as there are 2-element and 1-element sequences combined, as many 4-element sequences as there are 3-element and 2-element sequences combined, as many 5-element sequences as there are 4-element and 3-element sequences combined, and so on. But this is the definition of the famous Fibonacci sequence, each of whose terms after the second is the sum of its two predecessors. So the answer to the question is that there are 144 possible 10-element sequences of T's and F's having no 2 consecutive F's. Note that the "Fib" in "Fibonacci" acquires a new resonance.

Maybe to the polemical books listed above I should add Lying Politicians and the Convoluted Mathematical Truths They Reveal.[5]

Notes

1. "Bridge Facts," San Francisco—Oakland Bay Bridge, http://bata.mtc.ca.gov/bridges/sf-oak-bay.htm.
2. John A Paulos, *Innumeracy* (New York: Hill & Wang, 1988).

3. Thomas C. Schelling, *Micromotives and Macrobehavior* (New York: Norton, 1978), 62.
4. Francisca Kellett, "What Became of 'Mandela's Houses'?" *New African,* May 1, 2002.
5. Included with permission from Dr. Paulos. Taken from an e-mail to Robert Dodge, November 9, 2009.

THE PRISONER'S DILEMMA, COMPETITION, AND COOPERATION

CHAPTER 12

The Prisoner's Dilemma

The Prisoner's Dilemma is the best-known game in game theory and a model with wide-ranging applications. It has become a generic phrase for the competition between individual self-interest and group motivation, but the game represents a direct challenge to basic assumptions of classical market economics. Adam Smith taught that through pure competition "the invisible hand" of the marketplace would guide the factors of supply and demand so that goods and services were produced most efficiently at the lowest price. The Prisoner's Dilemma questions whether that is necessarily the case. Examples of the Prisoner's Dilemma can be seen in social interaction of all kinds. In this seemingly simple game, players have two choices: to cooperate, or not. In game theory, the term used for choosing to not cooperate is "defect."

Cooperating involves trust, and this makes the game complex. The Prisoner's Dilemma was first developed in 1950 at the RAND Corporation. John Nash had made an important discovery related to non-zero-sum games, those games where player's interests are not in complete opposition. Now known as the Nash equilibrium (Chapter 20), it involves proof of the existence of equilibrium points in every game. These equilibrium points are outcomes where the players have no incentive to change their decision.

Merrill Flood and Melvin Dresher developed a game to see whether people who had no knowledge of equilibrium points would tend to select these outcomes when they played a game. Armen Alchian of UCLA and John D. Williams of RAND played a game with each other repeatedly, using a simple two-by-two matrix where each could choose to cooperate or defect (Table 12.1).

The game is shown in Table 12.1.

This game has only one Nash equilibrium, or supposedly rational outcome where neither player would change his decision. It is the lower left quadrant. In each of the other quadrants either row or column or both could improve his outcome by changing his choice. The lower left is the stable equilibrium that Nash said always exists, which should be the solution to the non-zero-sum, two-person game. It is a simple and obvious solution, because both players have dominant strategies to follow. However, the upper right quadrant has better payoffs for both players and is the best collective outcome. Was the Nash equilibrium the rational solution to the game?

Table 12.1

		Williams	
		Strategy 1 (defect)	Strategy 2 (cooperate)
Strategy 1 (cooperate)		2	1
	−1		1/2
Alchian		1/2	−1
Strategy 2 (defect)	0		1

This simple game raised the question of whether it was always in a player's best interest to "act rationally" in game theory or rational choice terms. It set out in simple form the contrast between individual and group rational choice. Acting rationally, in game theory terms, means making the decision that would maximize one's personal utility. The simple two-by-two game being played at RAND demonstrated that acting in a manner that was strategically planned to maximize individual results could actually lead to poor individual results. That is, that "acting rationally" was not necessarily the truly rational choice, even based on maximizing individual outcomes. It appeared that when both players were attempting to maximize their personal outcomes, the rational thing for the two sides to do would be to cooperate. Though that might lead to better results, the game seemed to show that with rational actors, cooperation would not happen, and the best results would not occur. This obviously would be significant in a decision that had serious real world implications.

A Princeton mathematician who was once one of Nash's teachers, Albert Tucker, was visiting RAND when Flood and Dresher's experiment involving Alchian and Williams was taking place. Tucker had been invited to give a talk at Stanford University on game theory. He thought that the game in this experiment had broad applications that would interest his audience, but they lacked the background to understand the game theory. For that reason he came up with a story to capture the idea of the interaction and the problems it presented. The story he invented was the "prisoner's dilemma." Tucker's story has been retold often and a typical version is:

> Two men are arrested and put in prison because the police are sure they have committed a crime together, which they have, in fact, done. The two are placed in solitary confinement with no means of communicating with each other. The police are aware they do not have enough evidence to convict the two of the crime for which they were arrested. They can, however, successfully prosecute both on some lesser charge,

such as illegal possession of firearms, which carries a one year sentence. The only way to convict them of the more serious crime is for the men to testify against each other, so each prisoner is individually offered a deal: If he cooperates with the police and his partner fails to cooperate (defects), he will go free and his partner will get three years in prison. Each is told that the same deal is being offered to both, and if they both testify against each other, they both will be sentenced to two-year terms. Each prisoner is concerned only with his own welfare, which is minimizing his time in jail.

A prisoner could think, "Let's not testify, either of us. That way, we both get off with the light, one-year sentence for illegal weapons possession. We can't communicate, but my partner in crime probably has figured out we shouldn't testify. It's obvious. But if my partner has figured it out, and isn't going to testify, why not testify against him? That way I would be out free, while he goes to jail for three years. That's his problem. But wait . . . he is probably thinking the same thing. There's no way to know. Now what? And if we both testify against each other . . ." Now what? It is a dilemma. Each wants to do what is best for himself.

This has remained the standard telling of the story, but imaginative versions of this strategic game have been presented, such as the story in William Poundstone's *Prisoner's Dilemma*.[1] A summary of Poundstone's dramatic variation on the story is:

You stole the Hope Diamond and plan to sell to that malevolent and dangerous "Mr. Big" for a case full of $100 bills. He wants to exchange the money for the diamond in a deserted field. You are aware of Mr. Big's reputation and suspect that if you agree to the deserted field meeting, you will never return. Mr. Big will walk away with your diamond and his money, leaving you murdered in the secluded location.

You come up with a plan of your own that seems much safer. Why not two fields? He could hide the money in a field in North Dakota, and you could hide the diamond in a field in South Dakota. Once you had both done your hiding, you could call each other from public phone booths and exchange directions on how to find each other's hidden goods. He agrees to the idea.

Once you get to the field in South Dakota to hide the diamond an idea comes to you. What if I just keep the diamond? I could just wait here for him to give me my directions and I could give him his directions as though everything was going according to plan. Mr. Big wouldn't know anything had happened until he got to South Dakota. By then I would be in North Dakota. I could grab the money and get on a plane for Rio.

Then another thought comes to you: He must be thinking the same thing.[2]

The basic matrix for a prisoner's dilemma is shown in Table 12.2:

Table 12.2

		PLAYER A	
		Cooperate	Defect
		3	4
	Cooperate		
		3	1
PLAYER B		1	2
	Defect		
		4	2

This matrix represents the utility rankings for many situations. Assume you collect coins and you see one that you would like to buy offered for sale on an Internet site (not eBay). You make contact with the seller, who gives you an address to which you should send a check for $50. He says he will also send you the coin. You are in different countries, and the transaction is arranged only through this personal contact; there is no business address or company involved. Should you send the check? Should the other person send the coin? Both players have dominant strategies, which are "defect," so the game ends in the lower right quadrant. Many kinds of purchases are made on mutual trust of payment and delivery. While it is easy to see that both gain by cooperating, if you expect the other to cooperate, you gain more yet by defecting. This is the essence of the Prisoner's Dilemma, that it describes any situation where people benefit by cooperating but have the temptation of self-interest to defect both to get greater gain and to prevent being exploited.

Game theory is grounded on the foundation of the rational actor, one who acts in enlightened self-interest. The Prisoner's Dilemma demonstrates that in game theory terms, decisions that are rational from the point of view of an individual and decisions that are rational from the point of view of a group may diverge. This two-by-two game is the simplest possible illustration, but the commons (Chapter 15) and free-riders games[3] are multiperson versions of the same conflict between individual and group rational choice.

In the coin sale example you could both cooperate, and if you did the payoff would be what is sometimes referred to as the "trust" payoff in the upper left cell. If you sent your check and the other kept his coin, he would end up with both, which would be his highest outcome. Some analysts (e.g., Sugden) would refer to his payoff as the "nasty" payoff and yours as the "sucker" payoff. Those outcomes would be reversed if he sent the coin but you never wrote the check.

The sequence of values from worst to best for each player is:

1) Cooperate while the other player chooses to defect, the "sucker" payoff.
2) Defect while the other player chooses to defect.
3) Cooperate while the other player chooses to cooperate, the "trust" payoff.
4) Defect while the other player chooses to cooperate, the "nasty" payoff."

Prisoner's dilemmas can be found frequently on all levels, from personal interaction to the world stage. The decision by a professional athlete to take performance-enhancing drugs, such as steroids, can be a prisoner's dilemma. An athlete's choice is to take the drugs or not take the drugs. If he does, and others do not, he is likely to be more successful than his natural abilities warrant. If he does not, and others do, he is likely to be at an unfair disadvantage. If no one takes the drugs, or if everyone takes them, competition will be fair. Taking the drugs has side effects that are harmful to health, but that is a trade-off many obviously are willing to accept.

The Tour de France is a grueling three-week cycling race conducted in twenty single-day stages with each day's winner recognized. It covers a course of between two thousand and three thousand miles, mainly in France with excursions into Belgium, Italy, Germany, and Spain. It illustrates the Prisoner's Dilemma in sports, with cooperation throughout the day followed by defection as the finish line approaches as was reported in *Evening Hérault*:

> Take two riders in the middle of this afternoon's stage of the Tour de France from Marseilles to La Grande-Motte. They are way ahead of the peloton [the main group of riders]. The two lads are from different teams, and are competing against each other.
>
> Yet here they are, working together by taking turns to share the tough load of the front position—where there's no peloton, no team-mates, no shelter from the wind. In the prisoner's dilemma game, this is called "mutual cooperation".
>
> If they cooperate, they both win (for the moment). But if neither of them makes an effort to stay ahead ("mutual defection"), they'll be knackered and the peloton will soon catch up [once the two riders near the finish it is competition to the end]. [4]

Sometimes countries provide subsidies to producers of goods they hope to export to give themselves a competitive advantage in the international market, which can force other countries to do the same or take some other action in response or lose sales. The United States and China have differing views on what constitutes "fair trading practices." Each would like to see the other allow a completely unrestricted flow of its exports. However, both like to keep a measure of legal or procedural barriers to the importing of the other's products. Both are stuck in an inefficient equilibrium, in that neither is willing to unilaterally eliminate trade barriers, and allow cooperation. If both sides were forced to make their less preferred (but more efficient) choice, the consumers for both countries would receive cheaper products, but industries in each would be forced out of the market. In competition between individual firms there are decisions about making larger investments in advertising that can create a prisoner's dilemma for producers of the same product. If one company advertises more or lowers prices must its competitors follow suit? Prisoner's dilemmas are common in situations when airlines and automobile manufacturers get into promotion wars. Such aggressive competition may be good for the consumer, but carried to its extreme, does nothing good for either competitor.

During times of perceived danger from potential health threats, such as the avian flu scare and the anthrax fright that followed the discovery of several letters containing the substance in the mail in 2001, there were anxious people vying for vaccines and stockpiling antibiotics in a prisoner's dilemma that led to hoarding.[5]

On more familiar levels a couple might agree to work together on making arrangements for an upcoming vacation trip and when the day arrives to meet with the travel agent one calls at the last minute and defects, saying, "I'm too busy now, so you go ahead and make the plans on your own." Students often do their homework assignment and compare answers the following morning to see whether they agree. The morning comes and one says to the other, "I didn't have time to do mine. I'll just copy yours." Defection has taken place. Children agree to exchange toys but, as the game is played at an early age, one holds on to the toy he was to give away while taking the other. It is another example of cooperation paired with defection.

Does one tip less in an out-of-town restaurant, knowing he will never return? Does one cooperate by waiting his turn in a long freeway line, or defect by making a dash along the road's shoulder? When someone sneaks onto a bus, hops over the turnstile to get onto a train or a subway, or even watches public television without contributing, he is playing a form of the Prisoner's Dilemma. It is an n-person game with one person playing against a second player that is a group. This subset of the Prisoner's Dilemma is called the "free-rider dilemma," with the free rider defecting in the game with all who pay their share for the use of the systems. His "nasty payoff" is the free ride or the free television. It is being paid for by all of those "suckers" who did not defect. Their costs are greater because of him and others like him.

In the commercial arena, it is the fear of defection (in these cases called "default") that has led to the requirement of collateral on loans and payments of deposits for the delivery of goods or services. Those are safeguards against "sucker payoffs" of zero. In legal disputes the Prisoner's Dilemma has been significant in leading to cases rarely going to trial and commonly being settled in the United States by plea bargains.[6] A *Stanford Law Review* article that discussed the evolution of plea bargaining in America mentioned a nineteenth-century Massachusetts law that had made it legal for criminal defendants to testify at their own trials, commenting, "It ended up creating quite literal prisoners' dilemmas for defendants, especially for those who had a rap sheet."[7] In many countries plea bargains are not allowed, and the awareness of the Prisoner's Dilemma has been a contributing factor. Some feel plea bargains can impair fair outcomes. It can be seen that there are often situations where it is in the interest of each of those considered as suspects to confess and testify against the other, regardless of their guilt or innocence. In a case where only one of two suspects is guilty, the innocent one is unlikely to confess, while the guilty one is motivated to confess and testify against the other.

Whether it is competitors conducting business, couples negotiating understandings, or anxious citizens vying for flu vaccines, situations can often be illustrated as prisoner's dilemmas. The parties involved will often be better off collectively if each resists the temptation to go it alone and instead trusts or cooperates with the other person. Both parties' pursuing their own interests often leads to a worse outcome than do loyalty and cooperation.

As a model, the Prisoner's Dilemma has never had greater significance than during the arms race of the Cold War, and Schelling was a part of recognizing it and working to discover ways to demonstrate the wisdom in the "trust" payoff. In the fall of 1957, when Sputnik went up, Schelling's focus changed. As Paul Samuelson, first American winner of the Nobel Prize in Economics said, "Once the vital game of survival in a nuclear age challenged Schelling's attention, mere economics could no longer contain him."[8] He was back at RAND, then on to Harvard, and was soon the leading nuclear strategist of the time. A RAND document states, he "established the basic conceptual structure of deterrence theory. In fact, one could go farther. Schelling's ideas are at the heart of the complex, counterintuitive logic of mutually assured destruction, which has underpinned American nuclear and arms-control strategy for four decades."[9]

The year after Schelling moved to Harvard, 1959, John Kennedy was elected president. It was the most dangerous time in history, and at no time has the Prisoner's Dilemma been of greater consequence. This little-known strategist helped the world survive. Today there is great concern because North Korea has tested a nuclear device and Iran appears to be working on one. When Schelling became involved in nuclear strategy the United States was producing an average of seventy nuclear weapons per day. America's nuclear arsenal reached a high point in explosive power of 40 trillion pounds of TNT in the early 1960s. A pound of TNT would bring down a plane, and the United States had over thirteen thousand pounds of TNT for every man, woman, and child on the face of the earth. The Soviets had larger bombs but not quite as many and would catch and eventually surpass U.S. output.[10] As Einstein had observed at the beginning of the nuclear arms race, "annihilation of any life on earth has been brought within the range of technical possibilities."[11]

Schelling's struggle against the constant defection by each side in the prisoner's dilemma of the nuclear arms race was a testament to his ability to think strategically and to his understanding of how to deal with the dichotomy of individual rationality being at conflict with group rationality. It could all be reduced to a simple two-by-two matrix, and that was seen at RAND. Of Schelling's many contributions, perhaps his greatest success came with his arms control efforts and work to overcome the prisoner's dilemma that had locked the United States and the Soviets in an arms race for so long. Cold War fear had been so great that even though the "rational" thing to do seemed to be to cooperate, rational players would not do so out of fear of being exploited. So both the United States and the Soviets sought to gain superiority in arms when cooperation in reducing the expenditures would have been mutually advantageous. He worked to show that the efficient outcome for both sides, and one that could be monitored, was for neither to continue to try to gain superiority. Schelling's efforts and ideas, according to Al Carnesale, who was on the U.S. negotiations team for the Strategic Arms Limitation Treaty (SALT I) and the ABM Treaty, contributed greatly to the success of both treaties.[12]

The prisoner's dilemma that was the arms race led both the Soviet Union and the United States to continually defect and try to achieve military superiority. Schelling's idea to halting the defection was to find common ground in his "if and only if" approach. With satellite observation reducing secrecy in development, and expenses draining budgets, the sides could agree that they would introduce new weapons or delivery systems "if and only if" the other side did. This articulated limits that both sides were willing to accept and thus generated statements as to whether or not they would go ahead with further development. Reduction soon followed.

"Prisoner's dilemma" is one of the few terms from game theory and strategic studies to have entered general usage. A sampling of news items from around the world demonstrates the widespread use of the term and several of the stories further clarify the importance of the concept.

A December 2008 article in the *Bulletin of the Atomic Scientists* described the contest for control of oil prices that involves OPEC and has been partially driven by the growth of the Chinese and Indian economies, saying, "Most readers will recognize this situation as the classic 'Prisoner's Dilemma' in which the group is better off when each individual is worse off than he could be." The article continues, "This time imagine that you have three accomplices who are all waiting in their own interrogation rooms. Furthermore, imagine that your accomplices are Libyan leader Muammar Qaddafi, Venezuelan President Hugo Chavez, and Iranian President Mahmoud Ahmadinejad. Now that's a dilemma. Can you really trust those individuals to choose against their individual interests and sacrifice for the good of the group?"[13]

An article discussing competition among nations in setting their exchange rates for currency in the *Korea Times* opened by stating, "An increasing number of experts point out that the currency war involving the world's economic powerhouses is developing into a prisoner 's dilemma scenario."[14]

When there was threat the government would shut down unless compromise was reached in the spring of 2011 *Slate* reported, "There is no point in compromising before the very last second. President Obama has to promise not to sign a one-week measure, because he can't look like he's caving – liberals had their fill of that when he signed the tax cut deal last December. House Speaker John Boehner has to repeat, again and again, and again, that he's trying to get the 'biggest cuts' he can and will accept no deal that lacks the support of 218 Republicans. As the White House says no deal, it sets up meetings—there's another one with Boehner Wednesday night. As Republicans say no deal, they take meetings and revisit one-week stopgaps. In the prisoner's dilemma playing out now, it's important that everyone act as obstinate and offended and inflexible as he or she possibly can."[15] The Prisoner's Dilemma is now widely recognized as a general metaphor for self-interest harming the common good. Whether the reference is appropriately applied or the general population understands its use are different questions.[16]

Notes

1. William Poundstone, *Prisoner's Dilemma* (New York: Doubleday, 1992). Poundstone's book remains a popular introduction to game theory ideas but is also to a considerable degree a biography of John von Neumann.
2. Ibid, 103–105.
3. For an interesting study on how the free-rider problem is often overcome and what effects that has on the general group, see Peregrine Schwartz-Shea and Randy T. Simmons, "The Layered Prisoners' Dilemma: Ingroup versus Macro-Efficiency," *Public Choice*, Vol. 65, No. 1 (April 1990), 61–83.
4. "The 'Prisoner's Dilemma' in Cycling," *Evening Hérault*, June 7, 2009, http://irishherault.wordpress.com/.
5. See Jane Gross, "A Nation Challenged: The Doctors; Doctors Face Threat, and Fear, of Anthrax," *New York Times*, October 17, 2001, B1.
6. Jacqueline E. Ross, "The Entrenched Position of Plea Bargaining in United States Legal Practice," *American Journal of Comparative Law.* Vol. 54 (fall 2006), 717–732.
7. Reviewed works: Jennifer L. Mnookin, *Uncertain Bargains: The Rise of Plea Bargaining in America*, George Fisher, *Plea Bargaining's Triumph: A History of Plea Bargaining in America*, *Stanford Law Review* (April 2005), 1729.
8. Paul Samuelson, letter to Richard Zeckhauser, 1989. Copy given to Robert Dodge by Richard Zeckhauser.
9. David Jardini, "Commemoration of 50th of Project RAND" (diss., Carnegie Mellon University), 1996. Also see online at www.rand.org/publications/PAFbook.pdf.
10. Statistics involving the U.S. nuclear program over the years are available online at http://www.cdi.org/nuclear/facts-at-a-glance.cfm.
11. Albert Einstein, "Arms Can Bring No Security," *Bulletin of the Atomic Scientists,* Vol. 6, No. 3 (March 1950), 71.
12. Carnesale was a guest speaker for a course, International Relations, at John F. Kennedy School of Government in spring of 1990, when he made this comment. Carnesale reaffirmed Schelling's importance to theory of negotiations behind successful efforts during a telephone interview with Robert Dodge on July 28, 2000.
13. Kurt Zenz House, "OPEC and the Prisoner's Dilemma," *Bulletin of the Atomic Scientists* online (December 16, 2008), http:www. Thebulletin.org/web-edition/columnists/kurt-zenz-house/opec-and-the-prisoners-dilemma.

14. Kim Tae-gyu, "Korea Times: Seoul Hopes 'COEX Accord' to Bring Peace to Currency War," *Korea Times*, October 15, 2010.

15. David Weigel, "The Fleshy Part of the Budget," *Slate*, April 7, 2011.[16] For a memorable introductory experience with the Prisoner's Dilemma that requires four participants, try "Win as Much As You Can." Google gives over 400 million hits for the title, so it is common, but select one with a single tally sheet for choosing x or y and scoring, such as media.wiley.com/assets/manual/sample_download.pdf.

CHAPTER 13

Cooperation

The University of Michigan professor Robert Axelrod, foreseeing a lasting break-through in relations between the Russians and the Americans, wrote, "Once the US and the USSR know that they will be dealing with each other indefinitely, the necessary preconditions for cooperation will exist.... The foundation of cooperation is not really trust, but the durability of the relationship."[1]

It is clear that if the Prisoner's Dilemma is a one-time event, the rational strategy is mutual defection with a resulting low utility payoff. The question is different when one is likely to encounter the same opponent multiple times, and each player can consider what effect of his defection will have on the next encounter. Repeated, or iterated play of the Prisoner's Dilemma may lead some to consider the idea of cooperation, but the temptation of defection and its higher payoff is always luring players to seek more.

The arms race was a prisoner's dilemma that embodied the variation of the game that is exactly what Axelrod envisioned in noting the importance of engaging with the same opponent over time to reach the understanding that cooperation yields the best net outcome. The United States and U.S.S.R. knew that they would be dealing with each other for the long run—in effect repeating the game over and over again. In the area of arms control this ongoing engagement provided the possibility of knowing whether or not the other side was going ahead with development. This, in turn, permitted an agreement to slow development or halt testing, for example, if, and only if, the other side did the same. As well, it brought the gradual discovery over time that cooperation could result in spite of each individual country's self-interest.

Examples of cooperation emerging in situations that involved choices between cooperation and defection have been noted in a wide range of areas from armed combat to animal behavior. One now famous example is a story from the trenches of World War I, brought to public attention in July 2001 with the death of Bertie Felstead at 106. The *New York Times* noted Felstead's passing as the death of the last known survivor of the British battalion that on Christmas, 1915, near a small village west of Lille in France heard "All Through the Night" being sung one hundred yards away in the German trenches. Felstead's unit was soon singing "Good King Wenceslas." On Christmas Day shouts of "Hello Tommy, Hello Fritz," were exchanged, then a group of Germans left their trenches and started walking, heading for the British trenches. Many British emerged and went out to meet them. They exchanged cigars and cigarettes and communicated in sign language, French, English, and German, and they sheltered one another from the cold. A ball was brought out and a soccer game began in "no man's land" between the trenches. Nobody kept score; it was more just kicking the ball around with up to fifty on a side. After about a half hour a very upset major appeared and ordered the British soldiers back to their positions. Wounded the following year at the Battle of the Somme, Felstead commented later in his life, "the Germans were all right. There wouldn't have been a war if it had been left to the public."[2]

The story of the Christmas truce and soccer game had been familiar for some time, but awareness that such incidents were part of a pattern did not receive great attention until Robert Axelrod's *The Evolution of Cooperation*.[3] The book includes a case study that was a part of his focus on repeated play of the Prisoner's Dilemma and what the long-term outcomes of such repeated play was likely to be. To test what will happen and what strategies will survive in an iterated Prisoner's Dilemma environment, Axelrod conducted tournaments that would not have been a realistic possibility before computer assistance was available. These are likely the best-known Prisoner's Dilemma experiments ever conducted, and the findings were reported in 1984 in *The Evolution of Cooperation*. The first sentence of the book posed the key question: "Under what conditions will cooperation emerge in a world of egoists without central authority?"

The First Tournament

Axelrod set up a tournament and repeated it. In the first tournament there were fifteen entrants that included mathematicians, political scientists, sociologists, psychologists, and game theorists who submitted computer programs for strategies for playing the Prisoner's Dilemma. Each strategy was to play against every other strategy, including itself, in a round robin consisting of two hundred repeated games against each opponent. There was a system of payoffs for making the choice to cooperate or defect. The scoring was zero for one who cooperates while the other defects, one point for both players defecting, three points for mutual cooperation, and the big payoff, five for one who defects while the other cooperates. In the tournament one there were 240,000 choices that led to 120,000 moves. The strategies varied considerably in complexity, with some being long formulas that related to past performances by opponents or unpredictable, random defection at the maximum rate. Anatol Rapoport of the University of Toronto submitted the simplest of the fifteen programs, which also turned out to be the winner. His program started with cooperation, then did whatever the other player had done its the previous move. His strategy was called "Tit-for-Tat."

The Second Tournament

Axelrod ran a second tournament on a larger scale. All the entrants were aware that Tit-for-Tat won the first tournament. In the second tournament there were sixty-two entrants from six different countries, including people from the same five disciplines that were represented in the first contest but also evolutionary biologists, physicists, computer scientists, and computer hobbyists. All but one entrant submitted programs that were attempts to improve on Tit-for-Tat, and there were sixty-three contest rules. One rule involved a change from the first contest format in which each competition consisted of two hundred repetitions of the game. This fixed number of games had led to complex systems of back-ward induction, since if there was a finite limit to a contest, cooperation may unravel, as the final game's strategy would be to defect. Knowing your opponent will defect on the final game made it strategic for you to defect on the second-to-last game. But knowing that you would defect on second-to-last game made it rational for your opponent to defect on the game before, and so on. In the second tournament a new rule was that there was a probability of .00346 that games would end with each move, making the expected median length of games played two hundred moves, eliminating attempting backward induction for defection from the final stages of a contest. The actual average game turned out to be 151 moves.[4]

Among the many strategies were those that defected continually after an opponent defected, programs with probabilities for defection against other player based on their previous play, programs that used different strategies on odd numbers. Rapoport resubmitted his simple program, and once again, it won. The simple reciprocity of Tit-for-Tat succeeded without doing better than anyone with whom it interacted. It succeeded by eliciting cooperation from others, not by defeating them.

> Rapoport wrote of his winning program, "The interesting feature of this result was the fact that Tit-for-tat did not 'beat' a single pro-gramme against which it was pitted. In fact, it cannot beat any pro-gramme, since the only way to get a higher score than the co-player is to play more *D's* (defects) than he, and this, by definition, Tit-for-tat cannot do. It can only either tie or lose, to be sure by no more than one play. It follows that Tit-for tat obtained the highest score, because other programmes, presumably designed to beat their opponents, reduced each other's scores when pitted against each other, including themselves. The results of these contests can be interpreted as further evidence of the deficiency of strategies to maximize one's individual gains in situations where both cooperative and competitive strategies are possible."[5]

How Cooperation Takes Hold and Difficulties

Axelrod's book discussed Thomas Hobbes and his 1651 foundation work on government, *The Leviathan*, which presented a view of the state of nature in which man's life was famously described as being, "solitary, poor, nasty, brutish and short." Hobbes viewed the natural state of human relations as chaotic, and that the social contract necessary for a functioning society was that individuals would give up considerable freedom of choice and action to a strong central leader or authority in exchange for that authority imposing order on society. It is a way of overcoming the inefficient outcomes of prisoners' dilemmas that occur in many forms of social interaction, where allowing individuals to follow their own self-interest is counterproductive, so imposing cooperation by authority may have better results, whether or not one agrees philosophically with the loss of individual choice.

The results of Prisoner's Dilemma interaction in Axelrod's tournaments suggest an alternative to authority-imposed cooperation. They indicate that if there is a sufficient chance parties will interact again in the future and the parties are aware of it, cooperation is likely to emerge without the necessity of the imposition of enforced restrictions by an outside authority. Tit-for-Tat won the tournaments for a variety of reasons—all of which contribute to its simplicity and clarity. Tit-for-Tat avoids unnecessary conflict by cooperating, it is a "nice" strategy, never defecting first. It is not easily taken advantage of because it responds immediately when it is provoked in the face of uncalled for defection by defecting in return. It does not seek to punish, but forgives its opponent after it has responded to being provoked by a defection. Its clarity allows the other player to adapt to its pattern of play.

A critical point noted by Axelrod is that the future casts a shadow back on the present. He wrote, "The evolution of cooperation requires that individuals have a sufficiently large chance to meet again so they have a stake in their future interaction."[6] Knowing they will likely meet again affects players' current strategic actions. This is a form of "look forward and reason backward" thinking, where if they anticipate a single encounter defection is rational, but if future encounters are foreseen mutual defections can echo back and forth. "Thus a single defection may be successful when analyzed for its direct effects, and perhaps even when its secondary effects are taken into account. But the real cost may be in tertiary effects when one's own isolated defection turns into unending mutual recriminations."[7]

This danger in echoing is seen in situations where parties became locked into mutual defection. One could consider Palestine and Israel, where Israel raids are "in response" to Palestinian rocket attacks, which are "in response" to Israeli targeted attacks, and on and on. Axelrod wrote that a problem with Tit-for-Tat responding as it's opponent's last move, "is that once a feud gets started, it can continue indefinitely. Indeed, many feuds seem to have this property. For example, "in Albania and in the Middle East, a feud between families sometimes goes on for decades as one family's offense is repaid by another's and each retaliation is the start of the next cycle. The injuries can echo back and forth until the original violation is lost in the distant past."[8] Breaking these cycles can require other strategies, such as, "make the long-term incentive for mutual cooperation greater than the short-term incentive for defection...Large changes in the payoff structure can transform the interaction so that it is no longer even a Prisoner's Dilemma,"[9] or "A community using strategies based upon reciprocity can actually police itself. By guaranteeing the punishment of any individual who tries to be less than cooperative, the deviant strategy is made unprofitable."[10]

Knowing that going for the high payoff of a single defection can echo back and forth to mutual bad results down the line can cause players to restrain themselves before initiating the self-interest decision. That affects strategic choice and can lead to the "nice" strategies, those that are never first to defect, eventually being adopted by more and more players; and these strategies can protect themselves from clusters of other strategies as well as from individuals using "nasty" strategies. The strategies that survive in the long run in iterated play experiments are nice, provocable, and somewhat forgiving.

Robustness

The robustness of a strategy, whether competitive or cooperative is determined by whether it can protect itself from invasion by uncooperative strategies once it gets established by a small cluster of individuals. Tit-for-Tat is a robust strategy. It does well in a wide variety of environments and survives against a wide variety of strategies. It refuses to be bullied by responding immediately to defections, but does not do any bullying of its own.

As to analyzing the robustness of cooperative strategies and how they can protect themselves, Axelrod writes, "Evolutionary biology provides a useful way to think about this problem. Imagine there are a very large number of animals of single species, which interact with each other quite often. Suppose the interaction takes the form of a Prisoner's Dilemma: when two animals meet, they can cooperate with each other, not cooperate with each other, or one could exploit the other. Suppose further that each animal can recognize individuals it has already interacted with and remember salient aspects of their interactions such as whether the other usually cooperated."[11] He then interprets the average payoff from different strategies—ranging from aggressive, or "nasty," to random to cooperative that were included in his second tournament—that an individual receives as proportional to the number of offspring that individual is likely to produce. The new figures form the numbers for another generation of the game, which will again produce new numbers of offspring for the next generation of the game. As generations pass, the less successful of the original 63 strategies become more scarce or become extinct, while the more successful strategies compete more often. By the 500th generation, eleven strategies made up 96 percent of the population, and by the 1000th generation Tit-for-Tat accounted for the highest total, 14.5 percent of the total population, and also had the fastest growth rate at .05 percent per generation.[12]

However, the Prisoner's Dilemma, as it is played in myriad real-life situations, is not always identical to the simple, abstract game. The reality of the Prisoner's Dilemma is that the payoffs need not be comparable. For example, if someone in the government is thinking of leaking an inside story in hopes of having some policy presented favorably, he becomes a player who is ready to defect, and a journalist seeking the inside story before it is made available through channels to the press corps is another player. Getting the "scoop," the inside story, is a big payoff for the reporter, while getting the story out is also a big payoff for the government bureaucrat, but any of a number of reporters would do equally well. The two player's payoffs may not be identical, or symmetrical. There also are elements left out of the abstract game of Prisoner's Dilemma that may be present in reality, such as oral communication, the influence of third parties, implementing the choice that is made, and at times, uncertainty as to the other player's previous move.

Noise

"Noise" is another factor in the real world of Prisoner's Dilemma play. Noise is a reference to random errors in implementing choices players make. An example of such an error is discussed by Axelrod and Jianzhong Wu:

> An important feature of interactions in the real world is that choices cannot be implemented without error. Because the other player does not necessarily know whether a given action is an error or a deliberate choice, a single error can lead to significant complications. For example, on September 1, 1983, a South Korean airliner mistakenly flew over the Soviet Union. It was shot down by the Soviets, killing all 269 people on board. The Americans and Soviets echoed their anger at each other in a short, but sharp escalation of cold war tensions.
>
> The effects of error have been treated under the rubric of "noise." The best way to cope with noise has become a vital research question in game theory, especially in the context of the iterated prisoner's dilemma. Clearly when noise is introduced, some unintended defections will occur. This can undercut the effectiveness of simple reciprocating strategies."[13]

Introducing the noise factor into iterated Prisoner's Dilemma games has left Axelrod confident in his original belief that Tit-for-Tat is the road to cooperation. He now favors an even more generous Tit-for-Tat to accommodate noise.[14] He has proposed a modification to Tit-for-Tat called "contrite Tit-for-Tat" that has three stages, contrite, content, and provoked. It begins with content and becomes provoked if it is the victim of a unilateral defection, then it defects until the other player cooperates, when it returns to content. If it was content and became the defector (this is the accommodation for noise) it becomes contrite, and cooperates. It becomes content only after successfully cooperating. This only corrects one's own errors but can quickly restore mutual cooperation.[15]

Tit-for-Tat has had critics among game theorists,[16] but Axelrod remains convinced of the correctness of the importance of the findings of his experiments. He says:

> The only "flaw" that I see in TFT after 30 years is that it doesn't take into account "noise" (e.g. failure to detect correctly what the other side did, or failure to implement what you intended to do). I touched on this on pages 186–87 of EC (*The Evolution of Cooperation*), but didn't give it the exposition or emphasis it deserved. I came back to this issue, and resolved it to my satisfaction in a JCR (*Journal of Conflict Resolution*) 1996 paper.
>
> In short, a little generosity or contrition solves the problems of dealing with moderate amounts of noise. So I now recommend "generous TFT." I do not see (lack of) "end game awareness" as a flaw. As I say a dozen times, TFT (and its cousins) are suitable for games with long shadows of the future. That rules out end game awareness. I wouldn't recommend TFT if both sides know that the game will end in one move (of course), or even two moves (by backward induction). But as you see from Tournament 1, even when the submitters had common knowledge that it would end in 200 moves, only a few strategies took advantage of this knowledge—presumably because everyone thought (correctly) that no one was going to do backward induction over 200 moves (as Luce and Raiffa propose).
>
> In any case, I ran Tournament Two without a known ending, which avoids this wrinkle. I did this because I believe most of the real life examples of iterated PD do not have a known ending (at least not until one is very close to that ending e.g. the Cold War).
>
> In sum, one weakness of TFT is easily remedied (and I only regret that I didn't see this clearly enough when writing the book), and the other "weakness" is not a problem in situations with a long shadow of the future (which are the only ones I recommend TFT for anyway).[17]

Cooperation Examples

One example Axelrod gives of cooperation evolving is the arrangement Ron Luciano, a Major League Baseball umpire in the American League from 1968 to

1980, had with some catchers. When Luciano was having a "bad day" he would have catchers he trusted hold the ball in their glove if the pitcher had thrown a strike and throw it right back to the pitcher if the pitch had been a ball. Then he would make his call. The catchers and Luciano knew they would be dealing with each other repeatedly in the future and the catchers knew Luciano would have the opportunity to retaliate if he found he had been taken advantage of, so the system worked with the catchers he trusted.[18]

Cooperation has evolved in the animal kingdom. Symbiosis is an extension of reciprocity to biology, such as fig wasps' beneficial encounters with fig trees, and ants' relations with acacias. A striking animal example of cooperative behavior was reported in 1990 involving vampire bats. Vampire bats will starve if they go sixty bloodless hours, as without blood they are unable to maintain their body temperature. Altruistic sharing exists in the vampire bat community. If a bat has less than twenty-four hours remaining to survive without blood, other bats will give the bat blood and get nothing in return. The chances are that the donor bats will find themselves in the same situation in the future or have in the past and will be beneficiaries of other vampire bats providing them with blood in their time of need.[19]

Rapoport, the Tit-for Tat creator, sums up the significance of cooperation evolving from the Prisoner's Dilemma, saying, "Prisoner's Dilemma and its generalization, the Tragedy of the Commons, provide rigorous rationale for Kant's Categorical Imperative: act in the way you wish others to act."[20]

Supplement

Case Study: Evolution of Cooperation in World War I

The following case study is summarized from Robert Axelrod's *The Evolution of Cooperation*. The foreword to Axelrod's book was written by Richard Dawkins of Oxford, and begins with the line, "This is a book of optimism." The horrors of life in the trenches in World War I are known through such works as *All Quiet on the Western Front*,[21] but Tony Ashworth's research sheds a new light on the early conditions. The players he analyzed were typically battalions of one thousand men, with half in the front line. The first stage of the war had been highly mobile and bloody, but once the lines stagnated, spontaneous nonaggression occurred in many spots. Prisoner's dilemmas existed in small units that faced each other in immobile sectors.

To Allied headquarters the situation on the trenches called for a strategy of attrition. It was a zero sum game. To units, in the short run it appeared that the wise idea was to weaken the opponent to promote the possibility of survival if a major battle were to be ordered in the area.

Locally, where the same units were facing each other over an extended time there was a change in the strategic game from a single-move prisoner's dilemma, where defection was dominant, to an iterated game, where a stable outcome based on reciprocity began to emerge. Individuals could be simultaneously facing one, two, or three of the enemy regularly on the other side, so there were small units of prisoner's dilemmas.

Cooperation began emerging in the trenches in France and Belgium as early as November 1914. By Christmas, there was "extensive fraternization, a practice which headquarters frowned upon." In one area between 8:00 to 9:00 a.m. became reserved for troops to conduct "private business," and there were places in areas that had flags to mark places regarded as out of bounds by the snipers of both sides.

Direct truces were occasionally arranged by shouts of signals. Another way restraint sometimes got started was bad weather. As the study reports, "Often ad hoc weather truces emerged in which the troops simply did not shoot at each other. When the weather improved, the pattern of mutual restraint sometimes simply continued."[22]

The key factor was that if one side practiced restraint, the other might reciprocate. The sides demonstrated their ability to retaliate during periods of mutual restraint. German snipers would put on shows of how accurate they were by aiming at spots on the walls of cottages that the British and French troops could see. The artillery would also join at times and fire on something in the area to do great damage without threatening enemy soldiers as a warning of what they could be doing if violations of truce took place. The "evening gun" in one spot was fired every evening by the British at 7:00 in the same direction. In another sector the Germans had a predictable artillery pattern.

The truces were restraint, not weakness. Defection would be self-defeating. When defection occurred the response was more than Tit-for-Tat. Records indicate a response at a two-to-one or three-to-one ration was common, and "There was probably some inherent damping process that usually prevented these retaliations from leading to an uncontrolled echo of mutual recriminations."[23]

What destroyed live-and-let-live most of all was the tactic of raids on enemy trenches by anywhere from ten to two hundred troops. The soldiers were ordered to kill or capture, and there was no way to conceal what took place. The values of the prisoner's dilemma were altered, and ethics and revenge entered as major factors. Ethics and revenge dealt with care about other soldiers, duty, especially concern for fallen comrades and victims of required strikes. The soldiers' preference had been to cooperate rather than to compete, but the concern for fallen comrades and desire for revenge changed that. Their preferences were switched, and they no longer were interested in cooperating with those who had killed their companions. Changed preferences affected the outcomes and behavior, from cooperation to mutual defection, but in response to the tactic of forced change in behavior, the raids, that had affected preferences. The early war truces became a thing of the past.[24]

Notes

1. Robert Axelrod, "The Evolution of Cooperation," http://wwwee.stanford.edu/~hellman/ Breakthrough/reflections/reflections.htm.
2. Richard Goldstein, "Bertie Felstead, 106, Soldier Who Joined a Timeout in War," *New York Times*, July 30, 2001.
3. Robert Axelrod, *The Evolution of Cooperation* (Cambridge MA: Basic Books, 1984, revised, 2006).
4. Robert Axelrod, "More Effective Choice in the Prisoner's Dilemma," *Journal of Conflict Resolution* Vol. 24, No. 3 (September 1980), 383.
5. Anatol Rapoport, "Prisoner's Dilemma," in John Eatwell, Murry Milgate, Peter Newman, eds. *The New Palgrave Game Theory* (New York: Norton, 1989), 202.
6. Axelrod, *The Evolution of Cooperation*, 20.
7. Ibid., 38.
8. Ibid.
9. Ibid., 78.
10. Ibid., 134.
11. Axelrod, "More Effective Choice in the Prisoner's Dilemma," 398.
12. Ibid, 400–401.
13. Robert Axelrod and Wu Jianzhong, "How to Cope with Noise in the Iterated Prisoner's Dilemma," *Journal of Conflict Resolution* Vol.39, No.1 (March 1995), 183–184.
14. Robert Axelrod, e-mail to Robert Dodge, September 22, 2008.
15. Axelrod and Wu, "How to Cope with Noise in the Iterated Prisoner's Dilemma," 188.
16. See Avinash Dixit and Barry Nalebuff, *Thinking Strategically* (New York: Norton, 1991), on Tit-for-Tat, 108.
17. Robert Axelrod, e-mail to Robert Dodge, September 22, 2008.
18. Axelrod, *The Evolution of Cooperation*, 178.
19. William Booth, "Zoology: Vampire Bats Do unto Others," *Washington Post*, February 26, 1990.
20. Rapoport, "Prisoner's Dilemma," 204.
21. Erich Remarque, *All Quiet on the Western Front* (London: Little, Brown, 1929).
22. Axelrod, *The Evolution of Cooperation*, 78
23. Ibid. 80.
24. Case study included with Robert Axelrod's permission. From an e-mail to Robert Dodge, November 20, 2008.

CHAPTER 14

Coordination

In Britain and many former British colonies drivers keep to the left side of the road, while the United States follows the somewhat more common practice in which drivers keep to the right side of the road. About 34 percent of the world's drivers drive on the left side of the road while 66 percent drive on the right-hand side.[1] One might ask why this is so. The answer, at times, is offered in historical context and involves reigns and passing horses and ruts being deeper in roadways running away from quarries than those to them during the days of ancient Rome. Following the French Revolution it was ordered that the horse-drawn carriages that carried the elite through the crowded streets of Paris must pass on the right, while pedestrians pass on the left. The pre-Revolution custom had been the reverse, with the carriages on the left and the pedestrians on the right. Changing was symbolic of the new order established by the Revolution, and going on the left had been identified with privilege, while going on the right had been for the common man, so it was more "democratic," and appropriate that those with carriages embrace the sentiment.[2]

But the simple truth seems to be, people in most countries drive on the right-hand side of the road because everyone else drives on the right-hand side of the road. The converse is true in the third of the world where people drive on the left side of the road. That is, they do so because everyone else is doing so. This is a matter of convention, a generally agreed on way of doing things. People coordinate their behavior in a self-enforcing system, demonstrating that "orderly anarchy" is not a contradiction in terms. The machinery of state and rule of law are not always necessary to maintain social order. The idea of individuals governed by self-interest in a self-regulating market system, where the "invisible hand" of the institutions of the market promotes public interest, is no longer a view accepted by modern economists. Modern economists see the market as an imperfect system in need of varying degrees of government regulation and interference to limit the damage that can be done by individual actors in the market who have only their own interests in mind.

Schelling discusses self-enforcing conventions and how it is that things like one-way street signs need no enforcement by police. He believes that many rules, whether good or bad, are better than no rules at all, and conventions that help coerce orderly behavior are often very helpful. A simple example he uses to demonstrate this is when he asks how greatly many things in life would be complicated if we were to try getting along without alphabetical order. On the other hand, he concedes people can become trapped in self-enforcing rules that misdirect behavior, whether the rules are poorly designed one-way signs or traditions that separate men from women or whites from blacks, for example.

The inventor of traffic signals devised a brilliantly simple system of dividing all travelers into north-south and east-west, then reducing instructions on their behavior to a binary code of red and green lights. The lights, being incapable of granting favoritism, dispensed impartial justice, and order was established. There was no need for other enforcement once the system was established, as noncompliance carried its own hazards.

The traffic signal shows the essence of coordination, which is that people need to do the right thing at the right time relative to what others are doing. Schelling touts another great example of self-enforcing conventions: "The most ingenious piece of planning ever introduced into society may have been our common scheme for synchronizing clocks and calendars. I do not set my watch at zero every morning on arising and let it run through the day....I have a watch just like yours, one that I coordinate with everyone else's at remarkably little cost. And I know nobody who cheats."[3]

In his works analyzing conflict, Schelling discussed the impact of coordination extensively, writing in *The Strategy of Conflict*, "The coordination game probably lies behind the stability of institutions and traditions and perhaps the very phenomenon of leadership itself."[4] He found it related to focal points and tacit bargaining, bargaining done without words to find where boundaries will be drawn, when battles will end, the types of weapons that will be employed, the targets that will be considered out of bounds, and more. Gas was not used as a weapon in World War II on the voluntary basis of the parties knowing its use would be reciprocal. He says in disciplining children, business competitions, gang warfare, and limited war there is the phenomenon of thresholds. "They are conventional stopping places or dividing lines"[5] that are finite steps in enlargement of the conflict where tacit bargaining takes place, "This kind of conflict, whether war or just maneuvering for position, is a process of bargaining—of threats and demands, proposals and counter-proposals, of giving reassurances and making trades or concessions, signaling intent and communicating the limits of one's tolerance, of getting a reputation and giving lessons."[6] Schelling is well known for stressing the importance of signaling and tacit bargaining, and conducted war games in the 1960s to train government and military leaders to be more accurate in sending signals and interpreting the signals they received. Coordination was not possible without accurate signaling.

U.S. Secretary of Defense Robert McNamara sent his assistant, John McNaughton, to seek Schelling's advice in 1964 on whether an effective message could be sent to North Vietnam to stop infiltrating South Vietnam by initiating a short bombing campaign. While this has led to inaccurate claims[7] of Schelling being responsible for Operation Rolling Thunder, the massive bombing of North Vietnam, it indicates the regard held for Schelling's views on tacit communication. McNamara later noted this with the jest, "A story being circulated at Harvard during the 1960s was that a missed opportunity had occurred when Harvard failed to offer a scholarship to Ho Chi Minh, in order that he might have the opportunity to study with professor Schelling. If he had, according to the Cambridge pundits, he would have known that Washington was trying to send him a *signal* via the bombing. As it was, Ho and his colleagues, in their ignorance, thought the United States was trying to destroy their country."[8]

In his Nobel Prize speech, Schelling discussed what he considers to be a great achievement in coordination, the "taboo" that had been accepted internationally against the use of nuclear weapons and had for sixty years prevented their use in combat, though numerous opportunities had presented themselves to a number of countries.[9]

Schelling's view's on focal points and coordination proved basic to David K. Lewis, who wrote a fundamental work on convention, *Convention: A Philosophical Study*.[10] Lewis's acknowledgment says of Schelling, "it was he who supplied me with the making of an answer to Quine and White,"[11] in a reference to philosophers who had said language could not be considered in the framework of convention.

Also citing Schelling in making his case on coordination is Robert Sugden,[12] who discusses the development of coordination. Sugden argues that, contrary to the idea of Hobbes that strong rule is essential for order in society, if individuals live together in a state of anarchy, conventions or codes of conduct will evolve to reduce interpersonal conflict. The result would be what he calls "spontaneous order." Schelling presented Sugden's work in his course and added in his comments:

> Sugden's work is entirely deductive and is somewhat in the tradition of Western political philosophy. His own politics are somewhat libertarian, and he has an interest in demonstrating that government may not be essential to orderliness and cooperation, but his philosophical predilections do not get in the way of his theory. The readers should be aware of Sugden's political views as a Libertarian.[13]

Sugden makes no pretense about what he is doing, stating, "I shall investigate the extent to which people can coordinate their behavior—can maintain some sort of social order—without relying on the formal machinery of law and government."[14] Literal anarchy need not be equated with pejorative anarchy, as orderly systems of cooperation evolve without enforcement from authority.

Spontaneous order evolves with the establishment of conventions. A practice or policy has become a convention when everyone, or almost everyone, in a group follows a practice. Sugden puts it, "When we say a practice is a convention, we imply that at least part of the answer to the question 'Why does everyone do X?'

is 'Because everyone else does X.'"[15] More specifically a convention is a stable equilibrium in a situation that has two or more stable equilibria. It may be understood as a self-reinforcing rule. A self-reinforcing rule can be regarded as a convention only if a different rule could also have become self-enforcing, if it became established. The side of the road on which people travel is a perfect example—as either right or left could be chosen.

Sugden discussed how such conventions emerge, and he brought in Schelling and the questionnaire presented in Chapter 3 as one explanation. When there are two possibilities, and the people are playing the deductive reasoning of game theory, it can lead to an infinite regress of "he thinks that I think that he thinks that I think that…" on both sides. He reports that Schelling sent out his set of problems to forty-two people and on the question where they were asked to choose heads or tails, attempting to match what an unknown partner would choose who was trying to make a choice to match the person making the choice, thirty-six chose heads, or 86 percent correctly matched. On the question that instructed the participant to write any positive number that would match the number being written down by someone else, 40 percent chose one. The choices were not purely deductive and rational, but they were coordinated. Schelling's respondents also immediately converged on a meeting place in New York City, to a substantial degree. There was something Schelling explained as prominence about how people looked at choices and saw one as more conspicuous than others, whether by analogy, some sense of precedence, or some other factor that lent uniqueness to a choice. "Somehow they knew in advance which conventions were most likely to emerge. If people have some ability of this kind, even if imperfect, it may be very important in explaining how conventions first start to evolve—and hence which conventions establish themselves."[16]

To illustrate how conventions commonly emerge, Sugden developed a game called the crossroads game. In this game there are two drivers who are approaching a crossroads. Each has two choices: to slow down or to maintain current speed. In making it a game that looks at convention developments, several assumptions are necessary. The game involves a large community of drivers playing the game against each other repeatedly. All opponents are equally likely to meet. The game is anonymous, so the players do not remember each other as individuals.

The game can begin as symmetrical play, where player's payoff's are identical, illustrated in Table 14.1:

In the symmetrical crossroads game with the above payoffs, results are determined using mixed strategies, or randomization (Chapter 20). Equilibrium occurs when a player chooses "slow down" with a probability of p = 0. 8, or 80 percent of the time, where "slow down" and "maintain speed" both yield an expected utility of 0.4. The important point is in many cases (.8X.8, or 64 percent) both players both slow down, and in some (.2X.2 or 4 percent) they both speed up. That means the remaining 32 percent of the time one or the other would maintain speed while the other slowed down. In all cases where they do the same, the outcome is worse for both drivers than it would have been if one had given way to the other.

Table 14.1

| | | PLAYER A | |
		Slow Down	Maintain Speed
	Slow Down	0	2
PLAYER B			
	Maintain Speed	3	-10

If the community notices some asymmetry and looks at it as an asymmetrical game, things can turn out differently. The matrix for the asymmetrical game looks like this (Table 14.2):

Table 14.2

| | | B's Strategy (from left) | |
		Slow Down	Maintain Speed
	Slow Down	0 / 0	3 / 2
A's Strategy (from right)			
	Maintain Speed	2 / 3	-10 / -10

This has two stable equilibriums, each involving one player or the other slowing down while the other maintains speed. If the asymmetry originally came from drivers approaching the intersection from the right and drivers approaching from the left, one of the two will evolve as a convention that drivers from one side slow down while the others maintain speed. It will become self-enforcing and be a convention.

For a player to recognize asymmetry in a game requires an imaginative leap. For example, a driver must realize that his experiences at reaching crossroads could be grouped into two distinct classes of drivers, those approaching from the left and those approaching from the right, and realize this asymmetry might be significant. The question that arises is, what if only some players in the crossroads game recognize asymmetry, such as left-right? Sugden explains how the convention is still likely to evolve, by dividing players into those who can spot the asymmetry, whom he refers to as "smart" and those who do not see it, whom he rather callously labels as "dumb."

Another possibility is everyone recognizes some asymmetry in the game, such as drivers approaching from the left and drivers approaching from the right, larger vehicles and smaller, drivers on busier roads versus less used roads. With asymmetry one player may be called A and the other B. It is likely that not everyone will notice the same asymmetry, but Sugden argues that in the long run there is a tendency for the game to be played as though they do.

One or the other of the two possible conventions will establish itself among the players smart enough to recognize the asymmetry. As they adopt the convention, the "dumb" players will notice the change and gain the same benefits as the smart players. Communication is likely to speed up the process so that even if a "dumb" player does not understand the convention from his own experience, he will have plenty of people to explain things to him. There could be many asymmetries on which players might focus other than left and right, such as more important and less important roads, speeds of vehicles approaching crossroads, so the question becomes how one symmetry gets singled out. The group of drivers that will be most successful will be whichever is largest. As players become aware of more than two asymmetries they will be attracted to the convention followed by the largest number. Success breeds success, until in the long run there is a tendency for one convention to establish itself at the expense of the others.

Which convention evolves cannot be determined until a number of players, first, become aware they are playing an asymmetrical game and, then, focus on the same asymmetry. There must be some asymmetry in behavior or beliefs about behavior as alternative conventions in competition. Once one begins to evolve, everyone is attracted to it. If the asymmetry is embedded in the game itself, such as drivers on minor roads meeting those on major roads, the focus may come easily. The convention that evolves is not necessarily the one that is in the best interest of the community or the one that would yield the highest utility. It is just the one that gets adopted and noticed by enough people to be followed by others.

These conventions in society often are order established without the interference of political authority. Standardization of weights and measures, computer languages, rail widths for trains are all examples of conventions that have been successfully adopted. Forms of greeting are conventions, a piece of paper as money with the value to purchase goods and services is a convention, as are languages.

Sugden developed how conventions are a common part of everyday life and how there are cases where something between competition and imposed order that can exist and give society cohesion, though he never demonstrated that government was irrelevant. In his work he used as an example of one who failed to see this middle path, Kenneth Arrow. Arrow was described as a free market, self-interest defender who then switched to reliance on the necessity of government regulation. Sugden had the following to say about Arrow:

> Arrow is speaking for many fellow economists when he writes that the price system is "certainly one of the most remarkable social institutions" and the analysis of its workings is, in my judgment, one of the more significant intellectual achievements of mankind.... When Arrow writes about the economics of medical care, for example, he presents a long list of ways in which reality diverges from the ideal model for which, as a theoretician, he has such admiration; he concludes by remarking that a study of these divergences "force(s) us to recognize the incomplete description of reality supplied by the impersonal price system," and endorsing the "general social consensus ... that the laissez-faire solution for medicine is intolerable."[17]

Supplement

The Need for Government

All economists do not share Sugden's faith in the free market and his criticisms of Arrow's belief that the solutions for medical and other problems cannot be achieved without government interference. Paul Krugman wrote the following essay that appeared in the *New York Times* on July 25, 2009. Krugman has taught economics at Yale, MIT, Stanford, and Princeton and has written or edited twenty books. Since 1999 he has been a *New York Times* columnist and in 2008 was named Nobel Laureate in Economics.

Why Markets Can't Cure Health Care

Judging both from comments on this blog and from some of my mail, a significant number of Americans believe that the answer to our health care problems—indeed, the *only* answer—is to rely on the free market. Quite a few seem to believe that this view reflects the lessons of economic theory. Not so. One of the most influential economic papers of the postwar era was Kenneth Arrow's "Uncertainty and the welfare economics of health care," which demonstrated—decisively, I and many others believe—that health care can't be marketed like bread or TVs. Let me offer my own version of Arrow's argument.

There are two strongly distinctive aspects of health care. One is that you don't know when or whether you'll need care—but if you do, the care can be extremely expensive. The big bucks are in triple coronary bypass surgery, not routine visits to the doctor's office; and very, very few people can afford to pay major medical costs out of pocket.

This tells you right away that health care can't be sold like bread. It must be largely paid for by some kind of insurance. And this in turn means that someone other than the patient ends up making decisions about what to buy. Consumer choice is nonsense when it comes to health care. And you can't just trust insurance companies either—they're not in business for their health, or yours.

This problem is made worse by the fact that actually paying for your health care is a loss from an insurers' point of view—they actually refer to it as "medical costs." This means both that insurers try to deny as many claims as possible, and that they try to avoid covering people who are actually likely to need care. Both of these strategies use a lot of resources, which is why private insurance has much higher administrative costs than single-payer systems. And since there's a widespread sense that our fellow citizens should get the care we need—not everyone agrees, but most do—this means that private insurance basically spends a lot of money on socially destructive activities.

The second thing about health care is that it's complicated, and you can't rely on experience or comparison shopping. ("I hear they've got a real deal on stents over at St. Mary's!") That's why doctors are supposed to follow an ethical code, why we expect more from them than from bakers or grocery store owners.

You could rely on a health maintenance organization to make the hard choices and do the cost management, and to some extent we do. But HMOs have been highly limited in their ability to achieve cost-effectiveness because *people don't trust them*—they're profit-making institutions, and your treatment is their cost.

Between those two factors, health care just doesn't work as a standard market story.

All of this doesn't necessarily mean that socialized medicine, or even single-payer, is the only way to go. There are a number of successful health-care systems, at least as measured by pretty good care much cheaper than here, and they are quite different from each other. There are, however, no examples of successful health care based on the principles of the free market, for one simple reason: in health care, the free market just doesn't work. And people who say that the market is the answer are flying in the face of both theory and overwhelming evidence.[18]

Notes

1. "What percentage of the world drive on the left hand side of the road?" http:www. Brittany-internet.com/BrittanyNews/DrivingFrance/Drivingontheleft/tabid/841/Default.aspx.

2. H. Peyton Young, "The Economics of Convention," *Journal of Economic Perspectives* Vol.10, No.2 (spring 1996), 106.

3. Thomas C. Schelling, *Micromotives and Macrobehavior* (New York: Norton, 1978), 121.

4. Thomas C. Schelling, *The Strategy of Conflict* (Cambridge MA: Harvard University Press, 1960), 91.

5. Thomas C. Schelling, *Arms and Influence* (New Haven, CT: Yale University Press, 1966), 135.

6. Ibid.

7. See Fred Kaplan, "All Pain, No Gain: Nobel Laureate Thomas Schelling's Little-Known Role in the Vietnam War," *Slate* online, October 11, 2005, also Wikipedia: "John McNaughton (Government Official)," which includes a discussion of McNaughton's relationship with Schelling and states, "Together, they outlined a bombing strategy to intimidate North Vietnam in the spring of 1964, leading to the first phase of Operation Rolling Thunder." The fact is Schelling told McNaughton a short bombing campaign that McNamara proposed would not be successful, as the information of whether it was working would not be adequate and he made no proposal of any bombing campaign. He told McNaughton, "You should report that he couldn't accomplish what he wanted to accomplish in three months. That's what I would report." Shelling, interview by Robert Dodge, July 1, 2002. He made no recommendation of more extensive bombing, and that was clear to McNaughton.

8. Robert McNamara et al., *Argument without End: in Search of Answers to the Vietnam Tragedy* (New York: Public Affairs, 1999), 170.

9. Thomas Schelling, "An Astonishing Sixty Years: The Legacy of Hiroshima," Nobel Prize Lecture, Stockholm, Sweden, December 8, 2005.

10. David K. Lewis, *Convention: A Philosophical Study* (Cambridge, MA: Harvard University Press, 1969). New edition released by Wiley in 2002. Schelling especially recommends 5–8, 36–51, 53–80, 89–107.

11. Ibid., 3.

12. Robert Sugden, *The Economics of Rights, Cooperation, and Welfare* (Oxford: Blackwell, 1986).

13. Thomas Schelling, "Appendix to Seventh Reading Assignment," 1994, 102.

14. Sugden, *Economics of Rights, Cooperation, and Welfare*, 2.

15. Ibid., 32.

16. Ibid., 49.

17. Ibid., quoting Arrow from 1967, 1963, in passages.

18. Paul Krugman, e-mail to Robert Dodge, August 2, 2009. Used with permission.

INDIVIDUAL DECISIONS AND GROUP AGREEMENT

CHAPTER 15

Collective Choice and Voting

The common methods for collective choice involve voting. Voting brings to mind democratic decision-making, which is conventionally understood to mean reaching social decisions on the basis of majority rule. This understanding of voting and democracy is the basis of both classical liberal thought, as in Locke, and radical thought, in Rousseau,[1] and was the force behind the great democratic revolutions of the eighteenth century in the American colonies and France. As journalist and commentator Fareed Zakaria states, "We live in a democratic age. Over the last century the world has been shaped by one trend above all others—the rise of democracy. In 1900 not a single country had what we would today consider a democracy: a government in which every adult citizen could vote. Today 119 do, comprising 62 percent of all countries in the world."[2]

Voting is the common practice in meetings and organizations at all levels worldwide to arrive at collective choice. Votes are held to make choices in local and national elections; in the Security Council of the United Nations, where five members must vote in agreement; in board meetings of companies or charities, where there may be six to twelve people deciding policy; by text message for *American Idol*; by a show of hands in favor of an idea at school; and in a myriad other situations. Voting is a way of resolving controversies or reaching collective decisions that express a collective preference. It is a ritualized bargaining process, whether collectively agreed on by participants involved or imposed on them.

Voting in different circumstances follows different schemes, and the politics of contests between two parties may involve many familiar tactics, such as promises, threats, commitments, warnings. If more than two outcomes are possible, voting has the character of being a game in game theory terms. Strategic approaches may influence results when the game is played to one's advantage. An introductory problem from Schelling's course illustrates the importance of voting rules and the degree to which seemingly predictable rules can at times be manipulated by strategic action. Understanding how voting rules work can help in achieving decisions that reflect group collective will.

Introductory Problem

THE MOTION THAT PASSED

A fantastically wealthy company was owned and managed by thirteen share-holders who, owning one-thirteenth of the stock each, constituted the Board of Directors. According to the company's charter, the Board had full authority not only to govern the company, but to redistribute ownership shares and to determine Board membership.

All decisions of the Board were by simple majority vote. Voting was open, each member voting yes or no in his turn. The turns progressed clockwise around the table. No motion required a second. The voting on any motion started with the person to the left of the one who made the motion. The one who made the motion was recorded as voting yes on his own motion.

Among the provisions in the company's charter, one was unusual. It was designed to discourage constitutional change. "Constitutional change" was any change in the voting rules of the Board, and change in the membership of the Board, or any change in the ownership of shares in the company. It was based on the apprehension that a majority of the Board might gang up on a minority and pass a discriminatory law confiscating the minority's wealth or otherwise taking advantage of the unlimited power contained in the majority vote.

The rule was that if anyone offered a motion changing the voting rules, changing the ownership of shares, or changing Board membership and his motion failed, he would be deprived of his ownership rights and his membership on the Board, and his shares would be divided equally among the remaining members of the Board. Furthermore, anyone voting in favor of such a motion that failed would suffer the same fate as the one who made the motion, namely, lose his share in the company and lose his position on the Board.

This rule proved effective. Frivolous rule changes were never offered. In fact, no "constitutional" changes were ever proposed. It was so risky to vote yes and so safe to vote no, that no one dared offer even a compellingly attractive constitutional proposition, because it could always be voted down and possibly proposed later by someone else, after the first person's share had been divided among the rest of the Board and he himself had been removed.

At one of its meetings the Board went through the usual procedures for giving everybody the opportunity to make motions, and the final turn of the day fell to a member of the Board who surprised his colleagues by actually offering a drastic proposal for constitutional change.

The motion provided, in a somewhat devious way, for confiscating all of the shares of all of the other members of the Board, making the proponent sole owner of the company and sole member of the Board of Directors. The motion passed unanimously, and thereafter the former members of the Board, no longer having either wealth or the power to vote themselves any wealth, lived off such charity as their former colleague on the Board was willing, from time to time, to provide them.

What Exactly Was the Motion that Received Twelve "Yes" Votes? Schelling's Solution and Analysis

While this might sound like an impossible situation, the rules make it completely rational, as Professor Schelling explained: The motion provided that all the shares, together with the voting rights, of all the members of the Board be confiscated and then distributed as follows:

> If the number voting yes is exactly seven, the shares will be divided equally among all those who vote yes except that my own share goes in that case to the one who casts the seventh "yes" (who thus gets a double share), I and all who vote no thus being deprived of our shares and our membership on the Board.
>
> Otherwise, all the shares accrue to me together with sole membership on the Board, those who vote yes being eligible for modest charity at my expense, but not those who vote against the motion.
>
> The reason is that no one would cast a seventh vote of no on this motion.
>
> If there were already six no votes and six yes votes, the final voter gets two-sevenths of all the shares if he votes yes, and only one-seventh if he votes no. (If he votes no, the six who voted yes lose their shares, which are then divided equally among the seven voting no.)
>
> If there were six no votes and five yes votes, the twelfth voter knows that if he votes yes, so will the thirteenth voter, as we just saw. The twelfth voter then gets one-seventh of the assets and remains a member of the Board. If the twelfth voter votes no, the motion has lost and the thirteenth voter will also vote no, and each will receive one-eighth of the assets. The twelfth voter prefers one-seventh to one-eighth, that is, prefers out-voting six no votes and sharing in the proceeds with five yes. So the twelfth voter votes yes, making it six yes and six no, and the thirteenth makes himself the seventh yes.
>
> That being anticipated, the eleventh voter who faces six no votes and four yes votes knows that a yes gets him one-seventh of the assets, while a no will defeat the motion and be followed by a succession of no votes, with the exclusion of the four who voted yes, and the no voters getting one-ninth each. He prefers a seventh to a ninth, and votes yes. That being so, with three yes votes a no vote obtains only one-tenth compared with one-seventh; and so on back to six no votes and one yes vote. (Voting begins with one yes vote, the mover being counted as having voted in favor of his own motion.) Here again, the eighth voter can make it twelve to one against the motion or seven to six in favor, and he makes more money by voting yes.

The motion can't lose without a seventh no, so it will not lose. The first voter to the left of the man who made the motion may expect a unanimous vote of yes, in which case he doesn't care which way he votes. If he votes no, the motion will pass and his shares will be confiscated; if he votes yes, the motion will pass, probably unanimously, and his shares will be confiscated. Eligibility for charity will induce him to make it unanimous, and so on for the next voter.

This is merely *a* motion, not *the* motion, and if we keep trying we may find a variety of motions, simple and complicated, that create incentives that in turn generate strategies that lead to this unanimous surrender of wealth and power.

Note: As with most puzzles, this one is most easily approached by first working on a smaller or simpler variant. If you want to make it a three-man board the problem is simply to provide within the motion an incentive for the third person to vote yes if the second person should vote no.

Sincere and Strategic Voting

Schelling's problem demonstrates an extreme case of voting scheme exploitation, and more common ones will follow. What is perhaps best known from game theory is the influence of what is described as "sincere" and "strategic" voting. When people take others' votes into account and act in a way that will achieve their most desired attainable outcome, they are said to be engaging in "strategic voting." The alternative to this when there are more than two choices, is to vote strictly for one's preferred candidate, which is called "sincere voting." This seems straightforward, and often is when making a choice among several candidates for an elected office, but difficulty can arise in some cases in that unless an issue is formulated so that one has an absolute preference, one cannot vote in accordance with that preference. If a voter favors controlling inflation that will be appealed to on the local and national level, but just having that preference does not determine the candidate for whom one should vote, as all candidates are likely to voice similar concerns. If there are specific initiated measures of clearly spelled out approaches then sincere voting on the issue might be possible. The same is true of many other issues.

On the choice of presidential candidate, the differences between strategic and sincere voting choices can be of momentous consequence. In 1912, when former president Theodore Roosevelt failed to gain the Republican Party nomination, he formed his own party, the Progressives, nicknamed "The Bull Moose Party." He joined the contest against the Republican incumbent, William H. Taft, and the Democrat opponent, Woodrow Wilson. The two Republicans received more than a million votes more than their rival Democrat out of the fewer than fourteen million votes cast, the Democrat Wilson won 40 of the 48 states in the electoral college and began his first of two terms as president. He was not the choice of the majority, but sincere voting by divided Republicans put him in office.

Many would suggest the same was the case in the election of 2000 and the Green Party candidacy of Ralph Nader. Exit polls indicate that roughly 50 percent of those who voted for Nader preferred Al Gore to George W. Bush while only 20 percent preferred Bush to Gore, and 30 percent would not have bothered to vote if Nader were not a candidate.[3] If the Nader voters had voted strategically, realizing their candidate had no chance of winning the election, and cast their votes for one of the two candidates, Gore or Bush, who was going to emerge as the next president, the result would have changed. Gore would have won Florida, where Nader got almost 100,000 votes, about fifty times Bush's ultimate margin of victory in the deciding state, and he might also have won New Hampshire, where Nader received over 22,000 votes and Bush won by under 7,400.[4] A victory in either state for Gore would have made him president. The Nader voters were following "sincere voting" strategy and expressing preference while not attempting to gain their highest achievable outcome in the election. If those votes, given to a candidate with no chance of victory, had been divided between the candidates, one of whom was going to be the next president, there would have been no need for recounts and Gore would have been elected.

Sincere and strategic strategies may be illustrated in matrix form. Consider the following (Table 15.1):

Table 15.1

		PLAYER A	
		Column 1	Column 2
PLAYER B	Row 1	1 ... 2	4 ... 3
	Row 2	2 ... 4	3 ... 1

Player B chooses Row Two. Has this been a strategic or sincere choice? It is clear, if Player B considers the strategy Player A will adopt, that by choosing Row Two he has assured himself of his least desired outcome, in the lower right quadrant. But he expressed a preference for his most desired outcome, the one he has ranked as 4. This has been a sincere voting strategy, and its futility is apparent.

And the following (Table 15.2)

Table 15.2

		Player A	
		heads	tails
Player B	heads	2 / 4	3 / 3
	tails	4 / 2	1 / 1

In this case Player A chooses Column Two. Has he made a strategic or sincere decision? As can be seen, Player A's top choice is in Column One (lower left quadrant) but it is clear that if he makes a sincere choice for his preferred payoff, his actual payoff will be his third choice, valued at 2. Player B has a dominant strategy to choose Row One and Player A can achieve his second most highly desired outcome by playing strategically, so this would be strategic voting.

Secret Ballot

Presidential voting schemes have a certain symmetry, where all voters in each state have the same ballot and set of choices. This symmetry may not exist in elections if voting is not secret, or is alphabetical so that different information is available to different voters. If votes are counted but not named, so whom one voted for is not known, then only the number matters, which is the purpose of the secret ballot. Of course, the secret ballot is designed to prevent vote selling and coercion of individual voters, so they can vote for the candidate they truly favor. Schelling wrote, "In elections the secret ballot is mandatory, not as an optional privilege, so that no one can give evidence of how he voted and thus cannot be made to comply with a bribe or a threat."[5] However, this might not be true if there are side effects from voting where group rewards and punishment is involved, such as where housing improvements or school construction occurs first or how services get prioritized is based on voting patterns, even though no individuals can be identified for retribution for the way they voted.

A less discussed view on the ballot being secret is that it makes it difficult to market it as a commodity, since proving how it was exercised is difficult. That has not been sufficient to bring an end to bribery in elections. Tammany Hall ward boss George Plunkitt described that aspect in recalling his entrance into politics in New York, saying, "I had a cousin, a young man who didn't take any particular interest in politics. I went to him and I said: 'Tommy, I'm goin' to be a politician; can I count on you?' He said, 'Sure, George.' That's how I started in business. I got a marketable commodity—one vote. Then I went to the district leader and told him I could command two votes on election day, Tommy's and my own. He smiled on me and told me to go ahead."[6] Tammany is of the distant past, but vote buying is rampant in many developing countries and reports persist of its continuance in the United States.[9] Some statistics indicate the widespread practice of vote buying in influencing elections in more recent times: in 2002 about 7 percent of all voting aged adults in the Philippines were offered some form of payment for their vote in community level elections, and in 1999, 27 percent of the population surveyed in Taiwan's third-largest city admitted to accepting cash during past electoral campaigns. Of those who responded to a national survey in Cambodia, 40% said someone in their household had received a gift to vote for a particular party, while in Yerevan in Armenia, 75 percent reported in a random poll that a voting bribe had been offered to them, their relatives, or friends in the parliamentary elections of 2003. An estimated six million people were offered money for their votes in municipal elections in Brazil in 2000, while a national postelection survey following the 2000 election in Mexico found that about 15 percent of respondents received either a gift or assistance from one of the parties.[7] *The Economist* of London reported in 2008, "Whether Cambodia's general election on July 27th was a success or a travesty depends on what you compare it with.... There was widespread impersonation of voters, plus the usual vote-buying and glaring pro-government bias by broadcasters."[8]

   The secret ballot is desirable in situations where people are seeking public office, but not in situations where the voters are to represent us or be held accountable by us, such as public office holders or corporate officials who make the decisions where our wealth is being invested.

Characteristics Involved in Voting Systems

In U.S. presidential voting, although there are a number of candidates on the ballot, generally comes down to a choice between two. In many other kinds of voting there are a number of options to consider, and how the voting is done becomes especially important. In designing a voting system to achieve a result that reflects the will of the people involved, certain characteristics are critical. If several items are involved, the sequencing of voting must be considered. For example, if someone is against public housing and also against civil rights legislation, he might vote in favor of a civil rights amendment he despises being added to a bill on public housing, knowing that only with the amendment can the bill itself be defeated when it comes to a vote.

A second characteristic is whether voting is open or secret. A third is the initial information voters can find about each other's preferences before actual balloting. Can bargains involving incentives or penalties be made regarding issues not on the ballot? Can a person commit to threats or promises, such as, "I will vote for your proposal if you will vote for mine," or similar political trade-offs? One way of making bargains enforceable is to combine them in single package to be voted on as one vote. Sometimes this is considered illegal or unethical, but often the only way to "sell" a vote is to sell it in return for votes on other issues. The many earmarks that have been attached to congressional legislation amount to packaging for success in a single vote.

An ideal voting procedure for the situation you face, whether it is a club election, a corporate board election, a contest for county commissioner, or for president of a country, would discover and establish some unique collective will. An appropriate question is whether the vote actually arrives at this collective preference or merely determines an outcome already accepted in advance. Identifying a true collective will, or as Rousseau put it, the "general will" remains an ideal for which to strive but an elusive goal.

Arrow's Impossibility Theorem

The difficulty in finding an ideal voting solution was demonstrated in 1951 by Arrow's impossibility theorem.[9] Arrow did not look for an ideal voting procedure but formulated the principles on which a reasonable decision rule for voting systems that involved at least three choices would rest. He identified four conditions: transitivity, unanimity, nondictatorship, and independence of irrelevant alternatives. The voter's choices must be transitive, by which Arrow meant, if choice A was preferred to B and choice B was preferred to choice C, then choice A was preferred to choice C. Unanimity meant that if voters unanimously preferred a candidate or procedure ahead of another choice, that choice must be selected. Nondictatorship was that a single member must not dictate society's preferences. Arrow's fourth condition, the independence of irrelevant alternatives, was that the choice between two alternatives must not depend on the availability of a third alternative. This means that if there are more than two alternatives, the winning alternative should not lose in a one-on-one match with any other alternative.

These seemingly rational guidelines appear adequate for establishing an election framework. Arrow proved that no decision rule could satisfy all four conditions.[10]

Designing Voting Schemes

However, if the will of a majority of voters is known, it is often possible to design voting schemes that will lead to an outcome that expresses that will. This may sound like circular reasoning, but voting schemes can lead to voters who know they are in the majority not prevailing. If voters believe they are in the minority and they are voting for a preference that cannot be achieved, they might base their votes on a mistaken premise.

The criteria by which to judge voting schemes depends on what is desired, what preference is to be maximized. Preferences could include time lost voting, minimizing surprises, the programs to be implemented. One may want a scheme that, when applied to itself, confirms itself—if the voting scheme has to be voted on, will it, if employed, lead to its own selection? There are systems that minimize demands on strategy, systems that invite strategy, and systems that lead to different results.

To illustrate strategy being used to maximize preferences, consider the following problem. Notice the influence on voting and outcome illustrated by the decision on which of two statistical concepts, "median" or "arithmetic mean," would be the understanding of "average."

There is a club with a governing board of ten members and a budget of $10,000 to go to two projects, its library and its dining room. Six members want two-thirds to go to the dining room and four want two-thirds to go to the library. Their voting procedure calls for each member to write on a ballot an amount to go to the dining room, and the remainder will go to the library. Calculate the result first, by arithmetic mean: adding all amounts specified for the dining room and dividing by ten to determine an average. Everyone was aware of all other members' preferences.

Only one set of strategies has equilibrium quality, and it is the strategic voting choice, which, if everyone anticipates it, will lead to everyone adopting it. All six who favor the dining room will vote all the money to the dining room and the four who favor the library will vote all the money to the library. That leads to an average of $6,000 for dining room and $4,000 for library. If that were what everyone did, nobody would want to change his vote (making it a Nash equilibrium; Chapter 20). Nobody would have specified his true preference of two-thirds to one and one-third to the other. This vote would be strategic, as everyone voted for an outcome he disliked, but got nearest to what he preferred.

Now consider using a different type of "average," the median—the numeric value that separates the top half from the bottom half. Arrange the ballots in order of the amount specified for the dining room, then count down half way from top. Finding the middle point when there is an even number is a bit complicated, but the median in this case is clear. Six can vote to give two-thirds of the money to the dining room. They will have their way exactly, having voted "sincerely." The four who favor the library cannot affect the outcome in any way. Either one is in the middle position, casting the median ballot, and gets his preferred choice, or he is not. In a median-voting system nobody needs to bother with what anyone else prefers, except in even voting number, where some maneuvering might be considered.

This problem illustrates the difficulty in finding an ideal voting system that reaches an outcome uniquely in accordance with voters' preferences. With the latter method the majority imposed its will completely on the minority, while in the strategic voting, where a Nash equilibrium was achieved, they achieved an outcome that nobody would have voted for if expressing a sincere preference. If people had done what was originally instructed and written down their sincere requests of two-thirds for the arithmetic mean, there would be a third option to consider and another voting factor Arrow described would be involved.

Cyclical Choices

With three or more options people have "cyclical" preferences and will choose on the basis of which of the preferred options is most likely to succeed, rather than "transitive" preferences, which are one of the essentials of Arrow's theorem. For example, sincere voting might show a preference of choice A over choice B. The same group prefers choice B to choice C, but prefers choice C to choice A if those two are matched, making the outcome circular. According to Arrow's transitivity requirement for voting schemes, if choice A was preferred to B and choice B was preferred to choice C, then choice A was preferred to choice C. There are election examples where the "impossibility" is illustrated. Choices A, B, and C could be state presidential primary candidates, such as Republicans matching Romney, McCain, and Huckabee in the run-up to the 2008 presidential election.

Such a three-option choice might also appear, for example, in a group's position on an issue such as housing, with options being A, a nondiscriminatory housing program; B, a racially discriminatory housing program; or C, no housing at all. Assume the group's three sincere preferences were, A over B, B over C, C over A. Take any combination and hold a "sincere" election between the two, then pair the winner with the third, and the third is bound to win. If each voter knows the other's preferences and each knows that the winner on first ballot will be paired with the third alternative, the outcome can be manipulated. If the initial ballot is A against B, everyone knows the final choice will be C. Specifically, the one whose first choice is A will vote for B in order to get second choice, not third. This is easy to see on a voting tree or decision tree (Figure 15.1):

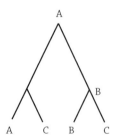

If a person acts tactically in this situation he can determine the results favorably. Suppose a person can commit his vote in advance. One who prefers C promises to vote for A on second ballot, then the one who prefers A can vote for A on first ballot. The one who prefers C could strike it altogether and the outcome would be A. The same tactics are available to one who prefers B. If everyone can do this, the voting ceases to matter. The outcome can be rigged in advance by any coalition of two voters who can reach a bargain. There is no uniquely stable coalition. The situation is symmetrical, and the coalition is such that the outsider willing to commit to a strategic vote to accept a second-best option can join the one member with that preference and can achieve it together.

Condorcet Option

An example of strategic maneuvering to avoid the least desired outcome dates back to voting in the Roman Senate and the case of Consul Afrinius Dexter, who was found dead. The cause of his death was uncertain; it could have been murder or suicide, or he may have ordered one of his servants to kill him. The Senate had power to decide what should be done with the free servants and it had three options: determine guilt or acquit, banish, or execute the freemen as they probably already had done with the consul's slaves. The factions in the Senate and their preferences were as follows (Table 15.3).[11]

Table 15.3

DECISION	SIZE OF THE FACTION	PREFERENCE
Acquittal (A)	45%	A > B > E
Banishment (B)	35%	B > A > E
Execution (E)	20%	E > B > A

In this situation, any procedure in which the voting takes place in pairs will result in a verdict of guilt and banishment. That would be the result if the Senate had used the contemporary practice of determining guilt first then sentencing. In game theory terms banishment, in this example, is a "Condorcet option or candidate"—that is, a choice that is preferred by a majority when matched against any other candidate or option individually. Condorcet was a French marquis who argued that any voting system that did not elect or choose the option a majority would select when it was paired against any other was flawed and should not be used; but history shows a number of cases where plurality winners have been elected when a third candidate siphoned votes from one who could defeat the others head to head.

In this case the presiding officer of the Roman Senate was Pliny, who favored acquittal and he foresaw the outcome that the preferences made a certainty. He demanded a three-way vote with the winner being the outcome, which would have been acquittal. The senators favoring execution were not outdone by his strategy and, rather than voting sincerely, they voted strategically and sided with those favoring banishment, giving them their second rather than their least desired outcome.

Positive Majority Sequential Voting Scheme

One way of attempting to see if a candidate or proposition is favored above all others is an alternative voting method called the "positive majority sequential voting scheme." For illustration we will return to the priorities used in Arrow's theorem, where if choice A was preferred to B, and choice B was preferred to choice C, then choice A was preferred to choice C. In this voting scheme proposition or candidate A is put to a vote and if a majority votes for A, A is the winner. If majority votes against A, proposition or candidate B is put up for vote. If B receives a majority, B wins. If B loses, alternative C is automatically declared the winner. The voting tree for this is shown in Table 15.2:

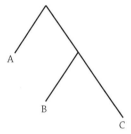

The first vote is really just A and B. Given the preferences of A over B, B over C, C over A, the majority prefers A to B, and A should win on the first ballot. If A loses first ballot, the final is B and C. Two favor B to C, so B would win on the second ballot. The system is symmetrical, and it can be inferred that whichever alternative is voted on first will win. Voting against preferences or dishonesty could alter the outcome, of course.

Consider five voters with preferences ranked from highest to lowest, left to right:

voter 1) CEDAB
voter 2) BDCEA
voter 3) DCEAB
voter 4) EDABC
voter 5) EDBCA

Now again employ the "positive majority sequential" voting scheme to see first if A receives a majority, and if not, then if B receives a majority, and so on through

D. If all fail, E is automatically declared the winning choice. The voting tree for the possible four ballots would be (Table 15.3):

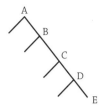

On the fourth ballot E would be preferred to D by a majority and since it would be the final ballot they would vote their true preferences and E would win. Anticipating that possibility, the choice on third ballot is between C and E and the majority prefers C to E. That means the second ballot is between B and C, with B preferred by the majority. The choice then gets to the first ballot, where if A does not win, B wins.

A wins this vote on first ballot because everyone knows everyone else's preferences and is thinking strategically. Strategic, rational decision making, but C was preferred to A by four of the five people, and everyone preferred E to A. The "rational" decision is extremely inefficient. This rational decision-making with an inefficient outcome is reminiscent of the Prisoner's Dilemma. Strategic voting led to this outcome. In this case "sincere" voting would have led to E, a fairly acceptable outcome. It would be inaccurate to draw the conclusion from this that if voters had the self-discipline to always vote sincerely, they will come out better than if they voted strategically.[12]

Here is another illustration of how procedure affects outcome. A committee of three with many options to consider carries on considerable discussion so all members are familiar with each other's preferences and rankings of the ideas. One might see this as somewhat analogous to a congressional committee that is confronting an especially divisive issue, where many competing proposals have been put forward. Here there are eleven proposals and a committee of three. They have labeled the proposals in alphabetical order. The voter's preferences in order, left to right are as follows:

1) C B A F E D I H G K J
2) A D C B G F E J I H K
3) B A E D C H G F K J I

A voting method involving paired comparisons that is similar to this took place in Scotland, where one candidate was excluded at each round of voting and the other moved on.[11] For simplicity's sake, the voting system is: start at the beginning of the alphabet and the winner of the majority vote between A and B is paired against option C. The winner of that vote is paired against option D, and the process continues until the apparently favored option emerges as the committee's choice. This head to head pairing sounds fair, but given the known priorities, sincere voting leads to a victory for option K. It seems unlikely that K should emerge as this committee's recommendation, since it is the last choice of one member and the second to the last choice for another and third to last for the third member. If the choice were to start from the right instead of the left and match pairs sincerely in the same way, there would be a considerably different outcome. In that case, the options would have continued to eliminate each other until it came down to B being paired against A, and B would emerge as the choice. This right to left sincere voting outcome would be much better in terms of efficiency, as it would be far more acceptable to the committee.

If the members started from the left and voted strategically, they would see that K would win once the voting reached J and K and reason backward to I, where H lost out by a 2:1 preference, and then they would have voted for G if they preferred it to I. This same logic can unwind all the way back to the very first ballot, where A would win 2:1. Sincere voting would have trapped them at K, but strategic voting permits them to foresee the downward spiral of preferences and anticipating it, foreclose on the first ballot.

Schemes that lead to selection of H, I, J, K are comparatively poor results because these are fairly low on everybody's list of preferences. It can be said they are "dominated" solutions and constitute "inefficient" outcomes. Any scheme that fails to select A, B, or C has in some sense failed.[13]

Efficient Voting Outcomes

The efficiency of the outcome is an issue in voting priorities. A voting result is considered "efficient" if no alternative outcome is unanimously preferred to the actual results. That was Condorcet's point, that voting systems should only be used if they yield a result that a majority would select if it was matched against any other option. There are important questions of whether voting schemes ultimately give rise to a choice of alternatives that would be unanimously rejected in favor of other alternatives. Some suggest the Electoral College scheme for presidential elections gives rise to a choice that would be rejected by other alternatives, or fails the Condorcet test. Four times a candidate has won the popular vote and lost the election: Andrew Jackson in 1824 (to John Quincy Adams), Samuel Tilden in 1876 (to Rutherford B. Hayes), Grover Cleveland in 1888 (to Benjamin Harrison), and Al Gore in 2000 (to George W. Bush). In 1969 a resolution calling for the direct election of the president and vice president passed the House of Representatives, but failed to pass the Senate.[14]

Robin Farquharson, who was early in applying game theory analysis to voting, concluded in 1956 that the restrictive nature of sincere preference makes elections more a test of skill than a measure of the will of the people and "in general, no voting procedure can be straightforward for all scales of preferences."[15]

Median Voter Theorem

The median voter theorem, first proposed by Harold Hotelling, is relevant in contemporary national elections. The theorem was formalized by Duncan Black and depicts political opinion as lying along a single liberal-conservative dimension, where voters could all be ranked from one extreme to the other. If everyone votes for the candidate closest to his favored position, then the candidate choosing the optimal position of the median voter wins. This applies when there are two candidates and a majority vote wins the election.

Consider an election involving 1,001 voters whose preferences are distributed in the following manner that originated in the National Assembly of the French Revolution. The distribution places the most liberal on the far left and the most conservative on the far right with the moderates occupying the center. This table ranks voters' preferences from 0 to 1, with 0.0 being the most liberal voter point of view and 1.0 being the most conservative (Table 15.4).

Table 15.4

Voter point of view	0.0	0.1	0.2	0.3	0.4	0.5	0.6	0.7	0.8	0.9	1.0
Number of voters	151	133	94	57	40	32	8	21	29	86	350

The median voter here is 0.5. According to this voting theorem, the candidate who wins voters at 0.5 wins the election. The thought is that each candidate represents an ideology that will win the voters on the extremes in a choice between two, but whoever has staked out a claim on the positions sought by the median voter will be victorious.

In countries like the United States, where there is a two-step process to presidential elections, that means there are two different median voters a candidate must win. "To win the party's nomination, the candidate is pulled toward the party median; the need to win the election pulls him back toward the population median."[16] This could lead to alienation and indifference among voters, as the choices no longer seem to represent sincere policy differences.

Slate carried an article attributing both Bill Clinton's and George W. Bush's first elections to strategy based on the median voter theorem, saying,

> The secret of Bill Clinton's campaigns and of George W. Bush's election
> in 2000 was the much-maligned politics of small differences: Find the
> smallest possible majority of electoral votes that gets you to the White

House. In political science, something called the "median voter theorem" dictates that in a two-party system, both parties will rush to the center looking for that lone voter—the median voter—who has 50.1 percent of the public to the right (or left) of him. Win that person's vote, and you've won the election.[17]

The median voter theorem presents a rational explanation for the rush to the center during the general election. As technology has improved media alternatives, it has become possible for campaigns to target separate audiences on single issues. So the median voter may be less the key, with voting blocks compartmentalized and reached by e-mail, Facebook, Internet blogs, cell phone messaging, Twitter, and similar forms of communication.

For all the strategies that can be applied to voting, achieving the ideal set out by the Greeks long ago remains a considerable challenge. and the march to a more democratic world continues but it is a daunting struggle for many.

Supplement: Struggling for Democracy

The difficulties of assuring that voting expresses the people's will is apparent as countries with no democratic tradition suddenly adopt democracy or have it thrust on them. Thomas Friedman has been a keen observer of such situations and is especially qualified to comment on struggles to achieve democracy. Friedman is a three-time Pulitzer Prize winner and a foreign affairs columnist for the *New York Times*, and his column is syndicated in one hundred newspapers around the world. He joined the *New York Times* in 1981, and his five books have sold extremely well. Friedman was named one of America's Best Leaders by *U.S. News & World Report* and was awarded the Order of the British Empire (OBE) by Queen Elizabeth II.

Hoping for Arab Mandelas

With Libya, Yemen, Bahrain and Syria now all embroiled in rebellions, it is not an exaggeration to suggest that the authoritarian lid that has smothered freedom in the Arab world for centuries may be coming off all 350 million Arab peoples at once. Personally, I think that is exactly what is going to happen over time. Warm up the bus for all the Arab autocrats—and for you, too, Ahmadinejad. As one who has long believed in the democracy potential for this part of the world, color me both really hopeful and really worried about the prospects.

I am hopeful because the Arab peoples are struggling for more representative and honest government, which is what they will need to overcome their huge deficits in education, freedom and women's empowerment that have been holding them back. But getting from here to there requires crossing a minefield of tribal, sectarian and governance issues.

The best way to understand the potential and pitfalls of this transition is to think about Iraq. I know that the Iraq war and the democracy-building effort that followed have been so bitterly divisive in America that no one wants to talk about Iraq. Well, today we're going to talk about Iraq because that experience offers some hugely important lessons for how to manage the transition to democratic governance of a multisectarian Arab state when the iron lid is removed.

Democracy requires 3 things: citizens—that is, people who see themselves as part of an undifferentiated national community where anyone can be ruler or ruled. It requires self-determination—that is, voting. And it requires what Michael Mandelbaum, author of "Democracy's Good Name," calls "liberty."

"While voting determines who governs," he explained, "liberty determines what governments can and cannot do. Liberty encompasses all the rules and limits that govern politics, justice, economics and religion."

And building liberty is really hard. It will be hard enough in Middle East states with big, homogenous majorities, like Egypt, Tunisia and Iran, where there is already a powerful sense of citizenship and where national unity is more or less assumed. It will be doubly hard in all the other states, which are divided by tribal, ethnic and sectarian identities and where the threat of civil war is ever present.

Not one was more divided in that way than Iraq. What did we learn there? First, we learned that when you removed the authoritarian lid the tensions between Iraqi Kurds, Shiites and Sunnis erupted as each faction tested the other's power in a low-grade civil war. But we also learned that alongside that war many Iraqis expressed an equally powerful yearning to live together as citizens. For all of the murderous efforts by Al Qaeda to trigger a full-scale civil war in Iraq, it never happened. And in Iraq's last election, the candidate who won the most seats, a Shiite, Ayad Allawi, ran on a multisectarian platform with Sunnis. Lesson: While these tribal identities are deeply embedded and can blow up at anytime, there are also powerful countertrends in today's more urbanized, connected, Facebooked Middle East.

"There is a problem of citizenship in the Arab world," said Michael Young, the Lebanese author of "The Ghosts of Martyr's Square," "but that is partly because these regimes never allowed their people to be citizens. But despite that, you can see how much the demonstrators in Syria have been trying to stay nonviolent and speak about freedom for the whole nation."

Lesson two: What was crucial in keeping the low-grade civil war in Iraq from exploding, what was crucial in their writing of their own Constitution for how to live together, and what was crucial in helping Iraqis manage multiple fair elections was that they had a credible neutral arbiter throughout this transition: the U.S.

America played that role at a staggering cost, and not always perfectly, but played it we did. In Egypt, the Egyptian Army is playing that arbiter role. Somebody has to play it in all these countries in revolt, so they can successfully lay the foundations of both democracy and liberty. Who will play that role in Libya? In Syria? In Yemen?

The final thing Iraq teaches us is that while external arbiters may be necessary, they are not sufficient. We're leaving Iraq at the end of the year. Only Iraqis can sustain their democracy after we depart. The same will be true for all the other Arab peoples hoping to make this transition to self-rule. They need to grow their own arbiters — their own Arab Nelson Mandelas. That is, Shiite, Sunni and tribal leaders who stand up and say to each other what Mandela's character said about South African whites in the movie "Invictus": "We have to surprise them with restraint and generosity."

This is what the new leaders of these Arab rebellions will have to do — surprise themselves and each other with a sustained will for unity, mutual respect and democracy. The more Arab Mandelas who emerge, the more they will be able to manage their own transitions, without army generals or outsiders. Will they emerge? Let's watch and hope. We have no other choice. The lids are coming off.[18]

Notes

1. Bradford Jones et al., "Condorcet Winners and the Paradox of Voting: Probability Calculations for Weak Preference Orders," *American Political Science Review*, Vol. 89, No. 1 (1995), 137.
2. Fareed Zakaria, *The Future of Freedom: Liberal Democracy at Home and Abroad* (New York: Norton, 2004), 13.
3. Akhil Reed Amar and Vikram David Amar, "The Fatal Flaw in France's—and America's Voting System, and How an 'Instant Runoff' System Might Remedy It," *FindLaw* online, May 3, 2002.
4. Ibid.
5. Thomas C. Schelling, *Choice and Consequences* (Cambridge, MA: Harvard University Press, 1984), 224.
6. Frederic C. Schaffer, *Elections for Sale: The Causes and Consequences of Vote Buying* (Boulder, CO: Lynne Rienner, 2007), 3.
7. Ibid.
8. "Cambodia's Election: Stability, Sort of," *The Economist* (London), August 2, 2008, 8.
9. Howard Raiffa, John Richardson, and David Metcalfe, *Negotiation Analysis* (Cambridge, MA: Harvard University Press, 2002), 358.

10. Scott Bierman and Luiz Fernandez, *Game Theory with Economic Applications*, 2nd ed. (Reading, MA: Addison-Wesley, 1998), 106.
11. Thomas C. Schelling, "Voting Schemes," unpublished lecture notes, 1975.
12. Robin Farquharson, "Straightforwardness in Voting Procedure," *Oxford Economic Papers, New Series*, Oxford University Press, Vol. 8, No. 1 (1956), 81.
13. Schelling, "Voting Schemes."
14. U.S. House of Representatives, Office of the Clerk, "House History: The Electoral College," http://clerk.house.gov/art_history/house_history/electoral.html.
15. Farquharson, "Straightforwardness in Voting Procedure," 80.
16. Dennis C. Mueller, "Public Choice, A Survey," *Journal of Economic Literature*, Vol. 14, No. 2 (June 1976), 409.
17. Chris Suellentrop, "The Vanishing Nonvoter," *Slate*, October 31, 2004.
18. Thomas L. Friedman, *The New York Times*, March 27, 2011, with permission.

CHAPTER 16

The Commons and Fair Division

Cooperation and coordination are related to what Schelling calls the social contract. Society consists of institutional arrangements to overcome divergences between perceived individual interest and some larger collective bargain. In the Prisoner's Dilemma individual self-interest is the natural choice at the expense of the common good. The social contract makes a bargain work where society benefits. The social contract may be achieved through experience of cooperation or coordination, but problems can exist when not everyone gains. He gave an example of defiance of the social contract, where responsibility to the group is secondary. In Schelling's example drivers are returning to Boston from Cape Cod on a Sunday afternoon. Traffic is creeping along, slowed by a mattress on the road that has fallen off the top of a vehicle. Hundreds of cars slowly inch ahead until reaching the mattress, wait for a break in oncoming traffic, swerve around the mattress and resume normal speed. If anyone bothered to move the mattress, the traffic problem would be resolved. But here self-interest wins the day, as nobody can remove the mattress until he has passed it and nobody gains anything by moving the mattress after having passed it.[1]

This situation resembles a well-known model that involves congestion and self-interest, and offers an explanation of situations where not everyone gains when self-interest is the motivation.

The Commons

Garrett Hardin's insight into the competition between public welfare and individual motives first appeared in his essay, "The Tragedy of the Commons."[2] The commons his title referred to is common land that existed in English villages and also New England. Common land was village property available for unrestricted use by both the villagers and their animals. What Hardin observed was that as more animals were put on the common land to graze, it became congested and there was less grass available for each animal, so the animals produced less milk and meat. However, as long as there was any profit to be made by grazing one's animals on the common, the villagers would be encouraged to do so. That was true even if individuals realized that the total amount of meat or milk the grazing animals produce might be higher if all the villagers restricted their use of the commons. There was no motivation for an individual to act on his own to do so, as he had nothing to gain personally from the self-restraint. Hardin said, "Each man is locked into a system that [causes] him to increase his herd without limit—in a world that is limited... Freedom in a commons brings ruin to all."[3]

Hardin returned to an interpretation first proposed by classical economist Thomas Malthus, whose *An Essay on the Principles of Population*,[4] originally published in 1798, asserted that population grows exponentially, while food production grows arithmetically. Hardin felt that overpopulation was the greatest problem, writing, "The most important aspect of necessity that we must now recognize, is the necessity to abandon the commons in breeding. No technical solution can rescue us from the misery of overpopulation. Freedom to breed will bring ruin to all."[5] Overpopulation is a commons problem because it imposes costs on all others in society by reducing scarce resources, just as in the village commons, each man who put his animal on the land to graze reduced the resources available to the group. "The direct psychic gains of parenthood are offset by economic losses channeled through the whole population,"[6] was how Hardin put it twenty-five years after the publication of his seminal essay.

The commons model captures a wide variety of situations in which people harm each other by pursuing their own personal interest, when the situation for the group would be better if they restrained, or cooperated, but there is no personal motivation for them to do so. Often, no one gains individually by self-restraint. Hardin mentions pollution, not as something taken out, but as something put in that affects all, where everyone is a member of the same commons. Factories may pollute the air and dump sewage in the water, and all might agree it would be better if that were not the case. But business is business, and others are doing the same. It could be a costly change for an individual factory to do otherwise, and a competitive disadvantage to act alone, so individual self-interest sets in.

Countries that share valuable resources can become commons examples. Oil deposits that cross boundaries are cases, as is water, an international law publication noted, "Since transboundary groundwater is a shared resource, and attempting to manage it unilaterally would be an exercise in futility, or worse: the consequences could easily amount to a tragedy of the commons."[7] Hardin uses overfishing as another example, writing, "Now the once unlimited resources of marine fishes have become scarce and nations are coming to limit the freedom of their fishers in the commons. From here onward complete freedom leads to tragedy."[8] The commons model has been evident in the ban on fishing in the hunting of whales, where an international agreement was reached in 1986 to ban whaling, but Norway, Japan, and Iceland defied the ban, giving them less competition and leaving the whales equally dead. In recent years the three countries have been killing about seventeen hundred whales annually, including some endangered species.[9]

Many instances of congestion and overcrowding, whether on the road, or attempting to get into an event or an elevator, exhibit commons characteristics. Things would go more smoothly and efficiently if people were to take turns, wait for the next elevator car, allow cars to change lanes by giving space, but during congested situations many are unwilling to make any personal sacrifice to improve the overall situation. A frequent attitude about commons problems is that it would be better if *others* cut back on their use of a shared resource or a given activity; but *I* really must continue, as I have nothing to gain, and might actually lose, by making a change.

Commons Characteristics

The commons is a multiperson prisoner's dilemma. This has led to it being referred to in academic literature at times as the "commons dilemma."[10] It involves the identical choice between individual utility maximization of benefits and group maximization. As the Prisoner's Dilemma demonstrated, the rationality that dictates seeking individual payoffs can be erroneous, as it can be in an individual's best interest to seek the best result for the group. Like the Prisoner's Dilemma, it challenges the underlying idea of classical free market economics and capitalism. Adam Smith, in his 1776 epic work, *The Wealth of Nations*, determined that the natural order of things is that self-interest leads to outcomes are the most positive possible. His "invisible hand," which was the market mechanism where a customer will only buy when the value to him of what he is purchasing exceeds the price he pays, and the seller will only sell when all his costs are covered by the price he receives. This supply and demand equilibrium works in some cases, but in areas where the commons applies, like clean air and water, and no price is set to exchange, it is not easily applied. The commons shows that in some such cases self-interest is counterproductive.

In the commons only those who use the commons are affected by the way it is used and they are affected in proportion to how much they use it. As well, the costs of overusing the commons are in the same "currency" as the benefits. Time lost in traffic congestion from all unwilling to yield in crowded intersections, is exactly the currency that is a benefit when saved by people abandoning self-interest and cooperating by yielding and allowing traffic to flow.

Fair Division

The commons demonstrates how resources will not be distributed in the interest of the group when self-interest is the dominant motivation. This section discusses social arrangements considered in rational choice that seek methods of dividing resources where those involved are satisfied with the outcome. Rather than pursuing self-interest, we will look to find methods for how to fairly divide and/or distribute things of any sort.

HISTORICAL FAIR DIVISION

Making the decisions involved and selecting the method appropriate for distributing something among a number of claimants has a long history in policy discussion. The topic is one that has been discussed since ancient times. Herodotus reported the solution the residents of Babylon found for the distribution of one of society's critical resources, brides. In the Western world marriage is generally a matter of chance encounter through the workplace, through interest in some common activity, attendance of the same institution, or seeking out a mate at some singles bar or online service. In the Asian subcontinent arranged marriages are still not unusual.

Herodotus wrote that in Babylon,

> In every village once a year all the girls of marriageable age used to be collected together in one place, while the men stood round them in a circle: an auctioneer then called each one in turn to stand up and offered her for sale, beginning with the best-looking and going to the second best as soon as the first had been sold for a good price. Marriage was the object of the transaction. The rich men who wanted wives bid against each other for the prettiest girls, while the humbler folk, who had no use for good looks in a wife, were actually paid to take the ugly ones, for when the auctioneer had got through all the pretty girls he would call upon the plainest, or even perhaps a crippled one, to stand up, and then ask who was willing to take the least money to marry her—and she was knocked down to whoever accepted the smallest sum. The money came from the sale of the beauties, who in this way provided dowries for their ugly or misshapen sisters.... No one could take home a girl he had bought without first finding a backer who would guarantee his intention of marrying her....Anyone who wished could come even from a different village to buy a wife.[11]

This sounds like an insulting and embarrassing practice by today's standards, and one wonders what it was like for the girl who was taken as a wife after the greatest amount of money was offered for someone to accept a bride. Before completely rejecting the idea as barbaric or a form of slavery, consider the equity and efficiency for society. Compare it with several alternatives, including women who are free to marry whom they please, the practice of fathers selling women as brides, which has been a historical reality in many places at many times, forced eugenic pairing, any other method you can imagine. Also consider all parties involved, including rich men, poor men, poor men with pretty daughters, and sisters of pretty girls.

Under this system all were married, and a poor man who might never be able to afford to have a wife might have one. There were also girls who, in the world of free choice would spend a life never chosen, would have husbands, rather than live with their family or alone. The rich would be paired with the beautiful in a sort of eugenic breeding, but that happens in some cases in any event. Fathers of pretty girls would benefit from the high auction prices, and fathers of unattractive girls would also benefit in that their daughters would no longer be their responsibilities, since they would be married. Social relations that existed in families might vanish after auctions, as sisters moved into different social classes. It is not a system that caught on and spread, but it had elements of social benefit in it and was not entirely negative. Free choice allows the option to not be chosen, and the long life without a husband, while Babylon's system guaranteed a life where all would become wives. What that meant might not be so clear in a time when concerns are more with population control than with population expansion, but it meant something.

When looking for examples of making choices about division and allocation one can go back to the days of Solomon in the Old Testament of the Bible for perhaps the most famous account. In 1 Kings 3 the story is told of two harlots before King Solomon, both claiming to be the mother of the same baby. One of them spoke first, saying,

> O my lord, I and this woman dwell in one house; and I was delivered of a child with her in the house. And it came to pass the third day after I was delivered that this woman was delivered also: and we were together; there was no stranger with us in the house, save we two in the house. And this woman's child died in the night; because she overlaid it. And she arose at midnight, and took my son from beside me, while thine handmaid slept, and laid it in her bosom, and laid her dead child in my bosom.
>
> And when I rose in the morning to give my child suck, behold, it was dead: but when I had considered it in the morning, behold, it was not my son, which I did bear.
>
> And the other woman said, Nay; but the living is my son, and the dead is thy son. And this said, No; but the dead is thy son, and the living is my son. Thus they spake before the king.
>
> Then said the king, The one saith, This is my son that liveth, and thy son is the dead: and the other saith, Nay; but thy son is the dead, and my son is the living.
>
> And the king said, Bring me a sword. And they brought a sword before the king.
>
> And the king said, Divide the living child in two, and give half to the one, and half to the other.
>
> Then spake the woman whose living child was unto the king, for her bowels yearned upon her son, and she said, O my lord, give her the

living child, and in no wise slay it. But the other said, Let it be neither mine nor thine, but divide it.

Then the king answered and said, Give her the living child, and in no wise slay it: she is the mother thereof.

And all Israel heard of the judgment which the king had judged; and they feared the king: for they saw that the wisdom of God was in him, to do judgment.[12]

Solomon's first pronouncement, to divide the child, is a common response for how to settle disputes over division of an object between two people and it seems fair. It illustrated not only who the real mother was, but also that dividing and being fair is not always a simple matter.

One Cuts, the Other Chooses, and Steinhaus

The method parents frequently use to achieve fair division with children when dividing a piece of cake or pizza is the "one cuts, the other chooses" approach. The idea is that the division will be fair, since the cutter will cut as nearly equally as possible, knowing he is going to get the smaller portion. It was long a policy regarding discoveries of ancient treasures in Egypt to make two piles and the Egyptian ministry chose the one it wanted.

Polish mathematician Hugo Steinhaus developed a method for expanding this cake cutting approach beyond two players. His rules call for an *n*-person division, with the players arranged in A, B, C... order to *n*, whatever number was involved. The division starts by A cutting but not taking an arbitrary slice, then B cuts a slice, followed by C, then D and so on in order with each player reducing the cake by an additional measured amount, but no one takes a slice. The process continues on to *n*, the "last diminisher," who must take what remains of the cake after all others have cut, or choose a piece that someone else cut. Following that, the process is then repeated, beginning with n-1 players and again A cuts a slice, followed by B, and so on, and when that is completed A again starts with n-2 players, and the procedure keeps repeating until the final two remain.

Of course, this is not a method for actually dividing a cake, as it would require somehow putting it back together after each round of cutting. It is for something where divisions could be made that could be represented by a diagram or on a map, whether it be a cake, a piece of land, overlapping claims to territory in the ocean within the coastlines of several nations, or anything similar. By making the divisions on a diagram or map, when a new round begins, an accurate representation of what remains could be depicted. That way player A could again make a reasonable decision on the size of the piece to divide from the whole, as can those who follow until the next last diminisher must take what remains or choose one of the divisions another player made. This process continues with one person being eliminated at each round until it becomes the children's cutter-chooser game between the final two remaining.

If one has to cut, he attempts to cut $1/n$ of what remains. This approach assumes that the players would seek ideal, equal shares and that whatever was being divided was continuous, so reducing it by an amount like a slice was possible. An equal slice among rational players was the best outcome they could achieve at their turn. The simple math was V = value of the whole entity and p = any fraction between 0 and 1. A player could reduce the entity by a slice worth pV at every cut, and the sum of the value of the parts (all pVs) would be equal to V, the sum of the value of the whole. Since it is an expanded version of one cuts, the other chooses, if at any stage of the procedure one must cut a slice, the strategy would be to cut what would appear to have a value of $1/n$th of whole value, but one would not cut at all if what remained already had what appeared to be that value or less. Greed, envy, or ignorance of others could not prevent one from obtaining $1/n$th of the entire value under Steinhaus's method. This is illustrated by the following cake/piece of property, which is divided by 10 people (Tables 16.1 and 16.2):

Table 16.1

| A |
| B |
| C |
| D |
| E |
| F |
| G |
| H |
| I |
| J, last diminisher |

The division at left has those dividing making differentiated selections, and the one at right has them making equal choices. J, the last diminisher in each case, must choose one of the divisions as his own. In the divisions above he will take division J, since it is the largest, while in the divisions below it makes no difference what choice he makes since all divisions resulted in equal shares. As can be seen, when the next round of divisions begin and I is the last diminisher, there is less remaining to be divided in the left rectangle, since the J division was larger than any division on the rectangle on the right. It is an extension of the children's cutter-chooser game where each player has no choice but to cut or divide $1/n$ as accurately as possible in his own self-interest. Equal divisions are in everyone's best interest.

Table 16.2

A
B
C
D
E
F
G
H
I
J, last diminisher

Adding Value

The "last diminisher method" applies to physically divisible objects like pieces of land, where cake is a realistic metaphor. If players were dividing things where they have different estimations of value, the possibility exists that everyone could get more than his seeming fair share. Steinhaus also devised a method for such division, where the sum of the individual shares that the players received could total in excess of what was the apparent total value of what was being allocated among those involved. Again at the most basic level we can use the division of a piece of cake between a cutter and chooser to illustrate the principle involved before expanding it to more complex divisions.

At the simplest level, the Steinhaus method for increasing value when preferences are dissimilar can be illustrated by a $1.00 piece of chocolate-marshmallow cake being divided by two people with differing tastes. "A" prefers the chocolate and "B" the marshmallow. Each gets half of the $1.00 piece, which means a value of $.50 apiece. The following diagram could represent their preferences (Table 16.3):

Table 16.3

	Chocolate	Marshmallow
A	.30	.20
B	.20	.30

The division that would be worth $.50 to each, would be Ch + M. But if the cake is cut for A, Ch + Ch, and for B, M + M, each gets $.60 in value. The $1.00 piece of cake then has a value of $1.20 to the recipients after the division.

By adapting the premise where individuals place different personal values on whatever is to be allocated among them, a procedure exists that can yield satisfying results. Though the procedure need not be limited to wills, Steinhaus exhibited this by discussing sharing objects among benefactors of inheritance, where heirs placed different personal values on objects to be divided among them, such as family heirlooms, works of art, animals, the family house. A percentage of the estate had been given to each heir and they were to divide the inheritance accordingly. In this method of division every participant writes down the value for each item to him personally. Estimates are arranged in rows (claimants) and columns (items). Each item's value is the total of the claims made on it, and items go to the participant or player who values them most highly. The value of the item to the person who claimed the highest value is computed by multiplying the combined estimates of its value times the percentage that expresses the share that person received of the bequest. This value to the person who claimed the highest value relative to the others may be greater than the value of his total share times the total bid on the item. If that is so, the minus claims give "differences."

"It is easy to see that positive difference is at least equal to sum of negative ones; thus having charged positive partners with payments to reduce their differences to zero and having covered out of this fund the deficit of the 'negative' partners, there will be left a remainder which has to be distributed among all partners proportionally to their ideal shares in the whole lot."[12] Following is an example of efficiency gained by subjective valuation in fair division (Table 16.4):

Table 16.4

	A	*B*	*C*	*D*
furniture	8	5	5	5
boat	5	7	5	5
car	5	5	6	5
total bid	18	17	16	15
share given	30%	40%	20%	10%
value received	8	7	6	0
share X total	5.4	6.8	3.2	1.5
value-claim	2.6	0.2	2.8	-1.5
give back	-2.6	-0.2	-2.8	+1.5

The numbers represent the personal subjective valuation in relation to others and not market valuation. Market valuation for the items is equal.

The procedure generated an efficiency gain of 4.1 in this example, as the bottom row shows. The 5.6 extra value gained by A, B, C (2.6+0.2+2.8) was reduced by the 1.5 shortfall by D. That is the advantage of the Steinhaus method of division, which can produce individual totaled value that is beyond 100 percent of expected value because of differing personal preferences. Steinhaus's scheme does not determine our relative claims. It assumes our agreement on equal shares or shares in proportion. The scheme is concerned only with translating an abstract formula for sharing into the concrete objects to be shared. It does not guarantee that everybody is equally satisfied. It accomplishes elimination of any valid basis for complaining afterward. Nobody can claim he got less than his "fair share."[14]

Two criteria are essential to fair division: fairness and efficiency. Efficiency in this case means that no other division of objects or cash should be unanimously preferred or would leave everybody better off. When this notion of efficiency is combined with a dissimilarity in relative valuations, different people give to different objects, it is possible to give everyone something that looks like more than his fair share. Objects can be distributed in accordance with "comparative advantage," with each going to the person who gives it the highest comparative valuation. An alternative rule for dividing the surplus that Schelling mentions is: everybody gets his share of his own total valuation, plus his share of the residue in the kitty. A second related possibility

Schelling mentions is: everybody gets his own claim (his fair share of his own valuation) augmented in the same proportion. In this method each player would get the same percentage of his own total valuation, and this percentage distribution would be more than 100 percent of value as a result of the kitty.

A third possible rule is: each gets exactly his share of total cash proceeds from sale of the items being divided, which is fair but eliminates the possibility of added value. The Steinhaus method assumes that with subjective valuation as in inherited family items there will be nonobjective factors involved that will cause certain individuals to place value beyond market value on selected items. What is the market value of a family pet to others? One heir might value it far beyond the painting that hung over the family mantelpiece. Another rule could be that everybody gets his fair share of his own valuation, but the "surplus," if one remained, would be distributed in accordance with some other criterion. That surplus would be what was left after everyone had received what he or she was obliged to consider a fair share based on personal valuation.

Lottery

Closely related to fair division is fair allocation when demand exceeds supply. A common method that is generally seen as fair is the lottery when there are more people who desire something than can have it, while auctions of some sort are sometimes used to allocate limited goods. In July 2009, about 1.6 million fans registered for a chance at fewer than nine thousand tickets to Michael Jackson's memorial service. Nobody seemed to have an unfair advantage in the procedure. However, there are situations, for example, the shortage of organs available for transplants, where there may be reasons to give an advantage to some over others. Some of the reasons for a preference in this situation may be more admirable than others.

Auction

Another method for distributing desired resources is by auction. A problem with some auctions is what is called the "winner's curse." The winner's curse applies in cases where the actual valuation of something being auctioned is the same to all involved. This can be true in big items like new oil fields. In these cases, there are overlapping bell curves. There is a bell curve of all those who have placed a value on the desired item with a normal distribution. A second distribution curve is the bids, which is a bell below the actual valuation. However, although the average of the bids is below the average valuation, the extreme high point of the bids is beyond the average valuation, and is where the sale takes place. The true value is the high point of the curve of the valuations, so the winning bid is above the value of the item sold.

This is true where items have actual, not subjective values. The bids are likely different because the bidders have different information, or all bids would be the same.

One approach to making auctions more accurate that Schelling says would lead to a dominant strategy to bidding actual value is the second prize auction. This approach is that interested parties bid for an object or rights to do something. The desired item goes to the highest bidder, who pays the second highest bid. This creates incentive for bidding true value and getting the profit of the difference between true value and second highest bid.

A Fair Division Problem

A way to process the various ideas involved in fair division/fair allocation is to consider a problem Schelling presented in his Conflict, Cooperation, and Strategy course. It deals with a situation many travelers have encountered. We know what solutions the airlines have selected in cases less extreme than this one. The problem is called Overbooked Airline Flight.

An airline oversubscribes a flight and has 120 passengers with valid reservations and only 100 seats. It is two hours before flight time. The airline has no record of who reserved their tickets when. What should it do?

a. Put all the people in a room for an hour, asking them to produce a list at the end of that time, stating who will be on the airplane and who will wait (at the airline's expense) in a motel.

b. Ask people whether they have to go urgently, and if so, why. Use their answers to order them in terms of personal priority and let the top 100 go onto the plane.

c. Raise the price in small steps, asking at each step who would be willing to pay to go at that price. Continue until 20 passengers fall out. Divide the proceeds from the additional payments among the 20 who do not get on the flight.

d. Issue boarding passes randomly by drawing names out of a hat.

e. Same as (d) except you then put everyone in a room for an hour and let them buy and sell the tickets, or make other deals.

f. Cancel the flight altogether.

g. Lower the price in small steps for tomorrow's flight until 20 people volunteer to go tomorrow.

h. Take women and children first, then elderly people, the blind and physically disabled, then randomize the selection of the remainder. You might also add the free market element as proposed in (e).

i. Deliberately delay the flight, allowing people to go to the motel at any point thereafter, and keep delaying until 20 people go to the motel.

j. You notice that people can be divided into groups according to whether they are young or old, male or female, married or not, left- or right-handed, black or white, Protestant, Catholic, or Jewish, and so on. Select a set of "relevant" categories, establish the percentage of the group in each category, and make sure the composition of the group that gets on the plane is similar to the composition of the whole group. Randomly select within categories if necessary.

k. Although you do not have the reservation dates for the people, make up a list of such dates on a random basis, without telling the potential passengers, and then, pretending it is a chronological list of reservation dates, apply the list to admit those who you say made their reservations earliest.

l. Have everyone hand in sealed bids for places on the plane. The highest 100 bids are selected, and the money collected. The amount collected over and above the regular price of the ticket is distributed among the group in a manner to be determined by you. You might give out equal shares to everyone, or only to those who did not get on, or whatever seems appropriate.

m. Choose 3 or 4 alternative reasonable procedures for deciding, and let people vote on the procedures. Select the procedure which gets the most votes.

n. Simultaneously raise the price of going tonight and lower that for going tomorrow, until you find a pair of prices at which:
   i. exactly 100 people wish to go tonight; and
   ii. you, the airline, break even; that is, your subsidization of tomorrow's passengers equals, in total, your surcharge on the ones for tonight. In other words, you have a balanced budget.

1. Which procedures on the list would be *more* acceptable if everybody knew in advance what the procedure would be in this situation?
2. Which procedures on the list would be *less* attractive if everybody knew in advance what the procedure would be in this situation?
3. Which procedures are likely, if they are the general rule for these situations, to induce the airline to book the right number of people for each flight? (What is the right number for each flight that the airline ought to book?)

This problem is included to provoke thought, as there are many options and value decisions to be discussed and weighed, and there is not one correct answer. The questions at the end raise important issues, but the points to consider are how to be fair, be seen to be fair, be efficient, and apply something that actually works in a complex system of competing interests.

Notes

1. Thomas C. Schelling, *Micromotives and Macrobehavior* (New York: Norton, 1978), 125. See pp. 127–133 for a discussion on social contract.
2. Garrett Hardin, "The Tragedy of the Commons," *Science*, Vol. 162, No. 3909 (1968), 1243–1248.

3. Ibid., 1244.

4. Thomas Malthus, *An Essay on the Principle of Population: An Essay on the Principle of Population, as it Affects the Future Improvement of Society with Remarks on the Speculations of Mr. Godwin, M. Condorcet, and Other Writers* (London: Printed for J. Johnson, in St. Paul's Church-yard, 1798).

5. Hardin, "The Tragedy of the Commons," 1248.

6. Garrett Hardin, "Extensions of 'The Tragedy of the Commons,'" *Science*, Vol. 280, No. 5364 (May 1, 1998), 682.

7. Stephen C. McCaffrey, "The International Law Commission Adopts Draft Articles on Transboundary Aquifers," *American Journal of International Law* (April 2009), 279.

8. Hardin, "Extensions of 'The Tragedy of the Commons,'" 683.

9. Juliet Eilperin, "International Whaling Commission Proposes Compromise on Ban," *Washington Post*, April 24, 2010.

10. For examples see Robyn M. Dawes, Jeanne McTavish, and Harriet Shaklee, "Behavior, Communication, and Assumptions about Other People's Behavior in a Commons Dilemma Situation," *Journal of Personality and Social Psychology* Vol. 35, No. 1 (January 1977), 1–11; Robert C. Cass and Julian J. Edney, "The Commons Dilemma: A Simulation Testing the Effects of Resource Visibility and Territorial Division, *Human Ecology* (December 1978), 371–386 ; Elinor Ostrom, "Institutional Arrangements for Resolving the Commons Dilemma: Some Contending Approaches," *Scientific Commons*, 1987, http://en.scientificcommons.org/23102465; Roderick M. Kramer and Marilynn B. Brewer, "Effects of Group Identity on Resource Use in a Simulated Commons Dilemma, *Journal of Personality and Social Psychology* Vol. 46, No. 5 (May 1984), 1044–1057; David Goetze, "Comparing Prisoner's Dilemma, Commons Dilemma, and Public Goods Provision Designs in Laboratory Experiments, *Journal of Conflict Resolution* Vol. 38, No. 1(March 1994), 55–86.

11. Herodotus, *The Histories*, translated by Aubrey de Selincourt (London: Penguin Books, 1954), 93.

12. I Kings 3:16–28, *King James Bible*.

13. Hugo Steinhaus, "The Problem of Fair Division," *Econometrica*, Vol. 16 (January 1948), 101.

14. For another example of bidding and fair division, the "Gap Procedure," applied to the housemate game of establishing the rent paid by different renters, see Steven J. Brams and D. Marc Kilgour, "Competitive Fair Division," *Journal of Political Economy* Vol. 109, No. 2 (April 2001), 418–443.

CHAPTER 17

Case Study: Overcoming Professional Basketball's Commons Dilemma

THE PHIL JACKSON STORY

In *Choice and Consequences*[1] Schelling discusses the incompatibility between rationality that focuses on individual incentives to maximize personal benefits and the collective rationality that causes people to make sacrifices that are beneficial to the group as a whole. He wrote of when people pursue self-interest, saying, "In these situations people are *individually* motivated to behave in such ways that they *all* could have been better if they had behaved differently."[2] One institution where this conflict between individual incentives and group outcomes takes place in a very public forum is professional basketball. Professional basketball teams in the National Basketball Association, the NBA, can be seen as individual commons, or multiperson prisoner's dilemmas. It is rational for players to act in their own personal interests but better for their teams if they cooperate. This is the "tragedy of the commons," or the commons dilemma.

This conflict has been analyzed by academic studies and in the press. One study looked at the individual contracts of every player in the NBA for a period of fifteen years and also the corresponding yearly statistics for each player, such as average points scored, rebounds, assists, and steals.[3] The conclusion from comparing the data was that in the year before a new contract was signed, players improved their performance in efforts to earn new more lucrative long-run contracts. Having signed their contracts, however, the players' overall performance declined, indicating that the incentive motivating improved play during contract years is self-interest. The study also noted individual performance incentives, and professional contracts are laden with them.

Individual performance incentives can promote team play, such as bonuses for making playoffs or winning the NBA title. However, incentives that can indicate success may promote individual self-interest. These latter performance incentives include such things as selection for the all-star team, number of points scored, most valuable player award. The value of winning special recognition was noted in research on professional sports that commented, "Most players in the highest professional leagues are well known to the public but only when they achieve star status their marketing value increases notably."[4] A recent study concerned how three top players reacted to each other when it was clear they were the only realistic candidates for Most Valuable Player, or MVP of the NBA. Winning this award could mean larger future contracts, valuable endorsements, and likely future hall of fame membership as well as the personal immediate prestige involved.

During the later stages of the 2008–2009 season it was apparent to all that LeBron James, Kobe Bryant, and Dwyane Wade were in a three-person contest for the MVP award. To find out whether the players were competing with each other for the award, an analysis was done of how the players reacted to each others' performances in the previous game, and what individual incentive this provided for them to perform better individually.[5] What was observed was that if Wade increased his scoring in a game, both James and Bryant increased their scoring significantly in response in their next game. James also increased his scoring significantly in response to Bryant having scored more in his most recent game. In all cases the players were scoring more because of a substantial increase in free throws attempted, which indicates they were playing more aggressively. While James seems to have been the most attuned to the others' performances, his altered behavior did not appear to have had adverse affects on his team's win-loss record. Still, the study indicated individual self-interest affected the team play of the MVP contestants.

Marcia Smith's article, "There Is an 'I' in Incentive,"[6] did a thorough job of outlining the commons dilemma in the NBA as well as in professional football's NFL. She wrote, "These incentives give star players extra earnings for reaching statistical benchmarks, playing-time thresholds, top rankings and league honors. The individual rewards challenge coaches who are trying to foster team unity.... Contracts for marquee American pro players, on average, reward individual more than team success.... Perhaps an NBA player would challenge more players one-on-one and attempt more shots rather than pass because a $1 million bonus for scoring average is at stake."[7]

One NBA coach has expressed strong feelings about the negative influence individual performance incentives can have on team unity. He is Phil Jackson, the most successful of all NBA coaches. His success has come because of his ability to get players to work together as a team, though there have been difficult moments. After the 2003–2004 season when "Jackson had a tough time getting four veteran All-Stars, each with incentive-laden contracts, to share the ball, playing time and attention,"[8] he said, "It's so inherent in today's game for players to think '[t]his is not going to last forever, so I'll have to make all the money I can and look out for myself.'"[9]

Jackson stepped down from his twenty years as a head coach in the NBA in May of 2011 when his Los Angeles Lakers were eliminated from the season's playoffs, after a career of unmatched success. As Jack McCallum of *Sports Illustrated* put it, "Jackson won 70 percent of his regular-season games and 69 percent of his playoff games, and there is the small matter of his 11 championship rings. That makes him perforce the most successful coach in NBA history (no objective argument to the contrary is possible), and I would argue that he is also the best."[10] His successor at Los Angeles acknowledged the challenge of following him, as he said, "I don't know what size shoes he wears, but I'm not here to fill his shoes."[11]

Successfully dealing with players and the commons dilemma is the unlikely hallmark of Phil Jackson's coaching career. That success put him in the NBA Hall of Fame in 2007 while he was still actively participating in the league, increasing his achievements. On June 14, 2009, the Los Angles Lakers defeated the Orlando Magic 99–86, winning the final game necessary to become champions of the National Basketball Association. Following the game Los Angeles coach, Jackson, lit a cigar in honor of the legendary coach whose record he had just erased. "I'll smoke a cigar in honor of Red," Jackson said. "He was a great guy."[12] He was referring to Red Auerbach, longtime coach of the Boston Celtics, who had led the team to nine NBA titles, a record Jackson had just surpassed, leaving him at the pinnacle as the most successful coach in professional basketball history.

Mike Wise, sports columnist for the *Washington Post*, described Jackson as "the greatest coach in the history of big-time pro sports in America…ahead of Vince Lombardi and Bill Walsh in the NFL, Joe Torre and Casey Stengel in baseball and Scotty Bowman in the NHL."[13] Wise continued, comparing Jackson with the legendary Boston Celtics coach Red Auerbach, who had been commonly considered the greatest in NBA history:

> Auerbach won his nine championships.…But Red's NBA had less than half the teams to go through for a title back then, and the idea that only Jackson had the greatest talent to work with is dispelled by Bill Russell, Bill Sharman, Bob Cousy and numerous other Hall-of-Fame Celtics. Red had horses too, and he hoarded them in his day.…Jackson's ability to get Kobe and Michael to bend their wills to fit the needs of a championship team is vastly underrated.
>
> The No. 1 talent of a coach in large-revenue professional sports is the managing of egos, and no one has done it better than Jackson. Because there are only 12 roster spots, an NBA player's salary on an average dwarfs salaries from football, baseball and hockey. Molding a genuine team from those players is what Rick Fox described several years ago.…"You're basically managing 12 CEOs, who are the head of their own companies and have their ideas about how the world should work because they've been given an inflated sense of their worth by their agents, their families and all that money," Fox said. "Around all that, Phil gets people to buy into something bigger than themselves."[14]

June 17, 2010, was the seventh and deciding game to determine who would be the year's NBA champion team, and the Lakers defeated the Boston Celtics 83–79, giving Jackson his eleventh title, increasing the distance between him and all other coaches in the history of professional basketball. Along with the eleven

NBA Champions rings Jackson has earned as a coach, he has two from his time as a player for the New York Knicks.

This success required bringing individuals together to cooperate, and Phil Jackson is an unlikely candidate to have attained such accolades and distinction. More than any other team sport, professional basketball is dominated by black athletes, most of whom are products of major urban areas. African American athletes, many from the inner cities, ghettoes, and urban housing projects constitute nearly 80 percent of the league's players.[15] Only about one out of five active players has completed college,[16] but the average salary for an NBA player in 2009–2010 was $5,854 million.[17] Many players have been found as high school stars or were lured from college early by the high salaries offered in the NBA. The jump from often poor, semifunctional families to instant great wealth can be a challenge. Jackson has a rare gift for transforming these individually motivated young men. As David Shields wrote in the *New York Times*, "One principal reason that Phil Jackson has been such a successful coach is that he has the ability to function as a subtly paternal rather than sadistically paternalistic leader of a group of young black men (many of whom grew up without fathers) who might have use for a mentor but have none for a tyrant."[18]

He has used his relationship with his players to alter the way they approach the game. He finds ways of working with players who grew up developing incredible individual skills. They were often players concerned with what they could do personally, and a basketball team is a form of the commons, where individual self-interest is not what is best for the group, the team. He convinced players they would be greater by sharing their talents with their teammates. Michael Jordan is the ultimate example, while Shaquille O'Neal and Kobe Bryant are similar cases.

What makes Jackson such an anomaly is that he is unsurpassed in relating to the diverse and disparate individual players he coaches and getting them to change their ways. This is a surprising and incredible achievement, as his background could hardly be more different from most of theirs.

Far from coming from a tough inner-city background, Phil Jackson was born in a very small town in the ranching country of eastern Montana, one of three sons and a half-sister of two Pentecostal ministers who had sworn oaths of poverty. After Jackson spent his early years in Montana the family moved to Williston in western North Dakota, which, with eleven thousand people, was one of the state's larger cities. With over 90 percent of the state covered by farmland, according to its state government North Dakota is the most rural state in the nation. The Native American Sioux, whom Jackson admires, had been largely confined to the state's five reservations, and diversity in North Dakota consisted more in whether one's heritage was Norwegian or German. The "whiter and brighter" that described North Dakota winters also fit the population. It was a tough world, with weather extremes that made day-to-day living a challenge and kept the population low.

Phil believes that growing up where he did affected him and he inherited a work ethic typical of the area, where struggle was a part of survival and working hard was normal.[19] It showed in the way he played basketball and in what he expects of his players: work hard at practice and at both ends of the court, playing defense and offense. Being gifted and a scoring star would not be good enough.

Phil's father preached Sunday morning services, and his mother preached Sunday evenings at the Assemblies of God church, and he was raised in a strict, uncompromising home. When he was four, a sign was hung over his bed, stating, "For God so loved the world that he gave his only begotten Son, that whosoever believeth in him should not perish, but have eternal life" (John 3:16). He describes his early years as rigid yet competitive, writing,

> Competition was a battle in my house. As a child of ministers and the last of 4 kids this was a positive outlet that was honored by my parents, altho they didn't let us participate in sports that conflicted w/church. However, if I played ball on Sunday I had to attend a church service any-where I might be playing that day. My mother was a player. My dad loved to play board games like caroms or scrabble. We did not have a TV. My mother told the story that when I was in my crib she used to come in and look at me sleeping and I would be catching balls in my sleep—strange behavior to her—she had to ask my sister 11 years older than I to come and identify my sleeping activity. Hmm.[20]

Through high school Jackson and his siblings attended church three days a week and were not allowed to go to movies or dances, or watch television. He thought he would become a minister after being led to the front of the church congregation and dedicating his life to future service of God, but had diffi-culties when failing to speak in tongues spontaneously as a teenager. As his athletic talents became more recognized his inquisitive mind was questioning not his parents' Christianity, but the absoluteness of their answers and their focus on the Book of Revelations. He accepted his parents' stern guidance to a remarkable degree, though he began sneaking out of some church services, as sports began to play a larger role in his life. His was a controlled upbringing unlike the backgrounds of many of the players he would later coach. He says he is uncertain about whether the strict paternal influence he felt as a young man was an influence on the paternal role he later came to play in the lives of many players he coached.[21]

While Jackson did not see his first movie until he was a senior in high school and did not attend dances while in high school, he and his brothers threw them-selves actively into athletics, where there was the freedom and opportunity to be with and like other young people. He played sports every season in high school, attempting football in the fall and basketball in winter. In spring he threw discus on the track team and when summer came he played baseball. There was little doubt as he grew that his body had been suited for basketball, and that was where he attracted attention. Very tall for the area at six-foot-six inches and growing, with a lean, angular, and lanky body that was all dangling limbs and broad shoulders, he was overwhelming against most teams.

Jackson was well known around the state his senior year and led his team to the state championship. He went on to the University of North Dakota, where future NBA coach Bill Fitch watched him grow two inches, stressed defense, and put together a team that did well in Division II competition. Six-foot-eight inches did not accurately reflect Jackson's height. He had exceptionally long arms that added great length and extension to what he could do. Fitch liked to show off Jackson's reach with "the car trick," where Jackson would sit in middle of the back seat of a large Buick and simultaneously open both doors. It was also said he could steer a Volkswagen while seated in the back seat behind the driver.

In the summer after his freshman year he visited his brother at the University of Texas and was introduced to the teachings of Zen. It took his life in a new direction. The idea of existing in the present moment would fascinate him, and he would find connections that existed among Zen, Christianity, and Native American thought. The philosophy and religion major became a voracious reader and began to assimilate some of the counterculture of the times. As he was changing as a person, his basketball achievements attracted notice.

Jackson had a left-handed hook shot that exploited his extreme reach as he shot it from around the basket fully stretched out, high in the air, his 39-inch sleeve-length arm extended. It was an unstoppable move that would make him a leading scorer in the conference, averaging more than 27 points per game when he was a senior. He was impressive enough that the New York Knicks chose him in the second round as the twelfth overall choice of the 1967 NBA player draft. Phil was very pleased with the money the Knicks were giving him—$15,000 salary plus a $3,000 bonus for signing. As an indication of how far he has come since then, in 2009–2010 he received a $12,000,000 salary plus a $2,000,000 bonus for winning the championship.[22] To a rural boy from North Dakota in 1967, being given $15,000 a year to play a game he loved sounded good.

Phil made the Knicks team, but found basketball in the NBA was not the same as it had been in college. The difference was evident his first year when he got into a game against the Philadelphia '76ers and went up for that unstoppable hook shot of his. The player opposite him was the most dominant scorer in basketball history, Wilt Chamberlain. Chamberlain, who averaged over 50 points per game in one season and once scored 100 in a game, did not block Jackson's hook or swat it away. As the ball looped high, Wilt just caught it in one of his massive hands. It was clear Phil was not going to be the offensive threat in the NBA that he had been in college, but he was intelligent. He became a fanatic on defense, where many NBA players slacked off. He adjusted and found how to add value to his team. "Head-n-Shoulders" or "Action Jackson," as New York fans called him, became a crowd favorite with his jerky movements and intensity as he relentlessly blanketed the players he guarded. His value as a role player earned him All-Rookie Team honors and a doubling of his salary.

Jackson spent thirteen years in the NBA, mainly as a reserve brought on for short periods, and played on two NBA Champion teams. After two years as a player- assistant coach for the New Jersey Nets, he left the NBA and eventually became coach of the Albany Patroons in the Continental Basketball Association, the CBA. He misses those years as coach of the Patroons, as there were no issues with personal incentive bonuses to incite the self-interest that can destroy the basketball commons. He drove the team in a van, and all the players received equal pay. The only bonus possible was as extra $25 weekly given to players who were married. Jackson recalls telling his players, "Everybody's going to get the same amount, so why don't we make it a team effort."[23]

Five years in Albany would result in his being named Coach of the Year and winning a CBA championship, which would make him the only person to ever coach winning teams in both the NBA and CBA.

He was always a different coach, less authoritarian than most. At one point Jackson took a personality test offered by the NBA. His top callings were first, Homemaker and second, Trail Guide. This hardly sounds like the makings of the most successful coach of all time, but perhaps it suggests that usual qualities are not the best match for the job. The job is definitely tenuous, as Chicago Bulls history demonstrates.

In the 1982–1983 season the Chicago Bulls had a 28–54 win-loss record under their new coach Paul Westhead, who was fired at the end of his first season and replaced by Kevin Loughery, who led the team to an even more dismal record of 27–55. An analysis of three NBA seasons concluded as they near the end there is a "race-to-the-bottom" incentive for teams that will not make playoffs to try to achieve poor records since this rank order of draft of future players has been based on a worst to best sequence for purposes of maintaining league competitiveness, directly through 1984 then by weighted lottery favoring the poorest records.[24] For their miserable season Chicago was rewarded with the third choice in the 1984 draft and the first two teams picked centers, the big men who often dominate the game.[25] Chicago went for a six-foot-six-inch Brooklyn-born, North Carolina–raised guard who had just finished his junior year at the University of North Carolina. As a freshman he had made a jump shot with eighteen seconds remaining in the NCAA College National Championship finals to give his team a one-point victory and the national title. In his sophomore year and again as a junior he was named College Player of the Year by the *Sporting News*. It was apparent that Michael Jordan had the phenomenal talent to rebuild Chicago's team.

In Jordan's first year in the NBA he was a starter in the All-Star Game and the Bulls also made the postseason playoffs, but were eliminated in the best-of-five first round series, 3–1. Coach Loughery was fired after the season and Stan Albeck was named the new head coach. When the new season began Jordan broke a bone in his foot and missed sixty-four games, but returned late in the season and managed to get the Bulls in the postseason playoffs, where they were immediately eliminated, and Coach Albeck was fired. The year 1986 saw Doug Collins as head coach and Jordan the league's leading scorer. Collins attempted to get Jordan to change his style to be more of a team player, but did not have the rapport to achieve success. While the team's record improved, they were eliminated in a 3–0 loss in the first round of the playoffs.

The next year Jackson got his job as assistant coach with the Bulls. Jackson says in his book that when he began as an assistant coach at Chicago, one of the other assistants called their offense, "the archangel offense." This was because when the situation was important the other players faded into the background and "waited for Michael to perform another miracle."[26] It looked like a good year, and their record improved, as Horace Grant and Scottie Pippen were added to the roster, giving support to Jordan, who again led the league in scoring and was the league's MVP. Chicago had its first playoff success in years. They won their opening series 3–2, but were defeated in the best-of seven Eastern Conference semifinals in a 4-–1 series.

The following year Jordan again led the league in scoring, and Chicago had promising results in the playoffs, winning the opening round 3–2 and the semifinal round 4–2, advancing to the Conference Finals for the second time in the history of the team's franchise. The Bulls got off to a 2–1 lead in the Conference Finals and winning would put them in the NBA championship series. They lost the next three games and were eliminated, and two months later, Collins was fired as head coach.

Phil Jackson was then named in 1989 as Collins' replacement. In the five seasons before Jackson became the head coach of the Bulls, Michael Jordan had improved the Bulls to where they had reached postseason playoffs every year and he was on the All Star team every season. Jordan had also been chosen for Most Valuable Player of the NBA, Defensive Player of the Year, led the league in scoring three years, and won the league's first two slam dunk competitions. In the critical playoffs during those years under three different coaches the Bulls had amassed a record of 14 wins and 23 losses. Changes were about to be made and history made along with them.

Jordan was aware of how good he was and he wanted to have control. Chicago Bull center Bill Cartwright spoke to the problem after he had been open under the basket on nine occasions during a playoff game and Jordan did not pass to him. Cartwright said, "He's the greatest athlete I've ever seen. Maybe the greatest athlete ever to play any sport. He can do whatever he wants. It all comes so easy to him. He's just not a basketball player."[27]

Under Jackson this commons dilemma that restrained Chicago was going to end and cooperation was going to come before individual motivation. He says he had learned team play came first from his personal experience as a player, and that his philosophy and religious practices fit with the idea of the primacy of team play. His years with the Knicks when they were at their best were great learning times. The transition on the Bulls to a more cooperative offense did not come easily and he describes the reaction to it as "mixed," adding, "MJ (Jordan) had to be convinced."[28]

Jackson put an emphasis on very aggressive defense, where the "Dobermans," as Jordan and teammate Scottie Pippin were known, exploited their superior athleticism and awareness of the court and made life difficult for opponents. He also did not assign new players to roles. Something he had learned from his own experience in the NBA was that a player could find the right role to help the team. In an age when the game was becoming more slam dunks and spectacular moves, many players liked to do things that called attention to themselves, but that did not add value to the team. His view was that aware players would find how they could benefit the whole, rather as he had done when he became a defensive specialist. He still says, "This is something I rarely do—require or dictate roles. I'd like Players to show me what their role is. . . . Bench players have to know if they are 8 min rotation men or just in to fill the gap."[29]

The big change came on offense, where he adopted what his assistant, Tex Winter, had used in college many years earlier, the triangle offense. The triangle suited Jackson ideally, as it was the right thing for his basketball and his philosophy and the two were intertwined. People may ridicule the "Zen Master" title so often associated with him, but the connection of the individuals to a group identity, their loyalty to each other, and mutual trust and involvement in the moment, where awareness is heightened, combined philosophy and sport. In strategic terms, it includes everyone in the commons, where shared values are ranked above individual values. The triangle was the vehicle designed for cooperation and depending on teammates; for it to work a real bonding of the team and the idea of quest were critical.

The triangle was a simple idea. Teams concentrated their defenses on Jordan, and Jordan wanted to show he could not be stopped. This offense made a triangle of three players spaced apart while the other two were nearer the basket. The triangle could be moved according to the defense being played, and the players were spread around enough that if the opposition doubled its coverage of Jordan, someone was left open. It also created space so there was room for Jordan to maneuver and do his magic. The triangle made it difficult for teams to focus their defense on guarding Jordan, and Jackson adds that it got Jordan to share the ball.[30] Getting Michael Jordan, and later Kobe Bryant, to adapt to this system and pass in the triangle offense rather than take all the shots depended on their trusting and depending on their teammates. But once the trust and sharing were established, the results were devastating.

So with such an incredibly successful offense that gets superstars to share and work as team players, why have NBA coaches other than the one who is the game's most successful not adopted this? Jackson says it is, "complicated and takes discipline; must be taught by teaching skills one-by-one."[31]

Jordan's scoring numbers dipped a bit, though he remained the league's leading scorer, and Chicago became a stronger team. It has been said the pivotal moment in turning Jordan into a team player came when the Bulls trailed the Lakers 91–90 in the fifth game of the 1991 NBA Finals and Jordan was determined to win the game by himself. Jackson called a timeout, then looked at Jordan and only asked, "Who's open?" When he did not get any answer he repeated the question and Jordan finally said, "Paxson." Jackson's response was, "Let's find him," and John Paxson scored 10 points in the final four minutes. The Bulls were NBA Champions for the first time in their history. Jackson agrees with the assessment of the significance of the incident, saying it was important that it be Jordan and not he that pointed out that Paxson was open because, "for him to change his style, he had to admit the team came first."[32] The commons dilemma was being resolved.

Jackson kept the unity of the team focused in many ways. He had brought teammate Bill Bradley with him to the Pine Ridge Reservation in South Dakota in 1973 and conducted a basketball clinic, which he continued for six years. Out of gratitude, the elders of the tribe gave Jackson the name Swift Eagle, and the Lakota Sioux's view of the way of the warrior became a theme for the Bulls to rally around for unity. It had been the Sioux warriors, being totally at peace with themselves as they went into battle and not trying to stand out from their fellow warriors, who represented what Jackson wanted the Bulls to be. He decorated their team room with Native American artwork, infused training tapes with scenes from *The Mystic Warrior*, a made-for-TV film based loosely on the life of Crazy Horse, and lectured them on Lakota ideals. During playoffs he frequently wrote them a passage from Rudyard Kipling's *Second Jungle Book* that encompassed his message, "For the strength of the Pack is the Wolf, and the strength of the Wolf is the Pack." Always the message was the individual was secondary to the group.

Jordan, described by Jackson as "Michelangelo in baggy shorts,"[33] bought into Jackson's system and ideas, as Jackson puts it "surrendering the 'me' for the 'we.'" Jordan would break loose at times and take over games, but he trusted his teammates and gave them opportunities to become better players. Jackson had several players take up meditation to help them live in the moment, as the practice allowed him to do, so they would react more instinctively on the court and not cloud their minds with continuous second-guessing. This living in the moment is why he allows the team so much freedom to function on its own, and is not one of the coaches who are continually instructing players on what they should be doing. The Bulls became a unit by that 1991 win, which would be the first of three straight wins, a "three-peat" for the team and the beginning of the legend of "Air Jordan" or "His Airness," the high flying star who could do anything but lose. Jackson gives details of his leading player's fame in his book, *Sacred Hoops*, writing, "The Associated Press reported that, in a survey of African-American children, Jordan had tied with God as the person they most admired after their parents. A radio station in Chicago asked listeners if Jordan should be named king of the world, and 41 percent of the respondents said yes. And fans were spotted kneeling and praying at the foot of Jordan's statue in front of the United Center."[34]

With a star that is so recognized and admired, how can there be equality? Jackson responded, "It is impossible to try to make everything equal. I've got a fine system in place for basic infractions of 'rules'... being on time, prepared to practice, etc. These are simple fines of small bucks, but if players continue to disregard the rules after 3 strikes the fines go up dramatically. These keep some equality in the game. There is jealousy, but . . ."[35]

The Jackson method of creating team value by getting the individual star to share and cooperate had been a great success, as would be expected in a multiperson prisoner's dilemma. Value had been created and something greater resulted when Jordan did not try to win everything by himself, but shared the ball, time of possession, and responsibility at key moments. Some say anyone could have done it who had Jordan, but that had not been the case before Jackson took control. Bill Bradley commented on this view in the forward to *Hoop Dreams* in 1995, saying, "I have heard: 'Anybody can coach a team led by Michael Jordan to the World Championship.' This comment signifies both unfamiliarity with Phil Jackson and with the game of basketball. . . . The Bulls are a team and not just one player. They won their three championships, without either a dominant center or an all-star point guard, because all the players worked together toward the same goal, sacrificing themselves for the betterment of the team."[36]

After three championships Jordan decided to leave basketball to try professional baseball. The first year he was gone, during the 1994 playoffs against the New York Knicks, another well remembered incident showed the unique Jackson coaching strategy. With 1.8 seconds remaining in the game Jackson sent his star player, Scottie Pippen, back into the game and Pippen refused to go. Following the game Jackson went into the Bulls locker room and rather than getting angry, said what had happened had hurt them and they had to work it out. He was giving them two minutes to discuss it softly among themselves. Asked why he handled it that way, he responded to, "emphasize the importance of being a team by forcing them to discuss it. Pip was a co-captain; his fellow 'co' was heartbroken. He made the plea for unity."[37] Always the group's interests came first.

Jordan returned to basketball and a team that was being rebuilt. It centered on Jordan's former colleague, Scottie Pippen, but a new, notoriously difficult to coach player had been added, Dennis Rodman. Rodman lived up to his independent reputation and missed practice during a playoff series to fly to Texas in support of the family of a black man killed by Ku Klux Klansmen. Many coaches would not have tolerated such insubordination, but Jackson accepted Rodman's priorities and the two were able to work well together.

With Jordan back, Jackson led the Bulls to three more consecutive championships in 1996–1998, establishing Chicago as one of the all time great teams. Jordan was recognized by consensus as the greatest player in the history of the sport, and was one of the most well known people on earth. After Jordan scored 63 points in a playoff loss to the Celtics, superstar Boston Celtic Larry Bird said, "That was God disguised as Michael Jordan."[38] The sports network ESPN voted Jordan as the greatest athlete of the twentieth century.

Jordan retired after the 1998 season, and Jackson also left the game. A situation similar to Chicago's beckoned a year later, however. The Los Angeles Lakers had the great talent but were not a great team. Their anchor since 1996 had been the awesome Shaquille O'Neal, standing 7feet 1 inch in his size 23 shoes and weighing 325 pounds. Shaq had been first choice in the player draft in 1992 and went to the Orlando Magic after his junior year in college. He had led Orlando to the playoffs the following year and the finals the next, when he was the league's leading scorer. The big man was dominant, but his teams were not having success in the playoffs, though there was considerable optimism in Los Angeles when teenage supertalent Kobe Bryant signed in 1998.

Before Jackson became the head coach of the Lakers in 1999, O'Neal was a seven-year veteran who had led his team once to the NBA Finals, where they were swept in four straight losses. O'Neal's teams were also swept out of the playoffs in 1994, 1996, and 1998. Excitement about the addition of Bryant to bolster O'Neal was dampened when the Lakers finished fourth in the Western Conference and lost 4–0 to San Antonio in the playoffs. Jackson was hired to be their coach, and the result was three consecutive NBA championships, another three-peat, never before achieved by Los Angeles, even in the years with Magic Johnson and Kareem Abdul-Jabbar. His method was again the triangle offense and getting everyone to be a part of the team. He wanted them to trust each other and see themselves as more than individuals, and then let the games happen. "Play the way you live your life, with your whole heart and soul," he has said, reflecting both the Zen exist-in-the-moment view he imparted to his players and the trust they developed that they were a part of something larger.

Jackson's strategy involves connecting with his team on a different plane. He wants them to believe there is more to life than basketball, and believes they can lose touch with reality by existing in the isolated world of celebrity stardom in professional sport. It is one way to help them bond, by encouraging activities of the mind and outside interests. While some coaches prefer boot camp–like sessions for attempts to get teammates to become close, Jackson thinks that is short-term at best and prefers things on deeper levels. He conducts regular ethics discussions and has handed out a modern interpretation of the Ten Commandments as a discussion starter. He remains a prodigious reader. Since his days after being drafted to play in 1967, when he made a visit to the big North Dakota city of Fargo, it was the used bookstore that first attracted his attention. Jackson is known for distributing individual books for his players when the team is on road trips. Some of his recommendations have been *Fever: Twelve Stories* by John Wideman, to Jordan; Langston Hughes's *Ways of the White Folks* for Scottie Pippin; *Zen and the Art of Motorcycle Maintenance* for John Paxson; Jack Kerouac's *On the Road* for Will Perdue. His choices have been surprising at times, notably when he gave Friedrich Nietzsche's *Ecce Homo* to Shaquille O'Neal.

Jackson has done other things, including take his team to visit the U.S. Senate, where Senator Bill Bradley greeted them. He took them for a tour of the Statue of Liberty during playoffs against the New York Knicks when they were scheduled to have practice; and he ordered pizza and beer delivered to their rooms to break the monotony of the NBA season life. All such activities unrelated to coaching were a part of building a unit.

He is known as the "Zen master" for his Zen beliefs in selflessness and elimination of ego; and his being a part of something greater translates to being a part of a team and not an individual. He turns over the game to his players to a considerable degree once the games have started and wants them to trust each other, for that is where there is strength. Like the great college coach, John Wooden, he calls few timeouts, and when he does he does not often tell players what they have done wrong. They know that and do not need to hear it from him. He said, "The most effective way to forge a winning team is to call on the players' need to connect with something larger than themselves."

Phil Jackson has managed to achieve sharing and cooperating where individuals play a part in being something more, a team. His methods are not easy to follow as a recipe but have succeeded. The Pentecostal son from the prairie has brought group awareness to inner-city athletes, and whether they ever would have achieved the greatness without him remains unknown.

For a final word on Jackson and strategy, the following is offered by Bill Bradley. Bradley is a former Princeton All-American, NBA all-star, U.S. Senator, and presidential candidate, as well as a longtime friend and former teammate of Jackson. This is his observation:

> Great basketball players can see the pass that leads to the pass that leads to the basket. Great strategic basketball coaches such as Phil Jackson know that perceiving the long term is the key to strategy. One event sets up the next and you have to see beyond the moment to what lies ahead. For example during the NBA finals in 2008, the Los Angeles Lakers were playing the Boston Celtics. It was the sixth game. The Celtics were ahead 3–2 in the series. By the second half the Celtics built up a 30-point lead. Phil urged his players to make a more intense effort, but the Lakers did not rally. It was clear they were going to lose. Instead of taking his first team off the floor Phil left them in the game so that they would have to absorb the maximum impact of defeat. Phil was already thinking ahead, knowing that he would use the blowout as a rallying cry the next season. When the 2008–09 season began the Lakers were still smarting from their embarrassment. Phil could summon up their determination by recalling that night in Boston and saying that this year they could redeem themselves only by winning the championship which required them to play intensely and unselfishly. In 2009 the Lakers once again became NBA Champions.[39]

Overcoming the conflict in the commons dilemma has led to great success in the coaching career of Phil Jackson.

Notes

1. Thomas C. Schelling, *Choice and Consequences* (Cambridge, MA: Harvard University Press, 1984).
2. Ibid., 208.
3. Kevin J. Stiroh, "Playing for Keeps: Pay and Performance in the NBA," *Economic Inquiry* Vol. 45, No. 1(January 2007), 145–161.
4. Tina Heubeck and Jochen Scheuer, "Incentive Clauses in Players' Contracts in Team Sports—Theory and Practice," *German Working Papers in Law and Economics* (2003), 19.
5. Andrew W. Nutting, "Individual Tournament Incentives in a Team Setting: The 2008–09 NBA MVP Race," *International Journal of Sport Finance* (August 2010).
6. Marcia C. Smith, "There Is an 'I' in Incentive: Many Pro Contracts Reward Individual Efforts, Sometimes at Team Expense," *Orange County Register*, Sports Section cover, January 30, 2005.
7. Ibid.
8. Ibid.
9. Ibid.
10. Jack McCallum, "Despite Sour Ending, Jackson Walks Away as Game's Finest Coach," *Sports Illustrated* online, May 11, 2011.
11. David Lassen, "Lakers' Brown Era Officially Under Way," *The Riverside* (CA) *Press-Enterprise*, June 1, 2011, B3.
12. "Finally Kobe, Lakers End Seven Years of Frustration," Associated Press, June 15, 2009.
13. Mike Wise, "Phil Jackson's Ability to Turn Malcontents into Champions Makes Him the Greatest," *Washington Post*, June 2, 2010.
14. Ibid.
15. "Study: 2010 NBA Racial and Gender Report Card," *Slam: Your Source for the Best in Basketball*, June 9, 2010, http://slamonline.com/.
16. Jonathan Abrams, "N.B.A. Players Make Their Way Back to College," *New York Times*, October 5, 2009.
17. David Aldridge, "Worldwide Recession Affects NBA Salary Cap for 2009–10," NBA.com, July 9, 2009.
18. David Shields, "The Good Father," *New York Times*, April 23, 2000.
19. Phil Jackson, e-mail to Robert Dodge, July 12, 2009.
20. Phil Jackson, e-mail to Robert Dodge, November 4, 2008.
21. Jackson, e-mail, November 4, 2008.
22. Marc Stein, "Jackson in Line for Bonus if Lakers Win," ESPN.com, June 15, 2010, http://sports.espn.go.com/los-angeles/nba/news/story?id=5289874.
23. Smith, "There Is an 'I' in Incentive."
24. Beck A. Taylor and Justin G. Trogdon, "Losing to Win: Tournament Incentives in the National Basketball Association," *Journal of Labor Economics* Vol.20, No.1 (January 2002), 23–41.
25. Houston Rockets selected 7' center Hakeem Olajuwon of University of Houston with first choice, Portland Trail Blazers, took 7'1" center Sam·Bowie of Kentucky with second choice.
26. Phil Jackson and Hugh Delehanty, *Sacred Hoops: Spiritual Lessons of a Hardwood Warrior* (New York: Hyperion, 1995), 84.
27. Sam Smith, *The Jordan Rules* (New York: Pocket Books, 1992), 249.
28. Jackson, e-mail, November 4, 2008.
29. Jackson e-mail, July 12, 2009.
30. Jackson, e-mail, November 4, 2008.
31. Ibid.
32. Jackson, e-mail, July 12, 2009.
33. Jackson and Delehanty, *Sacred Hoops*, 172.
34. Ibid., 17.
35. Jackson, e-mail, July 12, 2009.

36. Jackson and Delehanty, *Sacred Hoops*, xiv.
37. Jackson, e-mail, November 4, 2008.
38. Quoted in Fred Kiger, "Air Supreme," *ESPN SportsCentury*, http://espn.go.com/sportscentury/.
39. Senator Bill Bradley, e-mail to Robert Dodge, September 29, 2009.

PART

DECISIONS THAT MIX AND SORT POPULATIONS, DECISIONS BASED ON RANDOMIZATION

CHAPTER 18

Critical Mass and Tipping

The United States is one of the few countries that are neither on the metric system nor making progress toward converting to metric. The metric system originated in France and was first adopted by the French during their Revolution. From there it spread to much of Europe, then to the rest of the world. In 1989 Randy Moore reported in "Inching Toward the Metric System" that "Burma, Liberia and the United States are the only countries in the world that haven't converted to the metric system."[1]

The U.S. government's National Institute of Standards and Technology notes that it was not for lack of effort on the government's part.[2] In 1866, Congress authorized the use of the metric system in America, and in 1875 the United States became one of the original signers of the Treaty of the Meter, which defined the metric system and refined its accuracy. In 1968, Congress authorized a study on adopting the system, and the report's final 1971 study was entitled, "A Metric America: A Decision Whose Time Has Come."[3] Congress soon passed the Metric Conversion Act of 1975 that allowed for transition to the metric system through education and in a gradual, unforced manner. Road signs began to appear in kilometers, schoolchildren began to do math problems in grams and meters, and weather announcements gave us both Fahrenheit and Celsius. To remain internationally competitive in the expanding world market, in 1988 Congress passed the Omnibus Foreign Trade and Competitiveness Act that designated the metric system as the preferred system of weights and measures for United States in trade and commerce.

Since passage of the Metric Conversion Act most of the road signs have changed back; Sears still sells more socket wrenches and electric drills measured in 32nds of an inch than in centimeters. It looks as if, for ordinary citizens if not for the more scientifically oriented industries, "going metric" has petered out. "The United States is now the only industrialized country in the world that does not use the metric system as its predominant system of measurement,"[4] the National Institute of Standards and Technology reported in the early twenty-first century.

The metric system in the United States never caught on with enough people so that others were convinced to convert to it. It is an example of something that failed to achieve the momentum that carries it forward to ultimate success.

One thing caught on and had momentum briefly because of a joke by a popular late night television comedian. In 1973 there was an oil shortage in the United States as a result of an embargo by oil-producing Arab nations during the Arab-Israeli Yom Kippur War. In his December 19 *Tonight Show* monologue Johnny Carson joked, "You know what's disappearing from the supermarket shelves? Toilet paper."[5] His comment touched off nationwide panic.[6] People rushed out and bought toilet paper for the same reason they didn't convert to the metric system. They expected others were going to behave in a similar manner and were convinced to join in.

A model can be applied to the metric system's failure to catch on, the toilet-paper hording panic, and a diverse set of other circumstances; called "critical mass," it also known as the "bandwagon effect." This model captures the essence of game theory, for it is based entirely on interactive decision making, where an individual's choice is based on the decision he anticipates being made by others. It adds clarity to understanding the success or failure of events, ranging from the starting of new clubs, political rallies, the sale of new video games, race riots, and runs on banks. The name of the model, "critical mass," is derived from nuclear physics, where atomic energy is explained in the following general terms: Radioactive decay occurs in a substance like uranium, which emits neutrons. These neutrons fly into space, unless they hit other uranium nuclei before leaving the mass of uranium. If they do hit other nuclei, the collisions cause energy to be released, and more neutrons to fly into space, unless those neutrons hit other nuclei, in which case more energy and more neutrons are released, and so on. If the amount of uranium is large, there is a greater likelihood that a neutron will collide with other nuclei. There has to be enough uranium so that the released neutrons cause an equal or greater number of additional neutrons to be released for the reaction to carry on. This constitutes a "critical mass" of uranium. When that amount is present, the process will cross the critical point when it becomes self-sustaining. A self-sustaining reaction has "gone critical." Any smaller amount will result in the chain reaction fizzling out. A larger amount with each neutron producing more than one neutron on the average creates a more explosive chain reaction. The difference between achieving or failing to achieve critical mass in an atomic reaction is obvious—it determines whether the bomb explodes, or whether the plant produces electric power.

How this idea from physics relates to social science is that people often make decisions based on decisions other people have made or that they anticipate others will make. The social science critical mass model looks to determine accumulations of people that create self-sustaining human reactions, where the way a certain number of people acting is enough to influence others to act in a similar manner, and those people's decisions then influence others to act the same way, and so on, as the decision to act becomes self-sustaining. "Critical numbers," the number of others acting required to inspire a person to act, vary from one person to another. For each person there may be a different number or ratio of people making a related decision on a topic that is "enough" to compel the same decision.

School dances sometimes succeed or fail depending on whether students expect other students to attend. A school-sponsored Friday night dance may succeed if a substantial number of students are definitely going to attend and other students are aware of that. Then, more decide to attend, encouraging others to make the same choice; and their choices convince others to do likewise. In such a case the original group that was committed to attend constituted the necessary "critical mass" of students to begin a sustained reaction that led to a successful dance. Promoters who are aware that students are making their decisions on the basis of decisions made by others might do something to require or entice some original number to commit to attending. If nobody is aware that anyone else is definitely going to attend, there might well be an empty, decorated gym, as uncertain students find other Friday night activities more inviting.

When new products are introduced, the purpose of the initial campaign is to establish a critical mass of users. There are many marketing techniques for doing this, some involving claims about the product's superiority and how the consumer will be left behind if he does not purchase it. This can involve testimonials from famous athletes or others. If a product has been on the market, claims are sometimes made that imply a critical mass has been achieved, so the appropriate thing for the consumer to do is to get on the bandwagon with everyone else. Such claims might involve statistics that claim "four out of five doctors surveyed recommend" or "this outsells all other brands."

McDonald's marketing achieved critical mass much like a nuclear explosion. What began as a family burger stand in San Bernardino, California, in 1948 caught on and has become the leading retail foodservice in the world, with more than 32,000 restaurants located in 117 countries serving over 60 million people daily.[7]

Dick and Mac McDonald were looking for a way to increase earnings at their drive-in barbeque restaurant and they came up with the idea of doing away with carhops and limiting their sales to a small number of items they could mass produce and have people come in for quick counter service to pick up. When they reopened for business, it was soon clear they were on to something the public wanted. Their revenues rose and crowds of 150 were not unusual during peak times.[8] Their burger stand received publicity, and many requests for franchise outlets followed. The McDonald brothers agreed to open a franchise in Phoenix, Arizona, in 1953 and its design was a red and white tile building with "Golden Arches" that made it noticeable and memorable.[9]

The business took off when a former milkshake machine salesman named Ray Kroc joined McDonalds in 1954, gave it organization by adopting the operating format of QSC & V—Quality, Service, Cleanliness, and Value—and took over the expansion of franchising. By the end of 1956 there were fourteen McDonald's restaurants and total sales had reached 50 million hamburgers. Two years later the number of franchises had increased and McDonald's began bandwagon advertising in billboard form by adding a sign beneath one of its arches that proclaimed, "McDonald's Hamburgers: over 100 million sold." If 100 million had been eaten, wasn't it time you tried one? That number kept changing as the company engineered the growth of the fast food industry, and was 400 million in 1960. By 1963 growth was exponential, and McDonald's sales reached one million hamburgers a day, and their billionth burger was presented to Art Linkletter on his national television show.[10]

McDonald's went international in 1967, with outlets opening in Canada and Costa Rica. By the early 1970s they were in Japan, Holland, and Australia, and in the late 1970s a Brazil opening brought them to South America. McDonald's openings began making headlines, as in 1990, when an outlet opened in Moscow in what was still the Soviet Union. In Philadelphia the story was, "Thousands of queue-hardened Soviets yesterday cheerfully lined up to get a taste of 'gamburgers,' 'chizburgers' and 'Filay-o-feesh' sandwiches as McDonald's opened in the land of Lenin for the first time. The world's largest version of the landmark U.S. fast-food chain rang up 30,000 meals on 27 cash registers, breaking the opening-day record for any McDonald's restaurant worldwide, officials said. The Soviets, bundled in fur coats and hats, seemed unfazed, lining up before dawn outside the 700-seat restaurant."[11]

Kroc's emphasis on service was a part of the story as the *New York Times* covering of the Moscow record opening made clear, noting,

> Connoisseurs of fast food and human behavior were doubly satiated today as anxious crowds of Soviet customers engaged in traditional pushing and shoving to place 'Beeg Mek' orders at the nation's first McDonald's restaurant, only to be calmed by uniformed compatriots dictating that they have a nice day.
>
> As exotic as the food seemed, opening-day customers said they were most impressed at the simple sight of polite shop workers—Soviet workers—somehow having been trained in this nation of commercial boorishness to actually smile and say, "May I help you?" and "Thank you for coming."[12]

The record Moscow opening did not last long. Two years later McDonald's opened an outlet in Beijing, and according to the *New York Times*, the first day's attendance was 40,000.[13] Such a crowd was no surprise, given the comment made on opening day by McDonald's International president, who noted, "Our research shows that about 800,000 people pass by our corner every day."[14]

How broad the McDonald's expansion has been is seen in related fields. *The Economist* publishes a "Big Mac Currency Index" as a measure of the value of countries' currencies around the world. They do this by showing how much a Big Mac costs when paid for in local currency and that cost is converted to U.S. dollars, which they say "seeks to make exchange-rate theory more digestible." Thomas Friedman seriously discussed the theory that nations with McDonald's don't go to war with each other.[15] Through its aggressive development of its franchise program, the now seemingly ubiquitous McDonald's established a critical mass that carried on a chain reaction.

Establishing critical mass is sometimes the factor in deciding which of competing technologies or systems will survive in the long run.[16] One such competition existed in the years before DVDs, and it was a large-stakes game for the companies involved. In the 1970s technology became available for home videocassette recording, creating a new market for entertainment that potentially included all television owners worldwide. Sony was first to introduce a commercial product in 1975, its Betamax, and JVC followed a year later with the VHS. Both could record and play videotapes, but the systems were incompatible, so consumers had to choose one or the other. Sony, with its early lead and reputation, held the early edge in the worldwide struggle to control the videocassette market, but not for long. While Sony thought they could win the market on their own, JVC adopted a marketing strategy that involved giving away their technology to other electronics firms with good production skills and distribution and settling for a low profit margin. JVC's strategy proved effective, and VHS sales soon surpassed Betamax sales. Once they did, more products, like prerecorded tapes became available on VHS, and a critical mass of owners was achieved where most people began buying VHS. Because others were making that choice, the choice now offered them more—the chain reaction set in. By 1987, a full 95 percent of all VCRs in the world used VHS format.[17]

Critical mass is sometimes seen in politics when it is primary season before presidential elections and a candidate gathers momentum after early victories and voters "jump on the bandwagon" in support of the candidate who emerges as the favorite. On the larger political field of international relations no example is more dramatic in recent history than the changes in modern history set in motion when Mikhail Gorbachev became leader of the Soviet Union's Politburo in 1985. His policies of *perestroika* and *glasnost* opened the U.S.S.R. to many previously unknown freedoms and reforms. The discontent and dissatisfaction that existed below the surface began to gather voice and as some dared speak out and suffered no repercussions, others were encouraged to do so, which brought out others who were unhappy living under the communist system. By 1989 the Soviets were participating in their first openly contested elections since 1917, and soon a critical mass demanding democracy was achieved in Eastern Europe. With Gorbachev's encouragement of reform, democratic forces were unleashed in the Communist bloc. In 1989, to the continual shock of outside observers, revolutions overthrew the Communist regimes in Poland, Hungary, East Germany, Bulgaria, Czechoslovakia, and Romania. The loosening of oppressive control within the Soviet Union allowed the sustained reaction to carry on in the fifteen Soviet Republics, and in 1990, Lithuania became the first to declare itself an independent country. Others soon followed, and the leading state, Russia, lacked economic resources to prevent the deterioration. In 1990, the Cold War that had molded international relations and held the world hostage to nuclear destruction came to an end. The Communist bloc's rival alliance to NATO, the Warsaw Pact, was officially dissolved the following year.

Tipping

A subset of the critical mass model that Schelling wrote about in his 1978 *Micromotives and Macrobehavior* is "tipping." Whereas critical mass deals with one population, such as hamburger eaters, and is examined in absolute numbers, tipping refers to two populations, and their interaction and is often expressed in percentages. The term was first applied to the phenomena of neighborhood migration, when families of a minority race moved into a previously racially homogeneous neighborhood and the residents moved out, in part because of the minority members who had arrived and in part because of the anticipation that more were likely to follow. Their departure created openings that allowed more minority members to enter, which induced more of the original residents to leave, and so on. This was described as tipping, and the two processes were complementary, the "tipping in" of new residents and "tipping out" of previous residents who departed.

The "tipping point" is the precise level at which this process reaches a self-sustaining reaction that will carry on. It is rather like the fulcrum point of a teeter-totter in that an increase from the tipping point means self-sustaining reaction until some new stable point is reached, while a decline may mean a reduction that is likewise headed to an equilibrium point. "Tipping point" is an equally appropriate term for describing the point at which any critical mass situation can become self-sustaining.

Diagramming Critical Mass and the Tipping Point

Critical mass analysis and tipping points are easily visualized and analyzed when presented in diagram form. Situations can be illustrated by a simple graph that reveals at a glance whether critical mass has been achieved and the stability of the situation being graphed at any particular point.

Creating the graph requires several steps, beginning with gathering accurate information about individual motivation through studies such as polling and interviews, or making an educated estimation of the motivation of the population involved. As information is gathered it is recorded by frequency distribution, which is often displayed in tables or bar graphs as the following example shows.

There are 100 people who have made the same individual choice to do a certain thing—it could be to go on strike, to jaywalk, to sign a petition, to join a club, to start a revolution, or any of a vast number of options. For the most part, their decisions are interactive in that they are more likely to make a certain decision if enough others also make that decision. There are some people who will decide to take an action, regardless of what others do, whereas others may only follow if they are satisfied they are in a group that is sufficiently large.

In this instance, 4 people will take action, perhaps sign a petition to present to their employers, regardless of the consequences. This would be enough for 8 more to feel willing to join in. At that point there would be 12 all together. Twelve would be enough so that 10 more, who would never have acted out on their own, are now willing to join in the action. The total of 22 might be enough to attract 17 more, which would attract 16 more, and so on. Finally, we have the last 4 people joining in, bringing the cumulative total to all 100 people. Those final 4 were not willing to join in until 96 others had decided to do so.

In table form this would appear as follows (Table 18.1):

Table 18.1

Number of others acting	Number now motivated to act	Total number acting
0	4	4
4	8	12
12	10	22
22	17	39
39	16	55
55	15	70
70	13	83
83	10	93
93	3	96
96	4	100

If we were to graph the frequency distribution of people motivated to act along a horizontal axis, by looking at the middle column one can see the distribution is close to "normal," with the larger numbers crowded around the center and tapered off at the top and bottom. Such normal distribution yields a bell curve when graphed.

To be made useful this must be converted to a cumulative distribution curve, which is a curve of the total number acting. A cumulative distribution curve continually rises from left to right, unless congestion is being graphed. This curve compares the number actually acting, on the Y or vertical axis, with the number expected to act, listed on the X or horizontal axis (Figure 18.1).

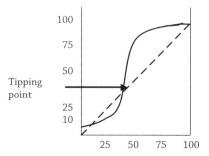

The 45-degree dotted line is included for convenience to show points at which "actual" equals "expected." It is where the number of people who are expected to take part in some activity is equal to the number who actually take part in the activity. This point is comparable to the point in a nuclear reaction where the release of one neutron causes the release of one more neutron. If the cumulative results continue above the 45-degree line, the reaction, or the activity carries on, but if it falls below the line, the activity fades out. That key point where the reaction is at the 45-degree point is called the "tipping point" because it signals the beginning of a successful chain reaction if the actual continues to exceed the expected.

To understand the tipping point, this graph should be visualized as a moving diagram as follows: Once actual exceeds expected, change continues away from the tipping point in a continual increase until it again reaches a point when actual and expected are equal. If change falls below the tipping point, it continues to reduce until it, likewise, reaches a point where actual and expected are equal. These points are called stable equilibrium points, and they are the outcomes of the tipping phenomena (Figure 18.2).

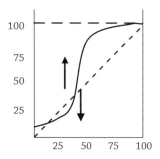

Figure 18.3 shows three curves that illustrate different circumstances of critical mass. Curve A fails to ever reach the 45-degree line, and critical mass is not attainable. Curve B has a tipping point and two stable equilibrium points that are far apart. It is the best illustration of how much difference the tipping point

can make, as the outcome will end at one or the other of the equilibrium points. Curve C begins with critical mass already achieved, as actual, the vertical y axis, is considerably greater than expected, the horizontal x axis, and there is one equilibrium point where actual and expected are equal.

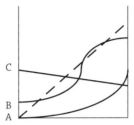

Critical mass diagrams make it clear that the fact that something fails does not tell us how close it was to success. Likewise, the fact that something succeeds does not tell us how close it came to failure. The question can be tipping, and perhaps some slight change might have caused the metric system to catch on. McDonald's clearly tipped, and recent expansion seems to no longer be at such an exponential rate, with failures in several countries, but it has found an equilibrium at a level of considerable success. As the women's movement gained strength, Ms. became a commonly used form of address, while the pronoun s/he had less success as a term to eliminate gender bias. Critical mass was achieved in one case and not the other, but by what margin is not apparent by end results.

Application: Los Angeles, 1992

A black man, Rodney King, was driving late one evening in Los Angeles. He was stopped by a Los Angeles police car containing four police officers, and told to get out of his car. Exactly what transpired between the officers and King at that time is disputed, but when he was out of his car, the police beat him repeatedly. As it happened, someone was watching, and videotaped the entire beating sequence. From the videotape, the beating appears to have been unprovoked, and on that evidence alone it was difficult to see it as anything other than extremely excessive, whether or not any sort of provocation was involved. The widely held view in the black community in Los Angeles was that it was just another incident in a frequently occurring pattern of police brutality and discrimination directed at them, except this time the police had been caught with evidence that was irrefutable.

A critical mass diagram could have been useful for predicting what might happen in Los Angeles, depending on the verdict rendered in the case. The variables being compared would be actual criminal activity or violence on the vertical (y) axis, and the expectation of such activity on the horizontal (x) axis. As anger built and agitation increased during the trial, incidents of crime and violence increased as well. The tipping point would come with the verdict, and the possible results were the return to a previous level with some crime, or a much higher level of crime as can be seen by looking at the locations on the graph in Figure 18.4 where the line crosses the 45-degree angle.

On this graph the actual level of crime and violence under normal circumstances was where the line crosses the 45-degree angle in the lower left of the graph, but as the verdict approached both actual and expected crime increased. The verdict was going to tip the level in one direction or the other (Figure 18.4).

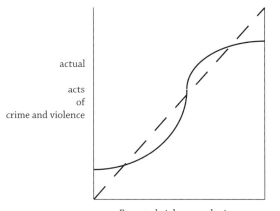

Expected violence and crime

When the verdict came in and the four officers who beat King were found innocent, critical mass was achieved, and rioting and looting took control of Los Angeles, leaving many dead and the city near anarchy. Something had to be done to prevent settling at a new equilibrium, and Rodney King as well as prominent black Americans made pleas to stop the rioting. Their calls fell on deaf ears, and minorities attacked minorities as the violence escalated. The mayor attempted to impose a curfew, but order was only restored when large numbers of troops occupied the city, reversing the self-sustaining reaction that was carrying the violence forward. That forced down the actual on the y axis, and as actual illegal activity fell, expected, on the x axis, followed. The situation was brought back to the tipping point and tipped in the opposite direction, but after considerable loss of life and much property damage. If the situation had been left to resolve itself, it could have resulted in near lawlessness as the norm, with armed bands of citizens defending themselves and looters feeling unrestrained. That would be the equilibrium in the upper right of the diagram, which depicts a very high crime rate.

Managing to control the tipping point and heading things in one direction or another is about more than selling hamburgers, but also about public policy.[18]

Notes

1. Randy Moore, "Inching toward the Metric System," *The American Biology Teacher*, Vol. 51, No. 4 (April 1989), 213.
2. "Measures/Metric Program," National Institute of Standards and Technology, May, 2002, http://www.nist.gov/metric.
3. "A Metric America: A Decision Whose Time Has Come," National Bureau of Standards Special Publication 345, U.S. Department of Commerce, Washington, DC, 1971.
4. "Measures/Metric Program."
5. Johnny Carson, *Tonight Show* monologue, NBC, December 13, 1973.
6. "Behavior: Hoarding Day," *Time*, June 18, 1979.
7. www.aboutmcdonalds.com/mcd/our_company.html, 2010.
8. Alan Hess, "The Origins of McDonald's Golden Arches," *Journal of the Society of Architectural Historians*, Vol. 45, No. 1 (March 1986), 60.
9. www.mcdonalds.ca/pdfs/history_final.pdf, 1.
10. Ibid., 3.
11. "Soviets Relish Their First 'Beeg Maks,'" *Philadelphia Daily News*, February 1, 1990.
12. Francis Clines, "Upheaval in the East: Moscow McDonald's Opens; Milkshakes and Human Kindness," *New York Times*, February 1, 1990.
13. "News Summary," *New York Times*, April 24, 1992, A4.
14. Lena Sun, "Chinese Get Burger Break as McDonald's Opens in Beijing," *Washington Post*, April 24, 1992.
15. Thomas L. Friedman, "Foreign Affairs Big Mac I," *New York Times*, December 8, 1996.
16. What is likely the most commonly used example of a technology achieving critical mass in game theory literature is the qwerty arrangement of keys for typing, beginning with typewriters and continuing to keyboards for computers. This arrangement was designed to reduce entanglement of striking keys on early typewriters, and when that was no longer a problem systems were devised that were intended to be more efficient for the letters used to increase speed. The rival system to qwerty that arose by the 1930s was Dvorak, which was claimed to be superior based on experiments and typing speed tests. This has been regularly reported this way, with the explanation that qwerty had established a critical mass of users and machines so the superior system was rejected. However, that was not the case, as was made clear in J. Liebowitz and Stephen E. Margolis, "The Fable of the Keys," *Journal of Law and Economics* Vol. 33, No.1 (April 1990), 1–25. Dvorak's claims to superiority were unfounded.
17. Jin Chyung, "New Rules for Setting Standards in Today's Hi-Tech Market: Lessons Learned from the VHS-Betamax War," October 8, 2008, http://besser.tsoa.nyu.edu/impact/f96/Projects/jchyung/.
18. Some examples that cite Schelling's work include April Linton, "A Critical Mass Model of Bilingualism among U.S.-Born Hispanics," *Social Forces*, Vol. 83, No.1 (September 2004), 279–314; Paula England et al., "Why Are Some Academic Fields Tipping toward Female? The Sex Composition of U.S. Fields of Doctoral Degree Receipt, 1971–2002," *Sociology of Education*, Vol. 80, No. 1 (January 2007), 23–42; Robert J. Sampson and Patrick Sharke, "Neighborhood Selection and the Social Reproduction of Concentrated Racial Inequality," *Demography*, Vol.45, No. 1 (February 2008), 1–29.

CHAPTER 19

Individual Decisions and Group Outcomes

The following edited question was posed by Schelling to introduce analyzing situations of individual decisions and group outcomes:

Consider a social event attended by fifty boys and fifty girls, held in a building that has two large adjoining rooms, either room large enough to hold them all and with easy access between the rooms and good visibility. Several alternative motivations toward companionship, gregariousness, and discrimination, are listed below.

For each set of motivations, state whether there is a unique equilibrium that can result, two or more possible equilibriums, or no equilibrium at all. Describe in each case the character of the equilibrium if any. "Equilibrium" is here defined as a situation in which nobody is motivated to change rooms as long as nobody else does.

a. Everybody wants to be in the room with the most people.
b. Everybody wants to be in the room with the fewest people.
c. Boys want to be in the room with the most girls; girls want to be in the room with the fewest boys.
d. Everybody prefers to be in the room that most nearly contains three-fifths of the total number of people.
e. Two-thirds of the boys like to be in the room with the most people; one-third of the boys like to be in the room with fewest people; girls like to be in the room with the fewest boys.
f. All boys prefer to be in a room that contains some girls, but not if the girls are a majority; all girls prefer to be in a room that contains some boys, but not if the boys are a majority.

Looking at this question shows how individual motives sometimes translate with little success when they are combined.

In choice a, "Everybody wants to be in the room with the most people," we have two equilibriums, one unstable and one stable. If at every stage along the way when people entered the rooms there were equal numbers and half went into each room, there would be fifty in each, which would be equilibrium. However, since everyone wants to be in the room with the most people, everyone can make that a reality by changing rooms and increasing the number in the other room to fifty-one. This is a tipping point. Once one person does this all others would follow, which leads to the second equilibrium, the stable outcome of everyone in one room. This would also result when early arrivers distributed themselves between the two rooms and later arrivals note a discrepancy and head to the room with a larger population. This would continue to reinforce the difference so that the others in the other room would also move to it and all would be in one room.

In b, "Everybody wants to be in the room with the fewest people," there is one stable equilibrium. This would resolve at fifty in each room, since a number below fifty would attract others because all desire to be in the room with the fewest and if it attracted more than fifty, the room they had come from would have the fewest and they would be attracted to it. Any disruption from fifty would return to fifty. With c, "Boys want to be in the room with the most girls; girls want to be in the room with the fewest boys," fifty-fifty with twenty-five boys and twenty-five girls in each room is the only stable equilibrium, since "most" and "fewest" are the same. This is unlikely to evolve through random mixing. The likely outcome in this case is no equilibrium, for if there are more girls in one room as the rooms begin to fill that will attract more boys, which will leave the other room with fewer boys, which would attract the girls, which would then attract the boys to again change rooms in pursuit and the girls to flee and a continuing cycle.

In d, "Everybody prefers to be in the room that most nearly contains three-fifths of the total number of people," there are two equilibriums, one of which is stable, depending on how the rooms fill initially. If initially there were forty people in each room and twenty more came and entered one room, the result would be the three-fifths that is most desirable. Yet, it would cause people in the room with forty to move to the room with sixty to get closer to their desired proportion. When ten have moved and it would be seventy–thirty, with seventy much closer to three-fifths, and the process would continue until all were in one room, the first equilibrium, which is stable. The second equilibrium is with fifty in each room, and everyone equally close to three-fifths. This might appear stable but it is not. Every one of the one hundred players has the temptation to change rooms because if he does, and others don't, the number in the room to which he moves becomes fifty-one, putting him nearer three fifths, and the process goes on until it gets to forty–sixty and there is no stopping it from carrying on to all in one room.

The next statement, e, "Two-thirds of the boys like to be in the room with the most people; one-third of the boys like to be in the room with fewest people; girls like to be in the room with the fewest boys" allows one unstable equilibrium, with fifty boys in one room and fifty girls in the other. The boys who want to be in the room with the fewest people will end up joining the boys who want to be in a group with the most people. The equilibrium is not stable because the two-thirds of the boys would have the temptation to make the girls' group larger by joining it.

The final statement was f, "All boys prefer to be in a room that contains some girls, but not if the girls are a majority; all girls prefer to be in a room that contains some boys, but not if the boys are a majority." The only possible equilibrium outcome is for there to be identical numbers of boys and girls in the two rooms, where neither is a majority. This is unlikely to result from natural, unplanned movement. If it is any other way, the group in minority status in the room would leave to increase the majority status in the opposite room, further causing the minority status in that room to leave, and the result would be boys in one room, girls in the other.

What these example illustrate is that individuals make decisions based on their own desires for outcomes, which Schelling labeled "micromotives," and when their decisions are combined, what Schelling termed "macrobehavior," the results can be inconsistent with the motivation. The common assumption is that free choice allows for the best outcome, but two of these options contradict that belief. Schelling would demonstrate what two of these situations illustrate, that there can be times when people's individual choices are better achieved by decisions imposed on them than by allowing them to make free choice and let the outcome fall where it will. That was the case in the situation where "Boys want to be in the room with the most girls; girls want to be in the room with the fewest boys." Assigned locations gave an outcome that was not ideal, but preferable to the continuous circling that would otherwise result. It was also demonstrated in the situation "Everybody prefers to be in the room that most nearly contains three-fifths of the total number of people," where requiring half the participants to remain in one room and half in the other would put all within 10 percent of their desired outcome, while allowing free movement would tip the rooms one way or the other in an attempt to get closer than 10 percent away and leave all in one room, 40 percent from their desired outcome.

The final statement, "All boys prefer to be in a room that contains some girls, but not if the girls are a majority; all girls prefer to be in a room that contains some boys, but not if the boys are a majority," is particularly instructive, as it introduces a basic lesson that Schelling made about segregation. It could have just as easily said blacks and whites rather than boys and girls, and the lesson is important. An identical statement would be "All whites prefer to live in a neighborhood that contains blacks but not if the blacks are in a majority; all blacks prefer to live in a neighborhood that contains whites, but not if whites are a majority." In this case we would have everyone expressing a preference for living in integrated neighborhoods but the result would be total segregation.

The kind of analysis being explored in this chapter is the relation between behavior characteristics of individuals who comprise some social aggregate and the characteristics of the aggregate. Sometimes we use what is known about individual intentions to predict the aggregate, or alternatively we try to figure out what intentions or motives of separate individuals could lead to a pattern that is observed.

There are easy cases where aggregate outcome is an extrapolation from individual decisions, such as drivers' lights going on at sundown on a highway being visible from the highway, one could conclude from his decision to turn on his lights that the behavior universally motivated by the same decisions being made by all drivers, that it improves their safety. But we learn to warn against jumping to conclusions about individual intentions from observations of aggregates, as in the final situation of the introductory problem, where both boys and girls preferred being in rooms with mixed genders, but the result was total separation with boys in one room, girls in the other.

Schelling describes behavior as both "purposive," having preferences and being in pursuit of goals, and "contingent," dependent on what others are doing. He notes that sciences sometimes ascribe motives when something behaves as if it were oriented toward a goal, as when it is said that water seeks its own level, or nature abhors a vacuum. But "nobody really supposes the water feels frustrated"[1] if it is poured in a J-shaped tube with the lower end closed so it cannot find its own level.

People seek to achieve preferences and to adapt and, through contingent behavior, doing vicarious problem solving, to make conscious decisions or adaptations in pursuit of their goals. The aggregate or macro results still do not necessarily represent the individual, or micromotives. Schelling says, "How well each does for himself in adapting to his social environment is not the same thing as how satisfactory a social environment they collectively create for themselves."[2]

This approach to social analysis has most in common with the social science discipline of economics. In countries with comparatively undirected economic systems, millions of people make billions of decisions every week, and most know very little about the whole economy and how it works, but they do know about the price of things they buy and sell and perhaps the interest rates at which they borrow or lend, and somehow all of the activities seem to get coordinated. Adam Smith said it was as if an "invisible hand" coordinated the decisions of buyers and sellers. Schelling compared the way the economic system works to that of an ant colony, with nobody "minding the whole store" and many players making choices in their own truncated little world that all add up to a meaningful pattern of aggregate behavior. He warns, "If we see pattern and order and regularity, we should withhold judgment ... and inquire first of all what it is that the individuals who comprise the system seem to be doing and how it is that their actions, in the large, produce the patterns we see. Then we can try to evaluate whether, at least according to what the individuals are trying to do, the resulting pattern is in some way responsive to their intentions."[3]

Schelling assigned a second problem on this topic that required looking at the interactive nature of decision making in the market. It involves the market for Christmas cards:

It has been observed that for many people an important criterion in sending or not sending a Christmas card to someone is whether or not they expect to receive one from the person. They would be embarrassed if they received one and had not sent one, but would rather not bother sending one unless they were going to receive one. They might also not wish to embarrass the recipient by sending a card he or she did not expect and implying that the recipient had been negligent. It may not be going too far to suppose that some people, in deciding whether or not to send a card, recognize that the other person, in deciding whether or not to send his or her card, is wondering whether or not he or she will get a card.

Draw a matrix corresponding to this situation, explaining your choice of numerical payoffs, and analyze the situation in familiar fashion.

Schelling provides an analysis of this problem. He says that the Christmas card market is interactive, also federally monopolized for sending them by mail. It is affected by custom and by expectation that others may send cards, by last year's cards received or not received, plus conditioned by the cost of cards and postage and the labor of selecting cards and adding inscriptions. People feel obliged to send to people from whom they expect to receive cards, often knowing they will be receiving them because senders expect to receive one in return. Cessation of sending a card might signal something. Some send cards early to avoid suspicion that they only sent them in response to having received cards. He concludes, "Sensible people who might readily agree to stop bothering each other with Christmas cards find it embarrassing, or not quite worth the trouble, to reach such agreement. If they could, they might be so pleased that they would celebrate by sending 'voluntary' cards, falling back into the trap!"[4]

A matrix illustrating this with ordinal preferences would be (Table 19.1):

Table 19.1

	Send cards		Don't send	
Send cards		3		1
	3		2	
Don't send		2		4
	1		4	

This matrix has no natural outcome but has a focal point solution in the lower right quadrant. However, it is not a strong focal solution and especially if it is a game that will be a repeated play game, the solution that is likely is that players will avoid their minimum, which in this case makes the outcome the upper left quadrant, or as Schelling says, "falling back into the trap."

The boy/girl problem that introduced this chapter illustrated mixing and sorting of both "discrete" variables and "continuous" variables. Discrete variables are those that represent different categories, such as race, religion, color, sex, or language. Continuous variables are those that fall on a continuum (comparative scale) within a discrete category, such as age, income level, or skill at an activity. In the introductory problem the continuous variable issues concerned wanting to be in a room with some specified proportion of boys and girls, while the discrete variable issues spoke to being in a room with the most or fewest people, no distinction made regarding gender.

Segregation and Integration

Within the discrete and continuous categories, the sorting (segregating) and mixing (integrating) of people happens in many fashions along many lines. There is segregation by gender, age, income, language, religion, skin color, personal taste, and accidents of historical location. While segregation may be a convenient general term to associate with sorting or separating, there is a related activity called "congregation" that serves a similar function.

Segregation occurs when people of some recognizable group limit the people with whom they are associated to those belonging to their own group. This is often associated with attitudes of status, privilege, and elitism, in which one group possesses benefits that another group is denied. In the present day, segregation first brings to mind race and racist attitudes, especially between blacks and whites.

Historically, however, segregation can be found in many contexts. It ranges from the fairly trivial to the morbidly disastrous. Among the obvious are "men only" clubs and organizations, the apartheid system of South America, the reservation policy applied to the Native American tribes, college fraternities and sororities, the Hindu caste system, the treatment of Jews by the Nazis, high school gangs and cliques, and serfdom and slavery in Europe and America. The common thread in these examples is that they all involve identifiable groups that collectively shun, or are shunned by, others.

A similar topic is congregation, which is the coming together of people, based on something that they have in common. Congregation is associated with the desire of people with certain qualities, interests, or beliefs to be around people who share those qualities, interests or beliefs. In congregation, people are not shunning others. They are seeking the companionship of others. People who attend the same church are sometimes referred to as the church's "congregation." Students with a great interest in computer games may spend time around other students with similar interests, not necessarily because they like each other personally, but because they have a shared common interest. People whose first language is Spanish or Mandarin may form their circles of friends from people with whom they communicate most easily. People with low incomes may end up congregating by virtue of the fact that they have no options about where to live other than available low-rent housing.

Both segregation and congregation involve discriminatory individual behavior. "Discriminatory" in this sense is being used to mean that the individuals have an awareness of factors that could affect segregation, congregation, or integration in some way, and that the awareness of those factors influences the decisions they make. For example, individuals may be aware, consciously or unconsciously, of age, religion, or skin color when they make choices about where to live, whom to sit by, whom to talk to, or what type of career to pursue.

Schelling, like many Americans, turned his attention to segregation during the era of heightened interest in civil rights in the late 1960s. His interest was not in "why," but "how." He wondered when individuals make choices on a discriminatory basis, what are the collective results? How successful are individuals in achieving their desired outcomes? Are individual motivations about discrimination and aggregate outcomes necessarily consistent? To what degree can we draw conclusions about individual preferences, or expressions of "popular will," from existing segregation? To answer these questions, he developed in 1969 what is certainly his most famous model, or "game," the Self-Forming Neighborhood Model. The answers this simple exercise provides are of importance in the analysis of race relations.

Schelling's simple game involved beginning with a population in a limited area that was a checkerboard with sixty residents. Thirty were from one group and thirty from another, and all residents preferred that it be integrated. It was originally intended to represent blacks and whites but could be applied as a model for divisions between men and women, French- and English-speaking Canadians, or any of many other situations involving two groups. Schelling used regular pennies and 1943 zinc pennies when he first did his experiment, but checkers or anything that can be found with thirty of one color and thirty of another that fits on a checker square works. Schelling used the experiment to analyze racial segregation, so whatever is being used, and for ease of descriptions we will say it is checkers, one color represents blacks, and the other represents whites. He later stated, "What I did not know when I did the experiments with my twelve-year-old son using copper and zinc pennies was that what I was doing later became known as 'agent-based computational models,' or 'agent-based computational economics.'"[5]

Each individual resident, or checker, is considered to be the center of a local three-square-by-three-square neighborhood on the checkerboard. His neighbors are any occupants of the eight squares surrounding him; so an individual could have anywhere from zero to eight neighbors. The introductory problem demonstrated that if both groups favor integration but want to be in the majority, the only result is complete segregation, as there cannot be two 51 percents. The racial tolerances assigned in this experiment are somewhat greater. If an individual has six to eight neighbors he must have three of his own race, if he has three to five neighbors he is satisfied with two of his own race, and if he has one or two neighbors, then one of them must be of his own race. Nobody is seeking majority status; they only want not to be in acute minority status.

Here is a checkerboard that meets everyone's expectations (Figure 19.1):

	X	O	X	O	X	O	
X	O	X	O	X	O	X	O
O	X	O	X	O	X	O	X
X	O	X	O	X	O	X	O
O	X	O	X	O	X	O	X
X	O	X	O	X	O	X	O
O	X	O	X	O	X	O	X
	O	X	O	X	O	X	

To examine the dynamics of motion from individual decision, we assume twenty individuals move away from the checkerboard neighborhood by removing twenty checkers using some method of random selection. Next, five newcomers with the same racial tolerance as all the others move in to randomly selected empty squares. In each case, determine whether the newcomer is white or black by a coin toss. At this point there are forty-five occupied squares and nineteen blank squares on the board. Forty individuals are where they were at the beginning, and there are five new arrivals. Finally, one by one in order from one corner, we move checkers to the nearest location that satisfies their requirements, observing how that changes the neighborhood in which it arrives, and what further movement that requires. The surprising and consistent result of doing this experiment is that the board develops into pockets of segregated neighborhoods, despite everyone's preference for integration. This simple game has been much analyzed[6] and has been computerized so that it is available online for viewing how segregated neighborhoods develop.[7] More sophisticated computer games with more than two ethnic groups have been developed and the results of the simulations compared with data to determine whether the models accurately determine that moderate individual attitudes tend to lead to segregation for the same reason as on Schelling's checkerboard game. A 2008 report concluded, "Mere tolerance and the absence of virulent housing discrimination will not produce integration under the prevailing patterns of ethnic preference, at least not in the short run. That the Schelling model has a physical analogue is interesting and theoretically illuminating is without question, but it is the social content of the Schelling model that gives it its power and importance."[8]

There have been attempts to prevent the development of self-forming neighborhoods by communities that have understood the nature of their development. The Housing Office of Shaker Heights, Ohio, refused to assist whites in moving into an area where whites were predominant or blacks into an area where blacks were predominant, and the Office admitted devoting, "the major part of its efforts to the introduction of whites into areas with a disproportionate minority population."[9] City officials in Oak Park, Illinois, took measures to prevent ghettos from developing by forcing real estate agents to abandon use of for sale signs, which sometimes sparked white flight, and encouraging the agents to route prospective customers to neighborhoods that would then become integrated. They expanded the police force and increased patrols in areas seen as less safe, and officials joined with local clergy in visiting neighborhoods to assure residents that integration was nothing to fear. There was a group that identified people who would be especially receptive to integrated neighborhoods and significantly, the town granted equity insurance to white home owners in newly integrated neighborhoods that guaranteed the price of their homes would not drop in value as black families moved in.[10] Things have been taken a step farther in Singapore, where segregation issues revolve around three ethnic groups, a Chinese majority and minorities of Malays and Indians. In the 1960s there was ethnic violence and the newly independent Singapore dealt with it in a manner that would be very difficult to achieve in the political climate of America. Singapore had launched a massive government housing project, and 85 percent of the county's population was living in government built facilities. The government adopted an "Ethnic Integration Policy," which required that the ethnic mixture of the population be reflected in all apartment blocks and neighborhoods included in its housing projects. Sale and resale of units in these projects was required to be on the basis of maintaining the racial balance prescribed by the government. Current Prime Minister Lee Hsien Loong had been a student of Schelling's at Harvard, and commented, "Schelling had analyzed this and we were therefore very conscious, that beyond a certain point, it changes very fast.... That gave us some impetus to move faster than we might otherwise have done."[11]

The dynamics that lead to segregation may reflect a variety of individual motives, as Schelling shows in his checkerboard game and the tipping that can result once a change begins. That is what the examples from the United States and Singapore hoped to prevent. While the term "tipping point" has only come into widespread usage in recent years, a *Harvard Law Review* article from spring 1980 that relies heavily on Schelling illustrates that it has been around for some time as an explanation of how individual motives may be overtaken by group results:

> As blacks enter a previously all-white community, black demand for housing in the community increases and white demand falls. This phenomenon, known as "white flight" culminates when the proportion of black residents reaches the "tipping point," the point at which white flight accelerates and leads to irreversible re-segregation.... The tipping point is often estimated at approximately 25% to 30% black, but the actual point for an individual community is determined by white

residents' and prospective entrants' expectations about changes in the character of the community, fear of a decline in property values and tolerance of black neighbors.[11]

Mixing and Sorting within One Variable

Similar analysis applies to how mixing and sorting takes place along a continuum, within a discreet variable. Again, people are responding to an environment that consists of people who are responding to each other. As they make choices they cause the environments of people they associate with to change, causing further responses. Outcomes are described in aggregates, as averages or by frequency distributions, but the outcomes result from individual decisions, unless people can commit themselves to organized or disciplined choices.

Age is a discrete variable. Within this discrete variable, young people may prefer to associate with other young people and older people may prefer to associate with other older people. Perhaps people share more common interests and experiences with people nearer their own ages, and are more comfortable with their company. In these cases segregation and congregation is taking place, just as it takes place between discrete variables.

If age is the variable of primary concern and there is an apartment for singles in a nursing home where nobody wants to stay if others are on average older than oneself, the situation unwinds. The younger people will move out and the average will rise, causing more to move out, again raising the average, and the process continues until all that remains are people who are tied for being oldest.

This same process would transpire if the variable on the continuum is skill and the group involved consists of members of a tennis club or other sports club where the poorest players find they don't enjoy being associated with the organization. If the bottom 10 percent felt that it was not worth continuing its membership and dropped out, there would be a new bottom 10 percent. If being in the bottom 10 percent was so unappealing that they, too, would drop out, that would create a new bottom 10 percent, and so on, until only the best players in the club remained as members.

Models in which people depart if their requirements are not being met are called "open-ended models." In such cases nobody can leave or join without altering everyone else's position. "Closed models" are those in which people will move to another location only if they expect to find that things are better or more desirable there—not a case of meeting absolute requirements, but rather, involving preferences.

Continuing to use age as our discrete variable, an example of the function of a closed model would be to deduce the outcome that results when only two options are available to suit the preferences of all the people involved. Imagine a population that is evenly distributed between the ages of 0 and 100. There are two adjacent rooms into which these people could go. They have no preferences about the rooms themselves, and there are no other rooms—they must be in one or the other. They all (including the 0-year-old) care about the ages of the people they are with, and will choose a room on that basis only. Their common preference is that everybody prefers the room in which the average age is closest to his own. A division that all 100 people would find preferable is not difficult to achieve. It is bound to result in a stable equilibrium with fifty people in each room. Say, for example, that originally the younger people would congregate in one room, and the older in the other. If the split took place at year 40, the average age in one room would be 20 (40/2), while in the other it would be 70 (140/2). The people age 40–45 in the older room would be closer to the average age of the people in the younger room, and would satisfy their preference by moving there. The effect of this would be to raise the average ages in both rooms (to 22.5 and 72.5). This would create another group who were now closer in average age to those in the younger room. This process would repeat until there was an even number of people in each room, with those above fifty in one, and those below in the other.

If we retained two rooms and 100 people, but change the discrete variable to people's attitudes about crowding, we can offer a different analysis. Some prefer crowded situations, some are more content with small groups, and some are happiest with solitude.

Suppose that all 100 people are going to distribute themselves between two rooms in some fashion or another, each individually choosing where to be on the basis of his personal preferences about crowding. If everyone prefers crowds, the bigger the better, it will be easy both to anticipate the outcome, and to anticipate the degree of satisfaction people will have with their choices. Everyone will end up in the same room, satisfied with their choices, because they will have achieved the maximum amount of crowding possible.

What if no one likes crowds? Everyone would then hope to be in the less crowded room. But as long as one room was less crowded, it would attract others to it. This would continue until there was no incentive for anyone to leave one room. The result would be two rooms with fifty somewhat dissatisfied people in each.

But what if everybody preferred a slightly more complicated situation? Say they all wanted to be in a room that contained a slight majority of the population, say 55 percent. What outcome will this lead to? If they were willing to settle for being close to their preference, everyone could come within five of their preference by dividing themselves fifty–fifty. But at fifty–fifty, people would be tempted to change rooms, because by doing so they could bring themselves nearer to fifty-five. If one person moved, the distribution would then be fifty-one–forty-nine, which would encourage more to move to the now slightly more desirable room, and so on. There would be a spiral that wouldn't stop until everyone was in one room, since the room with the larger number would always be closer to fifty-five than would the other room.

It would be possible for us to arrange for everyone to be closer to his preference by forcing some of the people in one room to move to the other. In fact, we could move any number of people between ten and ninety to the empty room, and everyone would be more satisfied than they would be with the results of their self-selection. What follows is the line of reasoning that determines this.

With everyone in the same room, everyone is forty-five away from his desired fifty-five in one room. If we were to move people into the less crowded room one at a time, the eleventh person we forced to move would be forty-four people away from fifty-five (fifty-five less eleven), instead of forty-five away, as he had previously been. He would then be slightly nearer his preference. The remaining eighty-nine people would be thirty-four away from their desired outcome (eighty-nine less fifty-five), instead of forty-five. If we keep moving people, we will find that it won't be until the ninetieth person is moved that anyone is forty-five people away from everyone's desired condition of being in a room with fifty-five people. We would also find that if we reached conditions that approached people's desired outcomes (anywhere from when both rooms are distributed between fifty-five and forty-five and fifty–fifty), then relaxed our restrictions and allowed them freedom of movement, people would not stay in these conditions, because they would be drawn to the room that is nearer their preferred outcome.

So, given these individual motives, even if we create a situation that comes as close as possible to satisfying all those involved, they will, in all probability, unravel that situation in a manner that is to their own detriment. This example raises social and political issues. What if a society has goals that are generally accepted by its population, but the effect of allowing the members of that society freedom of choice is to undermine the very goals it supports? Would those societies be better off accepting some more authoritarian rule that could prevent the unraveling of desired outcomes? The argument in favor of the efficiency of authoritarian rule and the dangers of its abuse is a longstanding one and perhaps there is no answer that is correct for all societies in all times under all conditions.

What remains clear is that it is not always safe to assume outcomes accurately express the individual decisions that brought them about, and being aware of the process of how decisions work is important in understanding results.

Notes

1. Thomas C. Schelling, *Micromotives and Macrobehavior* (New York: Norton, 1978), 17.
2. Ibid., 19.
3. Ibid., 22.
4. Ibid., 32.
5. Thomas C. Schelling, *Strategies of Commitment and Other Essays*, (Cambridge, MA: Harvard University Press, 2006), xi.
6. Abraham Bell and Gideon Parchomovsky, "The Integration Game," *Columbia Law Review*, Vol. 100, No. 8 (December 2000).

7. See SerendipSegregation, http://serendip.brynmawr.edu/complexity/models/secinteg/, http://web.mit.edu/rajsingh/www/lab/alife/schelling.html, http://sociweb.tamu.edu/vlabresi/sslite_us/_main.htm.

8. William A. V. Clark and Mark Fossett, "Understanding the Social Context of the Schelling Segregation Model," Proceedings of the National Academy of Sciences of the United States of America (March 18, 2008), 4114.

9. "Benign Steering and Benign Quotas: The Validity of Race-Conscious Government Policies to Promote Residential Integration," *Harvard Law Review*, Vol. 93, No. 5 (March 1980), 946.

10. "Oakpark, IL," *The Encyclopedia of Chicago*, http://www.encyclopedia.chicagohistory.org/pages/700000.html.

11. Lee Hsien Loong, interviewed by Robert Dodge, Singapore, August 29, 2000.

12. "Benign Steering and Benign Quotas," 942–994.

CHAPTER 20

Randomization in Decision-Making

This chapter looks at the role of randomness in decision-making and discusses the inclusion of a random factor in the solution to two-person, zero-sum games, which set the stage for the formal beginnings of game theory.

Decisions have long been made on the basis of randomness to be seen as transparently fair. "The tradition of making a decision by casting lots is ancient and has existed all over the world and at all times," writes John Lindblum,[1] as he notes its many uses in the Old Testament. Herodotus tells us that Darius of ancient Persia agreed to settle who would rule their great empire by meeting in a given place on a given day and seeing whose horse would neigh first, and his was first.[2] In ancient democratic Athens, where democracy was equated in many ways with equality, selection by lot determined membership in the Council and filled positions on the courts as well as determining who would serve as public officials. While particularly associated in Greece with the radical democracy of the fifth and fourth centuries BC in Athens, casting lots can be found in the earliest Greek literature, with references to it in both Homer's *Iliad* and *Odyssey*.[3] The word "decimate" comes from a disciplinary practice in the Roman Army that involved random choice, when units found to have been cowardly or to have retreated in battle were marked for punishment, and one man in every ten in entire cohorts was selected by lot to be murdered by his fellow soldiers.

The transfer of difficult individual decisions to chance was justified as being fair. From the time of the Old Testament until the early modern age lotteries were also used for the purpose of discovering God's will.[4] With the rise of Christianity in Medieval Europe there was for a time a turn to this second strain of random decision, relying on divine judgment in difficult cases, in the use of trial by ordeal. For most simple matters procedures existed for resolving differences and determining guilt or responsibility, but it would not be until cities had grown and trade revived that law had the structure to deal with complex cases. Society was based on oaths and duties between unequals. In some cases of crimes and serious disputes it was considered best to leave the final decision in the hands of God. Trial by ordeal was the method. Among the ordeals were thrusting arms in boiling water to retrieve some item, burning by hot iron, dunking of suspected witches, and armed combat between parties with disagreements. Casting lots was a lesser ordeal. With the burning of flesh, or "trial by fire," hot iron was applied to skin, which was then bandaged. If the burn healed in three days time, the person accused or charged was deemed innocent. Dunking suspected witches was based on the belief that water, the medium of baptism, would not accept them; so if they stayed under, they were deemed innocent. Trial by combat was battle between individuals, normally to the death. Perhaps the best-known example is seen in the Old English epic poem, *Beowulf*, when Beowulf sets off to save the Danes from the monster, Grendel. The reliance on God's wisdom is clear:

> When Beowulf is finally admitted to the presence of Hrothgar, the king of the Danes, he announces his intention of ridding Denmark of the terror of Grendel. He states his intention to settle the situation single-handed, and asks permission to do so (lines 424–426). He says he will fight with his bare hands, inasmuch as Grendel does not care about weapons; and in the coming struggle, he will rely on the judgment of God as to whom death carries off (lines 440–441).[5]

By early modern times the Church banned trials by ordeal, but casting lots remained important in making decisions. More recently, this could be seen in selecting soldiers for armies as an apparently fair way of seeing that those who are called to serve have equal opportunity. Another important use of random selection, or lots, has been in polling, where selecting a sample of people from certain areas or demographics can be extrapolated to determine the views of the general population. Random selection can also be applied to very difficult decisions such as who gets organs for transplants when there are shortages, which rifle the live bullet goes in on a firing squad for death penalties, random nuclear arms inspection. It is used in some countries for admission to schools, for spot checks by the IRS, to determine sacrifice, such as who doesn't get on the lifeboat. Some lotteries can be weighted lotteries to assure that those involved meet certain standards or are in certain proportions.

What is not as simple as it seems is what constitutes "random." Casting lots, rolling dice, and flipping coins are some simple methods of randomization. Programmed randomization cannot be truly random. There have been notable failures when randomization has been attempted. The U.S. military draft of 1940 stands out, as in the first 2,400 draws no number between 300 and 600 out of 9,000 was selected. The odds of this occurring are less than one in 15×10^{40} (which is less than one in 150,000,000,000,000,000,000,000,000,000,000,000,000,000,000, or highly unlikely).[6] The mixing of the containers of numbers was ineffective. Similar problems were encountered when the draft was introduced in the Vietnam War in 1970. A January 4, 1970, *New York Times* story on the draft began, "The new draft lottery is being challenged by statisticians and politicians on the ground that the selection process did not produce a truly random result."[7] Once again the problem was with the inadequate physical shuffling of the items to be drawn from, and large numbers came from the same pools.

Problems arose in jury selection in New Jersey when they used a fifth-letter alphabetization as a criterion of selection for randomness. This explained the large number of Jewish names included in the jury panels as many had the same fifth letter in their surname, such as Wiseman and Feldman, and also of many Italians being selected for the same reason, such as Ferarro and Dinardo. This method was held to be a violation of the defendant's right to a jury of a cross-section of the community.[8]

Similar problems have occurred with polling. A week before the presidential election of 1936 the *Literary Digest*, the only major polling agency to correctly predict the outcome of every presidential election since 1916, announced that Alf Landon would defeat Franklin Roosevelt. Their failure came from using telephone and car registration lists to create their mailing lists for postcards to receive information. That skewed the pool to a wealthy and Republican sample that did not represent the population. Roosevelt won in a landslide.

Still, randomness serves useful purposes in maintaining equality of duty and opportunity in many cases. Yet we are inclined to distrust the idea of arbitrary chance. We prefer to assign some meaning to random decisions and outcomes, whether it be religious intent or astrology or some other view that supports a system and a reason for things being as they are. Even when we have no reason to decide one way or the other we like to make a choice and to seek some framework in which one option has an advantage over the other.

Jon Elster explains, "The basic reason for using lotteries to make decisions is honesty. Honesty requires that we recognize the pervasiveness of uncertainty and incommensurability, rather than deny or avoid it. Some decisions are going to be arbitrary and epistemically random no matter what we do, no matter how hard we try to base them on reason. Chance will regulate a large part of our lives, no matter how hard we try to avoid it. By *taming chance* we can bring the randomness of the universe under our control as much as possible and keep free of self-deception as well. The requirements of personal causation and autonomy are reconciled by the conscious use of chance to make decisions when rational argument fails. Although the bleakness of this vision may disturb us, it is preferable to a life built on the comforting falsehood that we can always know what to do.[9]

While we may not like uncertainty in ourselves it can be a strategic advantage when one is involved in competition with another player. Understanding of this is what initiated the breakthrough thinking that created game theory.

There have been great milestones in the development of decision making by game theory and rational choice. An important breakthrough came with John von Neumann's 1928 proof concerning two-person, zero-sum games. Zero-sum games are games in which the players' interests are diametrically opposed; in the early years of game theory, these were the most studied form of decisions. In zero-sum games a gain for one player is a loss for the other. What was known was that there were solutions for games with dominant strategies, but whether there were solutions for games of mixed strategies had remained a mystery.

Von Neumann's *minimax theorem* proved that every finite two-person, zero-sum game has a rational solution. This was seen by many as the cornerstone of game theory, as it seemed to put it on a solid theoretical basis.

The rational solution to a precisely defined conflict between two people whose interests are completely opposite is reached through *maximin* and *minimax* strategies. There is a pure strategy that guarantees one player at least his avoidance of his minimum score. That strategy is called a *maximin* since it maximizes the player's minimum and guarantees his highest "security level," that is, the worst outcome the game could bring. While one player undertakes this strategy and the payoff is to be divided, his opponent can adopt a strategy that guarantees the first player that the most he can attain is the avoidance of his minimum score. This strategy is called a *minimax*, since it minimizes an opponent's maximum by limiting his "hazard level," that is, the best his strategies could bring his opponent. "The best you can expect is to avoid the worst" is the motivation of this combination.

The simplest example of this comes with the "one cuts, the other chooses" method of division used with children and a piece of cake. The person cutting knows the person choosing will take the larger piece so he cuts portions as close to equal as possible. He is attempting to "maximize his minimum" or maximin. The chooser does take the larger piece, which "minimizes the maximum" or minimaxes what the cutter will receive. Most zero-sum situations are more complicated, however, and Von Neumann's solution was to introduce randomization into the decisions.

A description of a boy in Edgar Allen Poe's *The Purloined Letter* shows randomizing and its advantages at the simplest level. The boy is about eight years old and is a great success at guessing in the marbles game of "even and odd." In the game one player holds a number of marbles in his hand and asks the other whether the number is even or odd. The guesser wins one if he is correct and loses one if he is wrong. The boy wins on repeated trials with his classmates and they term him lucky. The story continues:

> "It is merely," I said, "an identification of the reasoner's intellect with that of his opponent."
> "It is," said Dupin; "and, upon inquiring of the boy by what means he effected the thorough identification in which his success consisted, I received answer as follows: 'When I wish to find out how wise, or how stupid, or how good, or how wicked is anyone, or what are his thoughts at the moment, I fashion the expression of my face, as accurately as possible, in accordance with the expression of his, and then wait to see what thoughts or sentiments arise in my mind or heart, as if to match or correspond with the expression.' This response of the schoolboy lies at the bottom of all the spurious profundity which has been attributed to Rochefoucauld, to La Bougive, to Machiavelli, and to Campanella."[10]

Suppose you are playing Poe's wonder child and assume the worst: he can correctly anticipate your thinking in every case. Whether you choose odd or even you lose. You can change this. You could adopt a random method of making your choice. If you do, you would have adopted a "mixed strategy." You could flip a coin, with heads representing even and tails representing odd and then put your marbles in your hand. Then you would not have to reason or decide at all, so being out thought would not occur. That way you take control of the outcome away from your opponent. You could even tell him of your strategy. By randomizing he too can ensure an even chance of winning. The more capable your opponent, the more attractive the randomizing procedure.[11]

The rationale and use of randomization is illustrated in the following problem. Assume you purchased a $10,000 diamond and there is a burglar who knows you have it and plans to try to steal it this very night.[12] You know of his intentions, and he knows that you know; it is too late to put it in a bank vault, you will be leaving town for the evening and your house will be unattended. You have a small safe in your secluded home and another in your office, which is far away in the city. Both have combination locks that could eventually be opened by anyone with the patience and time to keep trying different combinations. Your home safe is a cheaper model, and if the burglar spends the night trying combinations, there is a fifty-fifty chance he will succeed. Your office safe is of higher quality and the burglar's chances of success are one-in-ten of getting it open with a night's efforts. The safes are too far apart for the burglar to get to both in one evening, and he is aware of the quality of each and of his chances of success at each location if he systematically tries different combinations.

So, the obvious choice is to put the diamond in the good safe. The burglar has only one chance in ten. But if that is so, then we should really put the diamond in the poor-quality safe, because he would have no chance, since he would not attempt to open it. We assume the burglar knows as much about people who have diamonds as we know about burglars, and he would have realized this. If he is going to know our decision and spend his night on the right safe, it is better to challenge him with the stronger safe.

But we can do better than that. Suppose the two safes are not unequal but, rather, are identical and of the quality of the home safe. This clever burglar knows this and that they offer him equal chances. Which safe should we put the diamond in? There is not much point thinking about a "right" place to put it and the decision could be made by tossing a coin. Tossing a coin does more than save the time of deciding. If we abide by the results of the coin toss, the burglar cannot outsmart us and guess which safe holds the diamond, and his chances are cut in half. If we had five poor-quality safes and rolled dice to decide which safe to put the diamond in, with the chances equal for all, there would be one chance in ten of the burglar getting the diamond.

Now back to the original strong safe at the office and poorer quality safe at home. Imagine the strong safe is a compartment containing five poorer quality safes. The burglar can open the compartment but must then pick one of the five safes he finds inside, with a fifty-fifty chance of success in opening it. Bring in a sixth poor quality safe, and it does not matter whether it is in the compartment with the other five or elsewhere. The burglar has to choose which among the six to spend the night on, the five which happen to be enclosed together, or the sixth one which is outside. He will think of himself as having to choose among six poor safes and we are in the same position.

Recognizing our strong safe as equivalent of five weak safes, we can roll dice to decide, perhaps labeling the home safe as 6. If the die comes up 1 through 5 the diamond goes in the office safe and if it comes up 6 it goes in the home safe. The odds are five to one that we will put it in the office safe. If we are smart enough to do this, the burglar is smart enough to know it is what we would do.

And from the burglar's point of view, if he goes to the office safe there is one chance in ten he will successfully crack the safe and five in six that if he does, he will find the diamond inside. That gives him one chance in twelve if he goes to the office safe. Spending the night at the home safe he has one chance in two of getting it open, but only one chance in six that the diamond will be waiting for him. Again he has a one in twelve chance of getting the diamond. Having the inferior safe adds to our protection, as his chances are lower than if we only had the higher quality safe. The burglar is indifferent between the two safes and might go to the more convenient or comfortable location. If we thought he would do that and slyly put the diamond in the other location, we are back to trying to outsmart the burglar and he might outsmart us. If we trust in randomizing, he has only one chance in twelve.

He can roll the die for his decision as well. We can guarantee that his chance of success is no better than one and twelve if we roll the dice and he can guarantee himself a chance of getting the diamond as good as one in twelve by rolling the dice. Either party can convert this strategic contest into a dice game, where the outcome is dependent on pure chance. If we lose the diamond it is not because we were outsmarted by the burglar, but because he was lucky.

In this case the problem is symmetrical, in that the burglar rolls the dice with the same five-to-one odds as do we. In other problems the burglar may choose from different odds than those from which we chose. We know in advance, though, that the odds of the burglar's ultimate success for his night's work must be the same for his procedure as for ours. We may arrange that he has one chance in "n" (unspecific number) of succeeding, regardless of what he does, and he can arrange it that we have one chance in "m" (unspecified number) that no matter what we do, "n" and "m" will be the same.

The problem is solved the same way with other topics. Imagine you are alone in a secluded house and the last phone call you get before your line is cut informs you that a murderer has been hired to kill you and he is waiting outside. The murderer knows you can escape if he tries to break in so he is waiting outside until you leave, then he will do his dastardly deed. You have two options for leaving, which eventually, you will have to do. If you can get to the woods that enclose your house you will be able to evade him, as they are very dense and you know how difficult it is to see pathways that a stranger could not find. As well, there are many tangled roots and low branches, and you are fit, while the murderer is less so. You glance out the front door and estimate that if the murderer is waiting on that side of the house, he has a fifty-fifty chance of killing you before you reach the woods. Next you check the back door, and estimate that if the murderer is waiting for you at the back of the house he has only one chance in ten of killing you before you would reach the much closer woods. If he's waiting on the wrong side of the house when you go out, he has no chance at all of harming you.

Again, this problem may appear to present an obvious choice: you should run out the back. However, like the safe and the diamond, the best strategy actually is to roll the dice with five numbers, perhaps 1–5, representing going out the back door and one, in this case 6, representing going out the front, then do what the dice dictate. This reduces the chances of success for the murderer to one in twelve.

It may be easier to do this rolling of dice and acting on the outcome with diamonds and safes than when one's personal safety is at stake. The normal tendency to rush out the "safer" side, or the hunch to outthink the assassin by going out the more "dangerous" side on the assumption that he will expect you to panic and the rush out the safer side may be irresistible. You might be tempted to say, "Best two out of three" if the more dangerous side comes up or something similar until you get the result you desire. At that point the advantages of randomization have vanished.

In both of these cases, the safe and diamond and you and the murderer, we used choosing odds to equalize expected outcomes. Both parties had chances of one in ten and one in two. If making the choice of where to put the diamond had been done by flipping a coin there would have been an equal chance it would end in either safe. In that case the burglar would certainly spend the night at your poor quality home safe with a one chance in four of leaving with the diamond. If you knew the robber was making his decision by flipping a coin, you would certainly put the diamond in the stronger office safe with one chance in twenty of losing it. By randomizing the choices as we did we chose odds to equalize the expected outcome for either choice the burglar might make and he chose odds that gave him identical chances, wherever we put the diamond. We maximized our minimum security level at one chance in twelve and he minimized the maximum of our hazard level, by limiting the degree we could protect our diamond at the same one in twelve level.

The burglar's or murderer's chance of success can be diagrammed. The graph is a function of both the odds of the random choice that is determined by the die and the choice of the safe the burglar chooses to attempt to open. "One" equals certainty on this graph and the strong office safe's line is graphed from right to left, while the home safe is graphed from right to left. Where the graphed lines intersect can be read with reference to probability, and it is .067 on the vertical axis, which indicates the likelihood of success for going to the home safe, while on the strong safe the value is .167. Here is the diagram (Figure 20.1):

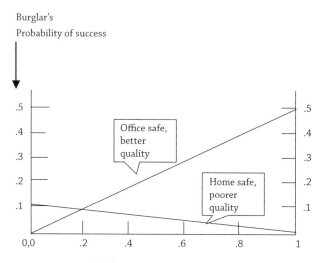

Probability of diamond in office safe

The lines cross where the odds we use in protecting our diamond are inversely proportionate to the odds of the burglar getting into the safe. At this point the burglar's best chance between going to the office safe and the house safe is minimized, as anything to the left of the intersection he does better at the house safe, and anything to the right he does better going to the office safe.

Game theory calls this making a choice in a zero-sum game by random selection with a choice of one in six the "solution" of the problem. The one in twelve chance the burglar has of success and our eleven in twelve chance of retaining our diamond is called the "value of the game." This probability of success, or expected value, is characterized by the facts that we need not settle for any less, we have maximized our minimum, and the burglar need not settle for any less than he is getting, he has minimized our maximum. If we behave otherwise the burglar's chances may be better or worse, but if we choose not to match wits we can hold him to one chance in twelve.

A similar form of problem, presented in *Thinking Strategically*, concerns duplicate bridge.[13] As described, the contest is actually known as barometer pairs, and groups of teams play the same hands against different sets of opponents in different rooms. You are playing for Team A and going into the final hand of the evening you are leading Team B, Goren and Zeck, and you will both play the same hand in different rooms. The cards you receive give you an almost perfect hand, one that guarantees that you make a bid of six no trump. Since you will get the bid, your opponent will lead, and based on the cards and early bidding it is equally likely the lead will be a club or a diamond. If the lead is a club, you will make a grand slam of seven clubs. Goren and Zeck are playing the exact same cards in another room. Since you are ahead going into the final hand, if you both bid six, you will both make it and you win the tournament. The same is true if you both bid seven and make it or if you both bid seven and fail. However, if you bid six and Team B bids seven and you both make your bids, they will surpass you and victory in the tournament is theirs.

The question becomes how to maximize your chances of winning. We will return to a different tool to analyze this situation. This matrix illustrates your team's chances for victory (Table 20.1):

Table 20.1

| | | Your team, Team A | |
		7 no trump	6 no trump
	7 no trump	0.75	0.50
Goren and Zeck, Team B			
	6 no trump	0.5	1.0

The matrix numbers are straightforward. If both bid seven no trump you win unless you fail and they make it. The odds are three to one in your favor (both have a 50 percent chance of making it, and a 50 percent chance club will be lead). If you bid seven and they bid six, you have a 50 percent chance of making it, and they will definitely make it. The same is true if they bid seven and you bid six; they have a 50 percent chance of making it, and they win if they do. If you both bid six, you win, since you enter this final hand with the lead. The easier method for calculating odds on how to play, called the "Wilson method," is to measure the difference in outcomes between rows or columns and then invert them, and you have random statistics for play. Your chance of winning using this method is the ratio (1–0.5):(0.75–0.5) or 2:1. You should bid seven no trump with a probability of 2/3 and six no trump with a probability of 1/3.

Playing this way you could expect to win two out of three times. If you bid seven no trump, the probability is 2/3 that your opponent will also bid seven no trump and 1/3 he will bid six no trump. That would leave you with an expected outcome of $(2/3)(3/4) + (1/3)(1/2)$, which equals 2/3. If you are willing to abide by the dictates of what the random selection picks, your opponents cannot do anything to make your outcome worse. If they knew for certain you were going for seven no trump they could increase their chances to 50–50 by going for six no trump, since they are sure to make this and you have only one chance in two of making seven, depending on the card led. If you are careful, and they know it, and bid six no trump, once again their chances of overtaking you have become 50–50, since they will bid seven, with an even chance of making the bid. It is only by randomization with uncertainty in your choice that you maintain your advantage.

Two experienced tournament bridge players were asked this question to see whether their answers would correspond to game theory play. Their responses mirrored to a degree the observations by economist Tim Harford that the play of experienced gamblers and that of gamblers who employed the lessons of game theory tended to resemble each other, as if what rational choice teaches is also learned by years of experience. The bridge players Craig Olson and Tom Fox[14] agreed that a good bridge player would immediately calculate the odds upon seeing the cards and felt there were other factors that would enter the decision. There is the psychological factor of the other team knowing it has a 75 percent chance of winning by bidding seven no trump and a possibility of zero chance of winning by bidding six, which they felt would mean most nonexpert pairs would bid seven. That would make your best choice a bid of seven, with a 75 percent chance for victory. You both bid seven and the prospects are 1) you both make it, 2) neither of you makes it, 3) you make it and your opponent does not, and 4) your opponent makes it and you do not. In three of those four scenarios you emerge as the winner. But, the following comment was added: "As the expertise of team B increases (Goren and Zeck), so in my opinion does making our choice more random."[15] While this does not spell out the method of randomization, it recognizes its place in the bidding process.

While he was at RAND Schelling presented specific applications of how randomization could be applied to the strategies he had outlined, of promises, threats, and commitments, with game theory analysis to justify his presentation.[16]

Following von Neumann and Randomization

While the minimax theorem provided a method for solving zero-sum games, solutions for the broader category of non-zero-sum games remained elusive. In 1950 John Nash came up with the formal concept, which showed that solutions exist for non-zero-sum, two-person games. He based his solution on the idea of "equilibrium points," outcomes where the players have no regrets. Given that there are points where players will have no regrets about the outcomes of games, it would be rational for them to choose those points. Nash's great mathematical achievement was to prove that every two-person finite game has at least one equilibrium point.

While the mathematics is complex, when illustrated on a matrix the concept appears quite simple.[17] An equilibrium point on a matrix is a quadrant where, if it were the outcome of a game and either of the players were given the opportunity to change his decision, neither would. Neither player could improve his outcome by changing the decision he had previously made. When the payoffs in a quadrant of a matrix are such that the players cannot improve their results by reversing their choices, the quadrant is called a *Nash equilibrium*. Consider the following matrices (Tables 20.2 and 20.3):

Table 20.2

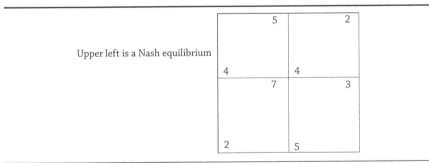

Upper right is a Nash equilibrium

Table 20.3

Upper left is a Nash equilibrium

The Nash equilibrium has been very important for bargaining, and one can see how problems sometimes arise. The following matrix depicts two competitive firms producing the same product and prices they could charge, along with anticipated sales (Table 20.4).

Table 20.4

		Firm A		
		$10	$9	$8
Firm B	$10	16 / 16	19 / 12	22 / 9
	$9	13 / 18	15 / 15	18 / 12
	$8	10 / 20	12 / 16	14 / 13

The Nash equilibrium is the lower right corner. That should indicate the out-come, since neither party could voluntarily change from that outcome and improve his position. However, it will be apparent to both firms that they are selling less for a smaller price at this outcome and there will be a tendency to collude, to coop-erate in price fixing likely at $10, even though both firms will need some sort of guarantee that the other will remain at that price and not go for a larger market share by reducing to $9. This has the makings of a duopoly.

Another common difficulty with Nash equilibria is, while Nash proved that every game must have one, that did not mean there would not be more than one. When that is the case, the question becomes which is the solution to the game. The following illustrates this situation (Table 20.5):

Table 20.5

	0	5
1		5
	2	1
2		0

The top right and bottom left are both Nash equilibria. Schelling observed that despite this, in many cases Nash equilibrium solutions were reached. He proposed that the reason for this was the existence of *focal points*. Schelling said there were properties that equilibria could possess that would tend to focus the players attention on those specific equilibria.[18]

An experimental two-person game conducted with college students and frequently repeated supports the focal point thesis. The game goes as follows:

Two college students are given a list of eleven U.S. cities, including Atlanta, Boston, Chicago, Dallas, Denver, Kansas City, Los Angeles, New York, Philadelphia, Phoenix, and San Francisco. Each city is assigned an "index" number, ranging from 1 to 100, reflecting its importance in a variety of areas. All the students knew was that New York was the highest and Kansas City the lowest. Each was told to independently make a personal list of cities (no specific number) using the given list, with no consultation allowed. One was told he must have Boston on his list, while the other was told he must include San Francisco. This much they both knew.

The payoffs were that if a city appeared on one student's list but not on the other's, the student who listed it received dollars equal to the city's index number (1–100). If a city appeared on both lists, each student *lost* twice as much as city's index number. If the two students managed to list all eleven cities between them without having any appear on each other's list, their total winnings were tripled. In pure strategies, this game has 512 Nash equilibria, so arriving at agreement of any sort without consultation would seem to be improbable, due to the abundance of "solutions." However, when the game was actually played, the students were surprisingly successful. The Boston list nearly always included New York and Philadelphia and frequently contained Chicago. The San Francisco list almost invariably included Los Angeles, Phoenix, and Denver, with Dallas frequently added.

Students quickly focused on geography without consultation in a sort of unspoken communication. The game seems to focus attention in this manner. If played by people with less knowledge of geography the focus could well be alphabetical. In some dual or multiple-equilibrium games, focal points present solutions.

Nash equilibrium solutions became standard solutions to non-zero-sum games. However, as with minimax, there were questions as to whether equilibrium solutions were intuitive. It was at the RAND Corporation, where so much of the development of game theory took place, that an answer to that question was first sought. This search led to the development of the Prisoner's Dilemma game.

All strategic thinking was about to face its most serious test, which is the subject of the final chapter.

Notes

1. Joh. Lindblom, "Lot-Casting in the Old Testament," *Vetus Testamentum*, Vol. 12, Fasc. 2 (April 1962), 164.
2. Herodotus, *The Histories*, trans. Robin Waterfield and Carolyn Dewald, (London: Oxford University Press, 1998), 207.

3. Richard G. Mulgan, "Lot as a Democratic Device of Selection," *Review of Politics*, Vol. 46, No. 4, October 1984), 540–542.

4. Jon Elster, *Solomonic Judgements: Studies in the Limitation of Rationality* (Cambridge, UK: Cambridge University Press, 1989), 50.

5. Morton W. Bloomfield, "Beowulf, Byrhtnoth, and the Judgment of God: Trial by Combat in Anglo-Saxon England," *Speculum*, Vol. 44, No. 4 (October 1969), 546.

6. Stephen E. Fienberg, "Randomization and Social Affairs: The 1970 Draft Lottery," *Science*, Vol. 171 (January 22, 1971), 255.

7. David E. Rosenbaum, "Charge Draft Lottery Was Not Random," *New York Times*, January 4, 1970, 66.

8. Elster, *Solomonic Judgments*, 48.

9. Ibid., 121.

10. Edgar Allan Poe, "The Purloined Letter," *Tales of Mystery and Imagination* (London: Dent, 1912), 463.

11. Presented in Morton Davis, *Game Theory* (New York: Basic Books, 1983), 28–30.

12. Thomas C. Schelling, "Zero Sum Games," Teaching Materials No. 15T. Public Policy Program, John F. Kennedy School of Government, Harvard University, August 1973.

13. Avinash Dixit and Barry Nalebuff, *Thinking Strategically* (New York: Norton, 1991).

14. Craig Olson won the North American Rookie Open Pairs in the 1970s when he was getting started with duplicate bridge and has over 1,000 masterpoints, Tom Fox finished second in the Reisinger Nationals and has 8,600 masterpoints.

15. Craig Olson, e-mail to Robert Dodge, December 9, 2008.

16. Thomas C. Schelling, "Randomization of Threats and Promises," P-1716, The RAND Corporation, June 5, 1959, available online, http://www.rand.org/content/dam/rand/pubs/papers/2006/P1716.pdf.

17. Schelling learned his game theory mathematics intricacies from an in-depth study of John von Neumann and Oskar Morgenstern's *Theory of Games and Economic Behavior* (Princeton, NJ: Princeton University Press, 1944), but found Duncan Luce, *Games and Decisions: Introduction and Critical Survey* (Hoboken, NJ: Wiley, 1957) more instructive, and Nash's work was included along with many other developments of the past ten years. For those with advanced mathematics backgrounds Roger Myerson's *Game Theory: Analysis of Conflict* (Cambridge, MA: Harvard University Press, 1997) has been considered a useful work and covers the formal math involved in both minimax and equilibrium solutions.

18. For an explanation of the development of cooperative game theory from Nash through Schelling and focal points see Vincent P. Crawford, "Thomas Schelling and the Analysis of Strategic Behavior," in Richard J. Zeckhauser, ed., *Strategy and Choice* (Cambridge, MA: MIT Press, 1991), 272–290.

CASE STUDY AND REVIEW

CHAPTER 21

Case Study: Cuban Missile Crisis

ANALYSIS AND REVIEW

Thirteen days beginning in late October 1962, were, according to historian Arthur Schlesinger, "not only the most dangerous moment of the Cold War, it was the most dangerous moment in human history."[1] Noam Chomsky agreed with that assessment.[2] Decisions of a new magnitude of importance were made. One can look back on all of history and find other times and events when some change in outcome or different choice would have led to monumental alterations in the direction of life on earth. While other crises had been dramatic, as Schlesinger added, "Never before had two contending powers possessed between them the technical capacity to blow up the world."[3]

Background

The Cuban missile crisis was the most dangerous event in the Cold War, the struggle that was born as World War II came to an end and two great powers remained: the communist Soviet Union and its Red Army; and the more democratic and capitalist United States, with its monopoly on the atomic bomb. Each side viewed the other as the embodiment of evil and strove to demonstrate the superiority of its system to the rest of the world, as well as to develop the military capability needed to advance its international interests against the other. The Soviets set up puppet communist states in all the areas they liberated from Axis control at the end of World War II. Germany was divided into sectors, with the Soviets controlling the east and the Western Allies controlling the west. Berlin, located in the Soviet sector, being similarly divided.

A crisis came in 1948, when the Soviet Union blockaded Berlin to try to force the Allies out of West Berlin and the Allies responded with a huge airlift to keep West Berlin's two million residents supplied with the necessities of life. The airlift continued for more than a year. The following year the United States joined the first peacetime alliance in its history as NATO was formed to halt westward Soviet advancement. That was also a year for communist gains. America's monopoly on atomic weapons vanished with Russia's explosion of an atomic bomb; and China, the most populous nation on earth, fell to Mao Tse-tung's communist forces, which had driven Chiang Kai-shek's government to exile on the island of Taiwan.

In 1950 the Cold War heated up when North Korea invaded South Korea. At the same time, in the United States, paranoia overcame fear as Senator Joseph McCarthy claimed "the State Department...is thoroughly infested with communists." A low point of baseless charges and name-calling began and led to thousands being fired and many more imprisoned or blacklisted. Congress passed an Internal Security Act along with a Communist Control Act as constitutional protections were sacrificed to panic. Loyalty oaths became common as concern about communist infiltration spread through scare tactics and name-calling. The witch hunt that followed lasted to 1954.

During that time the danger of the competition between the two superpowers escalated considerably with the dawn of the thermonuclear age. On November 1, 1952, "Mike," the first fusion bomb, or H-bomb, was exploded on the South Seas atoll of Eniwetok. The heat at the center of the explosion was five times as great as at the center of the Sun, and the blast was the equivalent of five million tons of TNT, or five "megatons" in the terminology of the nuclear age. Nine months after the U.S. test, the Soviet Union exploded an H-bomb in Siberia, and soon the race was on for delivery of the new weapons.

In 1954 President Eisenhower rejected advice to use nuclear weapons against Red China on five occasions in defense of two small islands, Quemoy and Matsu, claimed by both Taiwan and China. That same year the United States launched the first nuclear powered submarine, the *Nautilus*. Soviet Premier Nikita Khrushchev addressed visiting Western diplomats in 1956 with the chilling words, "We will bury you,"[5] and Russian tanks rolled into Hungary to crush an uprising against the communist government. The U.S. Army requested 151,000 nuclear warheads in 1956 and the following year.[6]

The Soviets made a shocking move forward on October 4, 1957, when they launched into orbit the first manmade earth satellite, Sputnik, demonstrating they had an intercontinental ballistic missile, or ICBM, that could carry a payload. This glaring symbol of Soviet supremacy in missile development shattered America's confidence in its technological superiority and strategic defenses as well as in its education system. Ben Pearse of the *New York Times*, summarizing America's national trauma, wrote "The national ego had not been so affronted since Pearl Harbor."[7] In another bit of bad news for the United States, the Viet Cong, communists supported by North Vietnam, began a guerrilla war against South Vietnam.

The space race was on, and the Soviets were in the lead. Nuclear warheads could be delivered to the United States from the U.S.S.R. within minutes, making their lead more frightening. The dramatic failure of the U.S. attempt to launch its own satellite two months after Sputnik with Project Vanguard led President Eisenhower to the decision to turn the missile development program over to Germans who had come to America following World War II, and on January 31, 1958, the United

States successfully launched a small satellite from Cape Canaveral, Florida. Later that year the United States deployed Thor missiles to England and Jupiter missiles to Turkey. The Office of Civil Defense began to promote building home fallout shelters and publishing guides and instructions for their construction. Fidel Castro launched a revolution in Cuba against the Bautista government and in 1959 he established the first communist government in the Western Hemisphere, ninety miles off the coast of the United States. Though they attracted little notice, the first U.S. casualties were suffered in Vietnam. Fear of communism and hope for survival were common American attitudes throughout the decade and a "delicate balance of terror" existed between the two great powers.

The first two years of new decade brought continued tensions. An American U-2 spy plane was shot down over Russian territory in May 1960, and in July Polaris missiles were successfully tested with underwater launches from a nuclear powered submarine. November saw the United States' youngest elected president, John F. Kennedy, who won a close election. Three months into Kennedy's presidency there was a botched attempt by CIA-backed Cuban exiles to overthrow Castro's government in Cuba at the Bay of Pigs. The next month the Soviets again demonstrated their lead in space technology when Yuri Gagarin became the first man to orbit the earth in a satellite. Kennedy responded by telling Congress that before the end of the decade, the United States should put a man on the moon and return him safely to earth. There was a crisis in Berlin that ended with the building of the wall that became one of the Cold War's most emotive symbols. In the fall the Soviet Union exploded Tsar Bomba, a 27-ton bomb with a 58-megaton yield, the largest of all time, equal to about 39,000 Hiroshima atomic bombs. The United States continued to make its own plans for Cuba, as a released document notes: "As desired by higher authority on November 30, 1961, the U.S. undertook a special effort 'in order to overthrow the Communist regime in Cuba.'"[8] This plan for the Cuban government overthrow was given the code name "Operation Mongoose." On December 2, Castro clearly proclaimed his alliance with the communist bloc, "I am a Marxist-Leninist and I shall be a Marxist-Leninist to the end of my life."[9]

The situation in 1962 was volatile. Castro anticipated another invasion from the United States and was looking for a way to protect his control of Cuba. In the1960 presidential campaign there had been much talk of a "missile gap" that favored the Soviet Union, but well-informed parties in both the U.S.S.R. and the United States knew that the United States had a considerable lead in missiles. As well, the United States had medium-range missiles deployed in England and on Russia's frontier in Turkey. In February the United States announced a complete embargo against Cuba. Deploying Russian missiles in Cuba appeared to Cuba and Russia to be a solution to their problems with the United States. On May 30 Castro accepted a visiting Soviet delegation's offer to provide Cuba with nuclear missiles, and Russian missiles began arriving in July. Officers in Cuba were given surprising latitude initially in their use of the weapons, as the U.S.S.R. Marshall of Defense wrote to the group commander in Cuba: "In the situation of an enemy landing on the island of Cuba...and there is no possibility of receiving orders from the U.S.S.R. Ministry of Defense, you are permitted to make your own decision and to use the nuclear means."[10] On September 28, U.S. Naval reconnaissance flights observed a Soviet vessel carrying bombers to Cuba, and three days later Secretary of Defense Robert McNamara discussed options with the Joint Chiefs of Staff, including a blockade of the island and a military strike.

While the U.S. Army's earlier request for warheads had not been met, the United States was well on its way to its largest stockpile of nuclear weapons in its history and was turning them out rapidly. The Soviet Union did not have as many, but had weapons of larger yield, and each side could destroy all life on earth many times over. "Overkill" became a term of the time. Another expression was MAD, or mutually assured destruction, which both prevented war from happening and made clear the results of the superpowers going to war, intentionally or accidentally.

In the fall of 1962 President Kennedy was facing great challenges on domestic issues as well as the international issue of survival. Especially thorny were efforts being made at desegregation, and the new leader inspired optimism in some. One situation involved James Meredith, who had taken out an application for admission to the all-white University of Mississippi the day after Kennedy was inaugurated; after a legal battle that ended with a Supreme Court decision, Meredith had won a court order to be admitted. Mississippi Governor Ross Barnett was determined to defy the highest court and assert states rights, proclaiming, "There is no case in history where the Caucasian race has survived social integration," and advised "any official who is not prepared to suffer imprisonment for this righteous cause" to resign.[11] On September 30, James Meredith entered the University of Mississippi under court order, accompanied both by National Guard troops Kennedy had nationalized and regular army troops. State officials attempted to block his way, and riots left two dead. President Kennedy went on television and radio that evening and addressed the nation, saying, "The eyes of the Nation and of all the world are upon you and upon all of us, and the honor of your University and State are in the balance."[12]

On October 2, Secretary of Defense Robert McNamara sent a memo to the Joint Chiefs of Staff, outlining situations that would call for direct military action against Cuba and asked that they prepare different military responses for them. Eleven days later State Department Ambassador-at-Large Chester Bowles had a long conversation with Soviet Ambassador Dobrynin, contending the United States had evidence that indicated some Soviet missiles were in Cuba. Dobrynin denied the claim, as the Kremlin had not informed him of the truth of the situation.

It was against this background that the events of October 1962 would unfold. **Sunday, October 14**: Early in the morning Major Richard Heyser piloted a U-2 flight over western Cuba and took photographs of medium-range ballistic missile sites.

Monday, October 15: Heyser's photographs were taken to the National Photograph Interpretation Center in Washington, and while the president hosted Prime Minister Ben Bella of Algeria in the State Dining Room at the White House the photographs were analyzed. They revealed twenty-three missile sites and also medium-range bombers being uncrated. This news was passed along to key Kennedy advisors that evening.

The Crisis Begins

Tuesday, October 16: At 8:45 a.m., National Security Advisor McGeorge Bundy told the president the news, and from that point on tension would be very high. The crisis had begun. By noon Kennedy had contacted his brother Robert and a former ambassador to the Soviet Union and had made the critical step of creating and convening the first meeting of a group called the Executive Committee of the United States National Security Council, commonly known as ExComm. This group would be there to help him make his decisions throughout the crisis. ExComm had twelve statutory members and a number of unofficial participants.

At the first ExComm meeting the members reviewed the U-2 photo evidence of the missile sites and ordered further flights. The missiles were first identified as nuclear tipped SS-3s, but that was corrected during the day to SS-4 medium-range ballistic missiles without nuclear warheads, and no nuclear warheads were reported in the area. A CIA expert said the missiles did not appear ready to be fired yet. There was an open discussion of response options that ranged from surgical strikes at the missile sites to a full invasion; and a blockade of the island was brought up. Kennedy commented, "I guess this is the week I earn my salary."[13]

The second ExComm meeting was that evening, and the committee was told the missiles in Cuba should be operational within two weeks though there was one that was ready to be fired "much sooner." McNamara presented three options, one political, calling for dialogue with Khrushchev and Castro; a second mixed, that involved a blockade and surveillance; and the third, a military invasion. There was no agreement on which was the best choice, though a military invasion seemed the favored option among the ExComm members.

Wednesday, October 17: The debate over options was taking place in several places, and positions were being taken. McNamara had heard from the Joint Chiefs of Staff that a surgical strike would require attacking all military installations in Cuba, and he had become the strongest advocate of the more moderate idea of a blockade. Former Secretary of State Dean Acheson, an unofficial member of ExComm, was critical of the blockade idea, wondering what would become of the missiles already in Cuba; and other blockade critics were concerned that by imposing the blockade, the United States would change the conflict from one between the United States and Cuba to one between the United States and the Soviet Union. A Soviet embassy official relayed a message to Attorney General

Robert Kennedy from Nikita Khrushchev that the Soviet missiles in Cuba were strictly defensive. ExComm learned of a medium-range ballistic missile (MRBM) site that would have a range of 2,200 nautical miles, enough to cover a significant portion of the United States when operational.

Thursday, October 18: At the morning ExComm meeting the Joint Chiefs of Staff presented their recommendation for an air strike against Cuban missile bases and other military targets. Robert Kennedy objected to a first strike on moral grounds. In the afternoon President Kennedy made the same moral argument in a meeting with Acheson and later met with Soviet Minister of Foreign Affairs Andrei Gromyko at the White House. Gromyko told Kennedy that any military assistance the Soviets were providing Cuba was purely defensive, and Kennedy did not disclose that he knew about the missile bases. Before Gromyko left Kennedy read him a statement he had made on September 4 that warned against deployment of nuclear weapons on Cuban soil. That evening there was another ExComm meeting, and consensus seemed to be forming around imposing a blockade. Legal opinions were sought to justify the operation, and there was a report that the MRBMs in Cuba could be launched within eighteen hours. The United States had carried out a high-altitude hydrogen bomb test in the Pacific during the day.

Friday, October 19: The idea of an air strike had been largely abandoned by the ExComm meeting of the afternoon, though military planning continued as an alternative. Theodore Sorensen agreed to get started on a speech to the nation in which President Kennedy could outline his Cuba quarantine strategy. It would take Sorensen until three o'clock the next morning to finish the speech, and it would be a historic one. During the day timetables were worked out for raising the military alert level, reinforcing Guantanamo Naval Base, and informing NATO allies, all of which were based on when the president informed the nation of the situation. During a questions session at the Defense Department regarding an article about missiles in Cuba, Pentagon officials denied any knowledge that they existed.

Saturday, October 20: Sorensen's speech was completed and amended and approved. The CIA sent a report on likely Soviet responses to U.S. actions, noting, "The most likely area for broad retaliation outside Cuba appears to be Berlin."[14] McNamara ordered four air squadrons to be readied for a strike on Cuba because there would not be time to ready them later if they were needed. In the afternoon all parties were called together and the president said the air strike proposals were not sufficiently surgical. A member of the Joint Chiefs suggested the use of nuclear weapons in any attack. The president called the idea of attack incompatible with American principles, and the full scenario for the quarantine of Cuba was covered. The time of the president's address to the nation was set for 7:00 p.m., October 22.

UN Ambassador Adlai Stevenson arrived late and proposed the president include in a settlement of the crisis withdrawal of U.S. forces from Guantanamo and removal of U.S. missiles from Turkey, but his suggestion was not popular. Kennedy agreed he would take the missiles out of Turkey and Italy if the Russians raised the proposal, but only at a later date. After the meeting adjourned at 5:10 p.m., Kennedy told Sorenson to revise the speech, indicating he was not sure whether he would be giving the blockade speech or a surgical strike speech. He would not know until he met with the Air Force once more the next morning. A new intelligence report stated that sixteen launchers of MRBM missiles were operational in Cuba and could be fired within eight hours of a decision to launch. The United States carried out another high altitude test of a nuclear bomb in the Pacific.

Sunday, October 21: In the morning Kennedy met with Secretary of State Dean Rusk and Secretary of Defense McNamara and finalized the quarantine plans. Following that he met with the commander of the Tactical Air Command and instructed him that any time after the morning of October 22 the military should be prepared to launch air strikes against Cuba to take out the missile sites and the MiG airfields. In the afternoon the president convened a formal meeting of the National Security Council at which Admiral George Anderson explained how the quarantine would proceed. Orders to stop would be given as a Soviet ship approached the line, and if the vessel did not respond a shot would be fired across its bow. If that was not enough to stop the ship, a shot would be fired to its rudder. Several newspapers, including the *New York Times* and the *Washington Post*, had pieced together what was taking place, and calls from the White House convinced them to keep the story quiet.

The Crisis Goes Public

Monday, October 22: Several Western leaders were briefed in advanced about the president's decision on a course of action for Cuba. A brief meeting of the ExComm members was held, and President Kennedy sent instructions to commanders of Jupiter missiles in Italy and Turkey to render them inoperable if any attempt to fire them was made without direct instructions from him personally. At noon the Strategic Air Command began a launch that kept one-eighth of its B-52 nuclear bomber force airborne at any time. In late afternoon Kennedy met with congressional leaders at the White House and while some supported his blockade/quarantine approach, others called for an air strike or invasion.

At 7:00 p.m. the president addressed the nation from the White House. This memorable and chilling speech, broadcast in black and white, was about a world both sides viewed in black and white and was straightforward in setting out the president's position. An excerpted version follows:

> Unmistakable evidence has established the fact that a series of offensive missile sites is now in preparation on (Cuba). The purpose of these

bases can be none other than to provide a nuclear strike capability against the Western Hemisphere.

The characteristics of these new missile sites indicate two distinct types of installations. Several of them include medium range ballistic missiles, capable of carrying a nuclear warhead for a distance of more than 1,000 nautical miles. Each of these missiles, in short, is capable of striking Washington, D.C., the Panama Canal, Cape Canaveral, Mexico City, or any other city in the southeastern part of the United States, in Central America, or in the Caribbean area. Additional sites not yet completed appear to be designed for intermediate range ballistic missiles—capable of traveling more than twice as far—and thus capable of striking most of the major cities in the Western Hemisphere, ranging as far north as Hudson Bay, Canada, and as far south as Lima, Peru. In addition, jet bombers, capable of carrying nuclear weapons, are now being uncrated and assembled in Cuba, while the necessary air bases are being prepared. This urgent transformation of Cuba into an important strategic base—by the presence of these large, long-range, and clearly offensive weapons of sudden mass destruction constitutes an explicit threat to the peace and security of all the Americas.... American citizens have become adjusted to living daily on the bull's-eye of Soviet missiles located inside the U.S.S.R. or in submarines.... But this secret, swift, and extraordinary buildup of Communist missiles...in violation of Soviet assurances, and in defiance of American and hemispheric policy—this sudden, clandestine decision to station strategic weapons for the first time outside of Soviet soil—is a deliberately provocative and unjustified change in the status quo which cannot be accepted by this country, if our courage and our commitments are ever to be trusted again by either friend or foe.... Our unswerving objective, therefore, must be to prevent the use of these missiles against this or any other country, and to secure their withdrawal or elimination from the Western Hemisphere.... We will not prematurely or unnecessarily risk the costs of worldwide nuclear war in which even the fruits of victory would be ashes in our mouth—but neither will we shrink from that risk at any time it must be faced. I have directed that the following initial steps be taken immediately: a strict quarantine on all offensive military equipment under shipment to Cuba is being initiated.... It shall be the policy of this Nation to regard any nuclear missile launched from Cuba against any nation in the Western Hemisphere as an attack by the Soviet Union on the United States, requiring a full retaliatory response upon the Soviet Union. I call upon Chairman Khrushchev to halt and eliminate this clandestine, reckless, and provocative threat to world peace and to stable relations between our two nations.... My fellow citizens: let no one doubt that this is a difficult and dangerous effort on which we have set out. No one can foresee precisely what course it will take or what costs or casualties will be incurred.... But the greatest danger of all would be to do nothing. The path we have chosen for the present is full of hazards, as all paths are—but it is the one most consistent with our character and courage as a nation and our commitments around the world. The cost of freedom is always high— but Americans have always paid it. And one path we shall never choose, and that is the path of surrender or submission. Our goal is not the victory of might, but the vindication of right—not peace at the expense of freedom, but both peace and freedom, here in this hemisphere, and, we hope, around the world. God willing, that goal will be achieved. Thank you and good night. [15]

The reaction to the speech was shock. Moments after it ended Secretary of State Rusk spoke to a meeting of all foreign ambassadors in Washington and said, "I would not be candid and I would not be fair with you if I did not say that we are in as grave a crisis as mankind has been in."[16] The lines had been clearly drawn, and nuclear war was at stake. The next morning, "The front pages of the nation's newspapers were dark with three-deck banner headlines and story upon story loaded with phrases such as the 'the risk of a major war,' 'threat of thermonuclear war,' 'offensive weapons able to rain nuclear destruction on all the Americas.'"[17]

Public obsession with the seriousness of it was apparent in the reaction, as described by longtime historian at the John F. Kennedy Library, Sheldon Stern: "The American public responded to JFK's speech with some signs of panic. Food and emergency supplies disappeared from supermarkets and hardware stores. Long lines were reported at gasoline stations, and there was a run on tires. People across America stood in silent, worried clumps around newsstands, anxiously reading the latest headlines. At the Phillips Academy in Andover, Mass. and at the Mount Hermon School to the west, students received phone calls from their parents urging them to come home to be with their families—just in case. Some 10 million Americans also left the nation's cities hoping to find safety 'far away from nuclear targets.'"[18]

One history of the period records,

Entire regions of the country now faced nuclear obliteration, and their residents prayed for peace. For Americans living in the northern sections of the country or in areas that Castro's missiles could never reach, their fear was focused on radiation sickness and not on obliteration. From Seattle to Boston, northerners flocked to the grocery stores, buying out every possible necessity to survive a long period of locked-up seclusion in their homes. Most civil defense authorities agreed that if the wind blew north from the nuclear-destroyed south, the radiation poisoning that came with it would remain intact for at least two months. The governors of northern states even stationed National guardsmen at certain grocery stores in order to protect food supplies, prevent total buy-outs by only a handful of people, and provide a sense of order and discipline. America's churches were open on weeknights so that the concerned faithful could make their peace with God. The once vigilant anticommunist America had become America the scared.[19]

A document from the U.S. Information agency captures the memory of the fear personally: "I was almost 13 when the Cuban Missile Crisis broke. How scary was it? That evening, after the President's address, my parents moved my bed into their bedroom and told me they wanted me to sleep with them that night. When I asked why, my Father said, 'Because, this may be the last night we ever spend alive together.'"[20]

Around the time of the speech much had taken place. A copy had been delivered along with a personal letter from the president to Premier Khrushchev in Moscow. In case of a reaction from Cuba, twenty-two interceptor fighter aircraft were sent airborne toward the island during the speech, and for the most serious threats ICBM crews were put on alert and Polaris nuclear submarines were dispatched to sea. Most U.S. forces went to DEFCON 3 when the President began speaking. In the Soviet Union, Colonel Oleg Penkovsky was arrested for having served as a spy for both the United States and Britain and he had two secret code numbers to call in the event of trouble, one if he anticipated arrest and another for an imminent Soviet attack. He called with the imminent Soviet attack code but intelligence officers decided not to give his warning credit. The Russians conducted a high altitude test of a hydrogen bomb.

Tuesday, October 23: At 8:00 a.m. the U.S. ambassador was summoned to the Soviet Foreign Office and given a letter from Premier Khrushchev to be sent to President Kennedy. The letter said, "I must frankly say that the measures indicated in your statement constitute a serious threat to the security of nations.... I hope that the United States Government will display wisdom and renounce the actions pursued by you, which may lead to catastrophic consequences for world peace."[21] A morning ExComm meeting decided that continued harassment of U.S. reconnaissance flights would probably lead to destruction of all SAM (surface to air missile) sites in Cuba. In late afternoon Adlai Stevenson first brought the situation up at the United Nations and was sharply attacked by both the Cuban and the Russian delegates.

At about the same time Fidel Castro began a massive mobilization of all military forces in Cuba that activated 270,000 forces to protect against a feared American invasion. A 6:00 p.m. meeting of ExComm made note of Soviet submarines that had moved into the Caribbean and of the added dangers they represented. President Kennedy sent a note to Premier Khrushchev admonishing that both sides show caution and requesting the Soviets honor the quarantine line. Shortly after 7:00 p.m. the president signed Proclamation 3504, formally establishing the quarantine and its line and making it official that the blockade of Cuba would begin at 10:00 a.m. the next day. That evening Castro gave a rambling, defiant 90-minute speech about U.S. imperialism and Cuba's right to arm itself. A Gallup Poll on the day showed that the quarantine had an approval rating of 84 percent while only 4 percent disapproved, yet about 20 percent anticipated the quarantine would lead to World War III. The Organization of American States (OAS) voted to support the U.S. quarantine of Cuba as new reconnaissance flights revealed Cuban missile sites ready to launch.

In the glorious Indian summer evening President Kennedy met with the British ambassador, who recommended he move the quarantine interception line closer, from eight hundred to five hundred miles from Cuba to allow the Russians longer to consider their response. Kennedy agreed and called McNamara to shorten the distance. Low-level reconnaissance flights were introduced to supplement the high-flying U-2s. Intelligence indicated the Soviet ships were headed for the confrontation line and Russian communications said that U.S. ships that damaged their vessels would be sunk. ExComm discussed how many of the 92 million people living in the 1,100 mile range of the Cuban missiles would survive a nuclear attack and concluded fewer than half would survive. The president presented the idea of evacuating cities before a U.S. invasion, but no one was interested in considering the chaos and panic. Moscow placed the military forces of the Warsaw Pact nations on alert. Some ExComm members were remaining in their offices and no longer going home at night.

Wednesday, October 24: A cable was sent to the U.S. ambassadors to Turkey and to NATO, saying a Turkey-for-Cuba missile swap was being considered. Turkey was upset with the prospect. William Knox, a U.S. businessman, was called in for a meeting with Khrushchev, and told that Khrushchev would give orders to sink U.S. vessels if they stopped Soviet ships at the quarantine line. The message was relayed, and President Kennedy expressed concern to his brother Robert. Khrushchev also sent Kennedy a letter saying he would not give orders for Soviet ships to honor the quarantine line. At 10:00 a.m., the official beginning of the blockade, two Soviet freighters drew near the quarantine line, 500 miles from the coast of Cuba. The Pentagon went to DEFCON 2 for the first time in history. All 1,400 of America's nuclear bombers went on 24-hour alert. In the Cabinet Room, Secretary of Defense McNamara informed the president that a Soviet submarine had moved between the oncoming Soviet ships and the *Essex*, the American aircraft carrier manning the boycott line.

McNamara told the president that the Americans would have to try to surface the sub with depth charges. As Robert Kennedy watched, President Kennedy put his hand up to his face and covered his mouth. He opened and closed his fist. "His face seemed drawn," RFK recorded in his diary, "his eyes pained, almost gray. We stared at each other across the table. For a few fleeting seconds, it was as if almost no one else was there and he was no longer the President."[22] There was a brief discussion about how this could unwind to nuclear Armageddon but at 10:25 a new message arrived that said there was information. Some of the Soviet ships had stopped dead in the water. President Kennedy instructed that no ship be intercepted for at least an hour while clarification was sought. Dean Rusk commented to McGeorge Bundy, "We're eyeball to eyeball, and I think the other fellow just blinked."[23]

Secretary General of the UN, U Thant, sent a message to both leaders urging restraint and proposed a voluntary suspension of the American quarantine for two to three weeks.

Thursday, October 25: The *Essex* intercepted the Soviet tanker *Bucharest* then allowed it to continue on its voyage to Cuba. Kennedy instructed U.S. Representative Adlai Stevenson to confront Soviet ambassador Zorin, and *Life* magazine described the historic event:

> Stevenson turned on him with magnificent scorn: "Do you, Ambassador Zorin, deny the U.S.S.R. has placed and is placing medium and intermediate-ranged missiles in Cuba? Yes or no?
>
> Don't wait for the translation. Yes or no?"
>
> Zorin then muttered something about not being in an American courtroom. Stevenson, cold and controlled: "You are in the courtroom of world opinion. . . . You have denied they exist and I want to know if I have understood you correctly. . . . I am prepared to wait for my answer until hell freezes over. And I am also prepared to present evidence in this room!"
>
> It was a moment of tremendous excitement. At Stevenson's order, aerial photos were spread on easels in the council chambers, showing the transformation of San Cristóbal from a peaceful country spot into a grim nuclear installation. Other pictures added further to the evidence. Zorin wanly denied the authenticity of the display. Stevenson wondered savagely why the Soviet Union did not test its denial by permitting a United Nations team to visit the sites. [24]

President Kennedy rejected U Thant's suggested suspension of the quarantine, while Premier Khrushchev accepted it. U Thant sent a second letter to both leaders asking them to avoid direct confrontations and that Soviet ships to stay out of the quarantine area. In late afternoon the *USS Kennedy* headed for the Lebanese ship *Marucla*, selected by the president as the first to be boarded.

Friday, October 26: President Kennedy had given orders that no actions be taken to provoke the Soviet Union into believing an attack on them was imminent or being considered, but there were blunders and lapses that posed possible dangers. As the new day began in Duluth, Minnesota, a security officer at a military command post spotted an intruder climbing the security fence and feared a terrorist attack by the Soviets, so he set off the base's alarms. That triggered a warning at nearby Volk Air Field, where nuclear-armed F-106A fighters were scrambled and had taxied to the end of the runway before being stopped, since it had been discovered that the intruder at the Duluth command post had been a bear. In an act that could have been seriously misinterpreted, the Air Force test-fired an intercontinental ballistic missile from California into the Pacific Ocean, following a test schedule previously arranged. There was near panic at the headquarters of the Strategic Air Command later in the day when another U.S. intercontinental ballistic missile was test-fired from Florida over Cuba and officers learned of it from an improvised radar site in New Jersey, where the report was that a missile had been sighted in the air and was apparently a Soviet missile heading toward Florida.[25]

The *Marucla* was allowed to pass after inspection found it carried only paper products. In the morning President Kennedy told ExComm he believed the quarantine alone would not succeed in getting Russia to withdraw the missiles from Cuba and that an invasion or a trade of some sort would be required. The CIA reported that the construction of the missile sites was continuing at an accelerated pace. *ABC News* correspondent John Scali was invited to lunch at a Washington hotel by KGB colonel and head of Moscow's U.S. intelligence operations, Alexandr Fomin. Fomin told Scali that Moscow would remove the missiles if Washington pledged not to invade Cuba, and Scali immediately passed the information along to government officials.

At 2:00 p.m. the U.S. ambassador to Brazil was instructed to meet with the Brazilian government to request that they have their ambassador in Havana meet with Castro and inform him that the United States was unlikely to invade if the missiles were withdrawn. The State Department received a letter from Moscow at 6:00 p.m. that was forwarded to ExComm. It was from Premier Khrushchev, and it proposed that the Soviets would remove their missiles if President Kennedy would publicly guarantee the United States would not invade Cuba.

ExComm was analyzing the letter from Khrushchev and Robert Kennedy held a secret meeting with Soviet Ambassador Dobrynin, during which he left the room to phone the president. When he returned he said the president would look favorably on the question of Turkey, and Dobrynin reported this to the Kremlin.

That evening Khrushchev received a cable from Fidel Castro, who was staying in a bomb shelter in the Soviet embassy in Havana. Castro anticipated a U.S. invasion and urged a nuclear first strike against the United States, saying, "I consider the aggression is almost imminent within the next 24 or 72 hours...that would be the moment to eliminate the danger forever through an act of clear legitimate defense, however harsh and terrible the solution should be."[26] Castro ordered antiaircraft weapons to fire at all U.S. planes flying over Cuba. The Soviet ambassador to Cuba asked Castro to rescind the order but he refused. The United States conducted a high altitude nuclear test.

Saturday, "Black Saturday," October 27: According to a 6:00 a.m. CIA report of the day, "San Cristobal MRBM sites 1, 2, and 3 Sagua La Grande sites 1 and 2 are considered fully operational. The remaining MRBM site, #4 at St. Crostobal

will probably be fully operational on 28 October."[27] Shortly after 10:00 a.m. a U-2
from a SAC base in Alaska wandered into Soviet airspace as a result of a naviga-
tion error and the pilot called for backup assistance. U.S. F-102 fighter aircraft
armed with nuclear air-to-air missiles were scrambled and sent to defend the
U-2, while Soviet MiGs took off to intercept it. The U-2 managed to escape to U.S.
airspace before an encounter took place. It was said that when McNamara heard
that a U-2 was in Soviet airspace he turned white and was hysterical, yelling that
it meant war with the Soviet Union. The day's troubles were far from over.

At 11:03 a.m. a new letter arrived from Khrushchev, this time offering to
remove the Soviet missiles from Cuba in exchange for a removal of the U.S. missiles from Turkey. At midday, while ExComm was debating how to respond to this
new proposal, another jolt came. A U-2 spy plane had been shot down over Cuba
and its U.S. pilot was killed. The inaccurate assumption was that this had been an
intentional Soviet escalation of the crisis. A low-level reconnaissance plane was
hit by antiaircraft fire over Cuba in midafternoon but returned home safely and
to the Pentagon's consternation, Kennedy decided not to order a reprisal attack
on the SAM site that shot down the U-2, but said he would do so in the event of
future attacks.

In the meantime, unknown to all the major players in the confrontation,
beneath the sea events were taking place that nearly led to Armageddon. Vadim
Orlov of Soviet submarine B-59 recalled,

> The Americans hit us with something stronger than grenades [depth
> charges]. . . . We thought—that's it, the end. After this attack, the
> totally exhausted Stavitsky, who in addition to everything, was not
> able to establish connection with the General Staff, became furious.
> He summoned the officer who was assigned to the nuclear torpedo,
> and ordered him to assemble it to battle readiness. "Maybe the war
> has already started up there while we are doing summersaults here,"
> screamed emotional Valentin Grivoievich, trying to justify his order.
> "We're going to blast them now! We will die, but we will sink them
> all. We will not disgrace our Navy!" But we did not fire the nuclear
> torpedo—Savitsky was able to rein in his wrath. After consulting Sec-
> ond Captain Vasili Alexandrovich Arkhipov [deceased] and deputy
> political officer Ivan Somenovich Maslennikov, he made the decision to
> come to the surface.[28]

Thomas Blanton, director of the National Security Archives, later observed,
"The lesson from this is that a guy called Vasili Arkhipov saved the world."[29] The
United States wasn't aware the Soviet submarines were carrying nuclear warheads
when they dropped depth charges on them and thus that if the Soviet submarine
commander interpreted the depth charge as a sign that was war had started he
would have to respond. Good luck won the day on October 27.

Discussion during the day centered on Khrushchev's offer, and Kennedy favored trading the Turkey missiles, but most of ExComm felt such an open concession would fragment the NATO alliance. The Joint Chiefs of Staff submitted a plan for an air strike and invasion, and the State Department submitted a letter rejecting the Russian proposal. The idea emerged that the United States should ignore Khrushchev's second letter and respond to his first, which only asked for a promise not to invade Cuba. Kennedy did not think it would work but was convinced it was worth a try. Theodore Sorensen and Robert Kennedy left the meeting to draft a response, and after forty-five minutes the letter was ready. It was sent that evening.

After most of ExComm left, the president remained behind with his brother, Sorensen, McNamara, Rusk, Bundy and Llewellyn Thompson. They agreed there should be a second letter to Khrushchev and an oral message passed through Soviet ambassador Dobrynin. They agreed Dobrynin should be told there would be military intervention if the missiles were not withdrawn from Cuba but the nonintervention pledge would be honored if that happened. Rusk suggested it should be made clear that there could be no public mention of any arrangement or deal over the Jupiter missiles in Turkey, but they would be removed after the crisis was resolved. This was kept secret from the other ExComm members.

Robert Kennedy met privately with Dobrynin at the Justice Department early in the evening and desperately presented his case, saying events were spinning out of control and there was great pressure on his brother to take more direct action, which he was sure would lead to Soviet response and could result in the deaths of millions of Americans and Russians. He presented the proposal for nonintervention if the Soviets removed their bases and added that the Turkey missiles were up for removal but it would take four to five months. He was insistent on the need for a rapid response to the proposal from Premier Khrushchev, as there were generals itching for a fight. The strain of the ordeal on the younger Kennedy was apparent to Dobrynin, who noted in his cable to the U.S.S.R. Foreign Ministry, "I should say that during our meeting R. Kennedy was very upset; in any case, I've never seen him like this before.... After the meeting with me he immediately went to see the President, with whom, as R. Kennedy said, he spends almost all his time now."[30] And as for conveying this critical information that had potential to end the most dangerous crisis ever, "The Soviet ambassador immediately wrote up his account of the meeting and sent it—incredibly, there was no other means of immediate transmission—by Western Union. A young boy came by on a bicycle from the telegraph agency to pick up the message. Dobrynin watched him pedal off into the night, praying that he would not stop off for a Coca-Cola or to dally with his girlfriend."[31]

When Robert Kennedy returned to the White House the president activated over fourteen thousand Air Force Reserve units in anticipation of possible military confrontation. At 8:05 p.m. the letter he had drafted earlier to Premier Khrushchev was sent to Moscow. At 9:00 there was an ExComm meeting to make plans for the next day, and the discussion included a possible air strike against Cuban missile sites, while Robert McNamara warned they had better have a government ready for Cuba and have plans in place for Soviet action against European targets. Later in the evening President Kennedy and Dean Rusk prepared a contingency proposal to be delivered to U Thant, asking him to initiate a public Cuba-for-Turkey missile exchange, but no others were included in the discussion.

The Crisis Comes to an End

Sunday, October 28: The CIA's 6:00 a.m. Daily Update announced that all twenty-four MRBM sites in Cuba were now fully operational. Khrushchev was informed that Kennedy was addressing the nation at 5:00 that afternoon and feared it would be to announce that an invasion of Cuba was underway. His speechwriter recalled how the premier rushed to make a morning radio announcement of his position, "This letter was not drafted in the Kremlin nor in the Politburo. It was drafted at Khrushchev's dacha, by a very small group. As soon as it was done, they ran it to the radio station. That is to say, they sent it by car, very fast; as a matter of fact, the car ran into some trouble on the way, an obstruction, which delayed it. When it arrived, the manager of the station himself ran down the steps, snatched the message from the hands of the man in the car, and ran up the steps to broadcast it immediately."[32] Khrushchev then sent it to President Kennedy, accepting his terms:

> Esteemed Mr. President:
>   I have received your message of October 27, 1962. I express my satisfaction and gratitude for the sense of proportion and understanding of the responsibility borne by you at present for the preservation of peace throughout the world....
>   In order to complete with greater speed the liquidation of the conflict...the Soviet government...in addition to previously issued instructions on the cessation of further work at building sites for the weapons, has issued a new order on the dismantling of the weapons which you describe as "offensive," and their crating and return to the Soviet Union.[33]

The message was received at 9:00 a.m. in Washington. Kennedy responded quickly with a letter sent that afternoon to the Soviet leader, beginning:

> I am replying at once to your broadcast message of October 28 even though the official text has not yet reached me because of the great importance I attach to moving forward promptly to the settlement of the Cuban crisis. I think that you and I, with our heavy responsibilities for the maintenance of peace, were aware that developments were approaching

a point where events could have become unmanageable. So I welcome this message and consider it an important contribution to peace.[34]

With Khrushchev's public statement the crisis had, in effect, come to an end, though some were unwilling to let it go. Some of the Joint Chiefs of Staff were unconvinced. General Curtis LaMay proposed the United States launch an attack anyway and another general complained the United States had "been had." At 11:00 on the morning of October 28 Robert Kennedy met with Ambassador Dobrynin at his residence and was told that the Soviet Union had complied with the request to dismantle the bases. He also said that Premier Khrushchev wished to send his best wishes to both Robert and the president. Instructions to dismantle the bases reached Soviet commanders in Cuba in the early afternoon and the dismantling of the bases began at 5:00 p.m. The Soviet Union conducted a high altitude hydrogen bomb test.

Fidel Castro, who had not been consulted by the Soviets, was especially upset. Upon hearing of the Soviet decision he publicly called Khrushchev a "son of a bitch, bastard, asshole" and days later in a speech at the University of Havana said Khrushchev lacked "*cojones*" (balls).[35] He went to an airbase to try to shoot down low flying U.S. reconnaissance flights personally, but to no avail.

Castro's reaction was an anomaly. As Christopher Hanson of Reuters recalls, "The world heaved a huge collective sigh of relief."[36] The banner headline of the *New York Times* shouted, "U.S. and Soviet Reach Accord on Cuba: Kennedy Accepts Khruschev Pledge to Remove Missiles under U.N. Watch," while the lead story on the BBC was "World Relief as Cuban Missile Crisis Ends." The Soviet bombers stationed in Cuba had not been mentioned in the terms of the communications, and the blockade remained in place after October 28. On November 20 the Soviet Union began packing up the bombers and shipping them back, and the following day President Kennedy formally ended the quarantine of Cuba.

In the aftermath there were important accomplishments. Khrushchev and Kennedy signed a treaty to halt nuclear testing in the atmosphere nine months after the crisis ended. The hotline that Schelling had been proposing since 1958 took on new life, as the importance of direct and immediate communication between the leaders of the superpowers was made evident. On June 20, 1963, it was approved and it was soon functioning as a direct connection between Washington and Moscow. Numerous conferences were held to discuss the lessons to be learned from the event, innumerable articles and books were written analyzing it, television shows, both documentary and dramatic, along with feature films relived the dramatic moments. Robert Kennedy, so intimately involved, wrote perhaps the most succinct summary of the lessons from those incredible thirteen days in October. He reduced the lessons to the following:

Take time to plan; don't go with your first impulse.
The President should be exposed to a variety of opinions.

Depend heavily on those with solid knowledge of the Soviet Union.=
Retain civilian control and beware of the limited outlook of the military.
Pay close attention to world opinion.
Don't humiliate your opponent; leave him a way out.
Beware of inadvertence. [37]

This last was known as "the Guns of August scenario," after Barbara Tuchman's book of that name that described the German mistake in 1914 of expecting Russia to back down because they had during the Balkans crisis of 1909.

Review and Analysis

The hawk, dove, and owl categorizations are now being applied to the political views of the principal advisors that surrounded the president. Harvard scholars defined the three positions: "Hawks see the proximate cause of war as one-sided weakness—weakness that temps an adversary to exploit advantage....For doves, the primary cause of war lies in the 'mad momentum of the arms race.'...To avoid war doves prescribe a policy of communication, conciliation and accommodation....Owls worry primarily about loss of control....Owls believe that crisis or conventional war could create the circumstances in which an unintended nuclear war might break out."[38] It is clear that John Kennedy and his influential brother Robert were of the owl persuasion, while they had powerful voices pushing them from the hawk side and lesser influence from the doves. Among the voices closest to the president was his long-time speechwriter, Theodore Sorensen, who was never in doubt that gradual tactics were preferable to direct military action. Sorenson supported the owl view of a measured response of a blockade coupled with the threat that an attack launched on the United States from Cuba would be considered an attack by the Soviet Union.[39]

This analysis will not attempt to make a judgment of the greatness of Kennedy or Khrushchev, but will focus on Schelling's ideas about decisions, especially those he presented in his Harvard graduate school course. Schelling was invited to the major reviews of the missile crisis that involved the people who had participated in the decisions at the time. There is reason to believe a number of the ExComm members were familiar with his ideas.[40]

We will use Schelling's views on decision-making as a guideline for looking at the decisions of October 1962. They will serve us as a reference for reasonableness as well as a means of reviewing the material presented in earlier sections of this book. Kennedy's speechwriter and confidant Theodore Sorensen, who was the final member of ExComm to pass away when he died on October 31, 2010, provided insight into this review. Sergei Khrushchev, son of Soviet Premier Nikita Khrushchev, also provides perspective. Dr. Khrushchev participated in the Soviet missile and space program from 1958 to 1968 and helped his father write his memoirs. He left Russia in 1993, following the disintegration of the Communist Party, to pursue an academic career in the United States.

Schelling's first lesson is that strategic moves impact the expectations of another. It is clear that the strategic moves selected by the United States during the crisis had an impact on the Kremlin, specifically Premier Khrushchev, and were carefully tailored to do so. The blockade with the veiled threat of military action set clear expectations for the Soviets without backing them into a corner that called for an immediate military response; it was confrontational and, given the nature of the superpower rivalry, total acquiescence was an unlikely response. The Berlin Crisis that had taken place the previous year and involved the same players, and it might seem reasonable to assume the United States began this new crisis with some understanding about how far the Soviets could be pushed. When asked whether that was the case, Defense Secretary Robert McNamara's emphatic response was, "No."[41]

Schelling stressed the importance of vicarious thinking, and Kennedy was certainly concerned with what was going on in the minds of the Soviet decision makers. The same can be said of Khrushchev and his concern about what was taking place in the United States. This vicarious thinking and its advantages were described in *Political Science Quarterly*: "During the crisis Khrushchev's confidence in deterrence wavered. He began to worry that Kennedy would be unable to control the militants in the military and the CIA who did not share his recognition of the futility of war and that the crisis might spin out of control. Kennedy, too, worried that Khrushchev would be ousted by militants determined to go to war.... He, too, then made the concessions necessary to resolve the crisis."[42]

Sergei Khrushchev takes issue with the statement that that the Soviets and the United States achieved vicarious understanding, saying, "I guess, that different from Schelling, they [Soviets] understood that it was and it is impossible to go 'inside minds of these...' as they represent different culture and different way of thinking, for example how Europeans, who had enemies at the gate all their history can understand way of thinking and reaction of Americans, who for centuries were protected by two oceans?"[43]

Despite this seeming protestation, his written account of the crisis has a sound of vicarious thinking on the Soviet Union's part. While describing the decisive moment when the deal was about to be struck that brought the crisis to an end, he said, "Later, in retelling the story of how Robert Kennedy looked when he met with Dobrynin, Father would always add with a smile: 'And we didn't look any better.' The President was asking for help; that was how Father interpreted Robert Kennedy's talk with our ambassador. The tone of the conversation was evidence of the fact that to delay would be fatal."[44]

"The President was asking for help," sounds like vicarious thinking, and indicates the importance of communication during the crisis; but the younger Khrushchev now says, "It was feelings that Kennedy can be overthrown and replaced (by a) hawk, who will push the button."[45] The younger Khrushchev believes the simple key to understanding the solution of the missile crisis is, "They were wise, prag-matic leaders that had no choice."[46]

The understanding was facilitated by communication between the adversar-ies. Understanding what is in your opponent's mind and thinking as he thinks is the key to rational decisions. Theodore Sorensen says the direct communication between the leaders was valuable in their understanding each other's motives and contributed to a solution.[47]

Schelling would look at this as a game theorist and see it as one of the best-known games in all game theory, the chicken dilemma. This offers a simple way of looking at the missile crisis. It could be said that in the chicken dilemma of the Cuban missile crisis Kennedy courageously drove straight while Khrushchev was "chicken" and swerved, and one would have a very simple, tidy explanation. There is some truth to this, and the common belief that Khrushchev lost his position in the government because of it would seem to support it. However, as Schelling knows well, Kennedy achieved his goal with a nuanced approach and more than the missile crisis was involved in Khrushchev's demise—he presided over eco-nomic weakness and agricultural failures. Kennedy relied on many tactics, not simply a head-to-head macho confrontation; and Khrushchev won a private victory, though he lost publicly.

Another apparent game theory situation that Schelling has discussed at length, warning of its interference with achieving rational outcomes in decision-making is the Prisoner's Dilemma. The missile crisis could be viewed as iteration, or repeated play, of the prisoner's dilemma game that dominated the Cold War rivalry. As we saw in Chapter 13, cooperation tends to develop with repeated play of the game. The most relevant defections were the Soviet installation of mis-siles following U.S. defection with the failed attempt to oust Castro at the Bay of Pigs. Cooperation emerged with the settlement of the crisis. Cooperation con-tinued following the crisis with the treaty to halt atmospheric testing and the establishment of the hotline.

Another Schelling view is that reaching agreement may require the use of specific tactics. Schelling notes that a person's ability to constrain or control his adversary may depend on the power to bind oneself, what he refers to as "burn-ing bridges." Kennedy used this tactic successfully when he went on television before the world and committed himself to the blockade of Cuba. He had put him-self in a position where he no longer had a choice in what he could do, and his public appearance made more credible his commitment to act in accordance with his announcement. As Schelling put it, deterrence often depends on getting into position where the initiative is up to enemy. By establishing the quarantine line, Kennedy had put the onus of initiating a confrontation on the Soviet Union. As was noted by many, this did not solve the problem of the missiles already posi-tioned in Cuba. That required the demand that they be dismantled.

Schelling's catalog of tactics also includes the use of teamwork for develop-ing credibility. The administration took pains to get approval for its quarantine from the Organization of American States and worked closely with the UN. Not only did Stevenson present a convincing case at the UN, but the UN also was involved in negotiations; and when an agreement was reached, the UN participated in the inspection of facilities to confirm compliance. Sorensen describes U Thant's and the UN's roles in the crisis as helpful.[48] A related tactic is the employment of mandated negotiating agents. In addition to the UN involvement, there were back-channel negotiations by agents who became mandated by approval of their actions from the highest authority, including *ABC News* correspondent John Scali and KGB colonel Alexandr Fomin, who helped to move things along.

Reasoning forward and looking backward is a basic approach to rational choice decision-making that is apparent in this case. The goal of removal of the missiles from Cuba peacefully was clarified first and steps to achieve it were developed. Once decisions, such as to increase surveillance, were deemed necessary, backward reasoning was done to analyze problems that could result, such as if the surveillance aircraft were shot down, what response was called for, and what Soviet actions various U.S. responses would invite. The point was to have thought of the possibilities and considered the consequences in advance, so no "shooting from the hip" would lead to disaster.

Schelling warned that competition in risk-taking could result when mutual threats were involved. A situation might get out of control and initiate a process that carries a risk of unintended disaster. Kennedy was cautious about escalating risks even when under considerable pressure from the Joint Chiefs. The October 26 Scali/Fomin lunch initiated by the Soviets offered a compromise, and certainly was intended to temper the escalation of risk as well.

Arthur M. Schlesinger Jr. recalls Kennedy's demeanor during the crisis and why he tried to avoid risk,

> He never had a more sober sense of his responsibility. It was a strange week; the flow of decision was continuous; there was no day and no night. In the intervals between the meetings he sought out his wife and children as if the imminence of catastrophe had turned his mind more than ever to his family and, through them, to children everywhere in the world. This was the cruel question—the young people who, if things went wrong, would never have the chance to learn, to love, to fulfill themselves and serve their countries. One noon, swimming in pool, he said to David Powers: "If it weren't for these people that haven't lived yet, it would be easy to make decisions of this sort."[49]

Schelling has described the strategic advantages of appearing to be unpredictable and out of control, "the mad man theory," and in this situation the person that best suited the role was Fidel Castro. However, Castro was of little tactical use, for as Sorensen says, "In our discussions, Castro was not a key player, in either the installation or the ultimate removal of the missiles. We later heard that his belligerence alarmed Khrushchev."[50]

Schelling argues that violence is most successful when it is threatened. When Robert Kennedy met with Soviet Ambassador Dobrynin and a U-2 had been shot down, he warned that there were U.S. generals were itching for a fight. He could use the threat of impending violence to push for a speedy response to the president's letter proposing a settlement agreement. The Soviets made use of the same tactic with the implication that violence against Cuba would be countered by action against West Berlin.

Being aware of the interrelation of commitments matters, Schelling points out, and that was clear in the resolution of this crisis. The Soviet Union had made a commitment to Cuba. As Sergei Khrushchev observed, "The defense of Cuba became a matter of prestige for the Soviet Union, something like West Berlin was for the United States. If you did not defend that small patch of land deep inside enemy territory that was allied to you, no one would believe in your willingness or, more important, your ability to defend your allies."[51] The United States also had a commitment to NATO and especially to Turkey. Turkey was being used as a bargaining chip along with Cuba for missile removal, and like Cuba, felt the loss of missiles threatened its security. When Sorensen was asked whether Turkey was ever consulted in advance about the arrangement, he responded, "I doubt it."[52]

By selecting the embargo, the United States broke down the confrontation with the Soviet Union into smaller units, allowing "salami tactics" to be adopted by both sides as they worked out a resolution and averted disaster. Kennedy announced the quarantine at eight hundred miles from Cuba, but the next day he moved it to five hundred miles, allowing Khrushchev more time to react. Khrushchev ordered the freighters to continue forward in apparent defiance, as they were in international waters, and when Soviet ships approached the blockade line and the cargo ships carrying military cargo were about to reach the line, he ordered them to halt and retreat. Other freighters and tankers carried on. Kennedy then allowed the first ship to reach the line, the *Bucharest*, to pass through. Each leader was taking small, cautious steps that signaled reasonableness to the other.

The threat and promise, a combination defined by Schelling, was basic to success. The threat indicated Kennedy's willingness to make a choice he preferred not making: a military strike to remove the missile sites. The threat's failure could be costly to Kennedy; he was uncertain what would follow, but disaster of some degree was likely. He accompanied this threat with two promises, one public and one private. Publicly he promised the United States would not invade Cuba and privately that the United States would remove its Jupiter missiles from Turkey and Italy in the near future. Promises are generally expensive when they succeed, and the United States was left with a communist neighbor ninety miles from its shores and without missiles in a NATO ally on Russia's border. Getting to this stage required careful work, what Schelling calls "moving in small steps." This allowed the Soviets to remove the missiles while not being humiliated, as they had been successful in their stated intent of guaranteeing Cuba's security.

Schelling presented behavior models, and two offer insight in this case. Each side was making costly investments that could not be recovered, the trap of the Dollar Auction. More directly, during the crisis the two sides continued to carry out atmospheric testing of hydrogen bombs, which appeared to be escalation of the threat each posed to the other if it allowed events to spin out of control. Surprisingly, Theodore Sorensen, who was intimately involved and was the last person with direct knowledge of the events, stated this was not strategic escalation, commenting, "I have no information on U.S. atmosphere nuclear testing at that time."[53] While the nuclear testing seems too strategic to have been completely coincidental, either it was the Pentagon's strategy or a fluke that added focus to the seriousness of the situation.

Behavior that followed the president's announcement of the crisis illustrates another model, the self-fulfilling prophecy. There are revisionists who feel that Kennedy created the crisis[54] when he announced in his speech to the nation, "My fellow citizens: let no one doubt that this is a difficult and dangerous effort on which we have set out. No one can foresee precisely what course it will take or what costs or casualties will be incurred." This prediction that things were going to be dangerous led to panic buying and hoarding and seeking out fallout shelter accommodations, so the times were difficult, and while the actual dangers were unknown, others were created by fear. Dr. Sergei Khrushchev says the same was not the case in the Soviet Union, where during the thirteen-day crisis, "It was calm on all levels: ordinary public and professionals, as myself, who knew all details."[55]

Two related topics discussed by Schelling that apply to the missile crisis decisions were coordination and fair division. The idea of coordination is that people can coordinate their behavior and maintain some sort of social order without enforcement from formal authority or machinery of law. In the case of the Cold War, coordination was embodied in the idea of "conventions," practices that are understood and followed by nations interacting. Among the effective conventions in the bipolar Cold War world was not violating the other great power's sphere of influence, the area a country found essential to its national security.

This relates to the Schelling concept, fair division. The post–World War II world was divided into the Communist Bloc, the Western Alliance, and the nonaligned world. While the U.S.S.R. and the United States dominated this as the two great powers, they were in competition for support among countries in the nonaligned group. Fair division meant that within the countries in each superpower's sphere of influence, the other would be seeking trouble in overtly attempting to interfere or challenge for a change in alliance. Each side's sphere of influence was its "fair share," as the "containment" policy recognized, and the nonaligned world was the grounds for competition. The convention of remaining out of what the United

States viewed as its sphere by fair division was clearly articulated by Kennedy in his speech to the nation: "In violation of Soviet assurances, and in defiance of American and hemispheric policy—this sudden, clandestine decision to station strategic weapons for the first time outside of Soviet soil—is a deliberately provocative and unjustified change in the status quo."

Critical mass and its pivotal spot, the tipping point, were also at work throughout the crisis. Critical mass is achieved when a certain number of people acting one way is enough to influence others to act in a similar manner, and those people's decisions then influence others to act the same way, and so on as the decision to act becomes self-sustaining. The tipping point is the precise level at which this process reaches a self-sustaining reaction that will carry on. In the missile crisis this can be seen with the argument to launch a military strike against the missile sites and bases in Cuba. There was always support for this with the Joint Chiefs of Staff and with some members of ExComm, but not enough to achieve critical mass. When Kennedy went to Congress a second time he found there was more support, but it was still not enough to put him past the tipping point. He was close on October 26, the day before the most dangerous day of the crisis, when he told ExComm he believed the quarantine alone would not succeed in getting Russia to withdraw the missiles from Cuba and that an invasion or a trade of some sort would be required. It turned out that the trade was the solution.

The question of how close the United States came to going to war was based partially on CIA intelligence reports of Soviet missiles and their readiness in Cuba. As to the reliability of the intelligence ExComm was receiving, Sorensen describes it as, "Very valuable."[56] However, while valuable, the information appears to have been incomplete. In the October 27 CIA daily briefing a report was passed along of a conversation Khrushchev held with an American businessman, William Knox, three days earlier, in which Khrushchev stated, "We have anti-aircraft missiles and we have ballistic missiles, with both nuclear and high explosive warhead already" in Cuba.[57] It has been assumed and Soviet generals have testified to that being the case, but Schelling is among those who does not believe there were nuclear warheads married to missiles in Cuba. Sorenson agrees there was no certainty. He commented, "No one knew whether the Soviets had nuclear warheads in Cuba. But a prudent President and ExComm necessarily proceeded on a worse-case assumption."[58]

The situation could have "tipped" several times, as there were events that could have caused enough people to favor military action that a critical mass supporting the idea would have been achieved. Sorensen describes the danger as "uncertain" when the United States first confronted Soviet ships at the quarantine line, "increased" when the U-2 was shot down on October 27, and "extreme, but unknown" at the time when the USS Beale dropped depth charges on the Soviet submarine B-59.[59]

According to Sergei Khrushchev the most dangerous moment came with the initial confrontation at the quarantine line, where the Soviet submarines posed a danger if their commanders felt Soviet shipping was at risk. He wrote,

> At first Father ordered Soviet freighters to continue forward, despite Washington's threats. After all, they were in international waters. They were accompanied by submarines, each armed with one nuclear torpedo along with conventional torpedoes. The submarines' commanders had instructions to act according to circumstances. If the ships they were guarding were attacked, they could use their weapons—even the nuclear torpedo. On the morning of October 24 no more than half an hour separated us from nuclear war.
>
> Fortunately, the time granted the Kremlin for reflection was sufficient. At literally the last moment Father decided not to take the risk; after all, missiles and nuclear warheads were already in place in Cuba. Minutes before the confrontation all Soviet transport ships carrying military cargoes were ordered to halt and turn around. But the other freighters and tankers continued on their way.[60]

Though there were pressures on Kennedy, the owl, he chose the middle path, and a critical mass for military action was never achieved among ExComm members or the public that could tip him from his original decision to follow a path of determined confrontation with minimal risk of war. Khrushchev followed that same path, and nuclear war was averted. And how close was war? Schelling recalls, "Kennedy was said to have said he thought the chance of nuclear war was one in three, and my response to that is Kennedy just doesn't understand fractions."[61]

One reason the situation was volatile and unpredictable was because it contained elements of randomization. In game theory, randomization is intentionally introduced to solve zero-sum games, where player's interests are completely opposite. By introducing probability in their choices, players with strictly opposing interests can achieve a higher "expected utility," or anticipated outcome than by simply avoiding their poorer option. The missile crisis might seem appropriate for a randomization, or a minimax solution, since one could look at it as having two parties with completely opposing interests, each with one choice: for Russia it was to remove the missiles or not; and for the United States it was to use military action or not. This would be a simple but inaccurate characterization of the Cuban situation. The crisis is better classified as what Schelling described as "mixed motive," meaning it has elements of competition and cooperation. Randomization is not the solution for mixed motive games. Both players, the United States and the Soviet Union, were interested in cooperating in avoiding nuclear holocaust, while the competition was about hemispheric hegemony. They had much in common in their effort to prevent the situation from getting out of control.

While Kennedy and Khrushchev both sought to keep the crisis under control, not all elements were totally in their hands, and random events threatened what they could achieve. That was illustrated by the actions of Vasili Arkhipov in convincing his captain not to launch a nuclear torpedo against U.S. ships. Dangers came not only from the Soviet side. Efforts were made during the crisis by some U.S. Minuteman missile engineers to hot-wire missiles, bypassing safety controls and the command links that authorized that they could be launched. At Incirlik Air Force base in Turkey, pilots of nuclear weapons–equipped F-100 fighters sat for hours in their cockpits, and a former commander of the fighters there said that nuclear weapons control "was so loose, it jars your imagination."[62]

Conclusion

President Kennedy and ExComm's handling of the missiles in Cuba will continue to be looked at through changing prisms in the future as new generations bring different values to the analysis and seek new meaning in the event. What this discussion has sought to do is look at how it was handled, not in terms of Kennedy's personality or political interests or in relation to the times in which he lived, but in terms of rational choice. The rational choice standard has been the teachings of Thomas Schelling.

There is considerable evidence that the process and decision-making by Kennedy and ExComm during the Cuban missile crisis was by and large similar to much that Schelling taught as wise methods for rational choice. The president was aware of what his decisions would do. Kennedy approached the decisions vicariously and employed a range of tactics that Schelling considers to be effective. It is fortunate that his adversary, Nikita Khrushchev, came to adopt a similar mode of thinking,[63] and that the individuals and incidents beyond the two leaders' control did not spark anything to alter the course beyond safe passage. [64]

Notes

1. Arthur M. Schlesinger Jr., *A Thousand Days: John F. Kennedy in the White House* (New York: Mariner Books, 2002), xiv.
2. Noam Chomsky, "Reasons to Fear U.S.," *Toronto Star*, September 7, 2003.
3. Schlesinger, *A Thousand Days*, xiv.
4. Winston Churchill, "The Iron Curtain Speech," Washington, DC, The Churchill Centre, http://www.winstonchurchill.org/learn/in-the-media/churchill-in-the news/842-anniversary-of-iron-curtain-speech.
5. "Foreign News: We Will Bury You," *Time*, November 26, 1956.
6. Stephen I. Schwartz, ed., "50 Facts about U.S. Nuclear Weapons," Brookings Institution, July 3, 2010, http://www.brookings.edu/projects/archive/nuweapons/50.aspx.
7. G. Calvin Mackenzie and Robert Weisbrot, "Kennedy v. Khrushchev: How an Inexperienced President Changed Nihilistic Cold War Policy," American Heritage.com, October 10, 2008.

8. Brigadier General Edward Lansdale, "Review of Operation Mongoose," Phase One, July 25, 1962," in Laurence Chang, comp., and Peter Kornbluh, ed., *Cuban Missile Crisis, 1962: A National Security Archive Documents Reader* (New York: New Press, 1999), 40.

9. Robert Daniels, *A Documentary History of Communism*, (London: Tauris, 1986), 294.

10. U.S.S.R., draft directive, Directive to the Commander of Soviet Forces in Cuba on transfer of Il-28s and Luna Missiles, and Authority on Use of Tactical Nuclear Weapons, September 8, 1962, The National Security Archive: The George Washington University, http://www.gwu.edu/~nsarchiv/nsa/cuba_mis_cri/620908%20Memorandum%20from%20Malinovsky.pdf.

11. "The South: This Righteous Cause," *Time*, September 21, 1962.

12. "Radio and Television Report to the Nation on the Situation at the University of Mississippi. September 30, 1962," *Public Papers of President Kennedy, 1962*, JFK Link, http://www.jfklink.com/speeches/jfk/publicpapers/1962/jfk19_62.html.

13. Schlesinger, *A Thousand Days*, 818.

14. CIA Special National Intelligence Estimate, "Major Consequences of Certain U.S. Courses of Action on Cuba," October 20, 1962, 9.

15. "Radio and Television Report to the American People."

16. "A Halloween to Remember: The Cuban Missile Crisis," About.com, US Government, October 31, 1997, hhtp://usgovinfo.about.com/library/weekly/aa103197.htm.

17. Claudia Smith Brinson, "For a Week in '62, War Was Thinkable," *The State*(Columbia, S.C.), October 26, 1992, 1A.

18. Sheldon M. Stern, *The Week the World Stood Still: Inside the Secret Cuban Missile Crisis* (Palo Alto, CA: Stanford University Press, 2004), 91–92.

19. Maga, Timothy P. "Cuban Missile Crisis." Something about Everything Military, http://www.jcs-group.com/military/navy/1962cuban.html.

20. "A Halloween to Remember."

21. "Chairman Khrushchev's Letter to President Kennedy, October 23, 1962," *The World on the Brink: John F. Kennedy and the Cuban Missile Crisis*, John F. Kennedy Presidential Library and Museum.

22. Evan Thomas, "Bobby at the Brink," *Newsweek*, August 14, 2000.

23. Ibid.

24. "Thousand Days," *Life*, November 12, 1965, 123.

25. Jeffrey Smith, "Missteps by U.S. Military Posed Threat during Cuban Missile Crisis, Book Says—'Unordered Risks-Taking Cited in Handling of Nuclear Weapons,'" *Washington Post*, September 20, 1993, A11.

26. Prime Minister Fidel Castro's letter to Premier Khrushchev, October 26, 1962, quoted in Chang and Kornbluh, *Cuban Missile Crisis, 1962*,199.

27. CIA daily report, "The Crisis USSR/Cuba," October 27, 1962, quoted in Chang and Kornbluh, *Cuban Missile Crisis, 1962*, 204.

28. U.S.S.R., Memoir, "Recollections of Vadim Orlov (USSR Submarine B-59): We will Sink Them All, But We Will Not Disgrace Our Navy," (2002), Cuban Missile Crisis.info – DeclassifiedDocs, http://cubanmissilecrisis.info/pdf-secrets docs/20.pdf.

29. Marion Lloyd, "Soviets Close to Using A-Bomb in 1962 Crisis, Forum Is Told," *Boston Globe*, October 13, 2002.

30. U.S.S.R., Cable, TOP SECRET, Dobrynin Report of Meeting with Robert Kennedy on Worsening Threat, October 27, 1962, in The National Security Archive: The George Washington University.

31. Thomas, "Bobby at the Brink."

32. Daniel Ellsberg, "The Day Castro Almost Started World War III," *New York Times*, October 31, 1987, 28.

33. Ernest May and Philip Zelikow (eds.), *The Kennedy Tapes: Inside the White House during the Cuban Missile Crisis* (Cambridge, MA: Harvard University Press, 1997), 630–631.

34. Ibid., 636.

35. Chang and Kornbluh, *Cuban Missile Crisis, 1962*, 380.

36. Christopher Hanson, "Legendary Face-off: 25 Years Ago Missile Crisis Gripped World," *St. Petersburg Times*, October 12, 1987, 1A.

37. James G. Blight, Joseph S. Nye Jr., and David A. Welch, "The Cuban Missile Crisis Revisited," *Foreign Affairs,*Vol. 66, No.1 (fall 1987), 172.

38. Graham T. Allison, Albert Carnesale, Joseph S. Nye Jr., "Hawks, Doves and Owls: A New Perspective on Avoiding Nuclear War," *International Affairs,*Vol. 61, No. 4 (autumn 1985), 581–589.

39. Theodore Sorensen, e-mail to Robert Dodge, October 17, 2008.

40. Robert McNamara wrote, "This [Schelling's] view permeated civilian leadership under Kennedy... to a remarkable degree." Robert McNamara, et. al., *Argument without End: In Search of Answers to the Vietnam Tragedy* (New York: Public Affairs, 1999), 169. The *Washington Post* wrote, "It was in John Kennedy's Camelot that Schelling really first burst upon the Washington scene." "Game Theory Suggests Quick Action on Greenhouse Effect Is Remote," *Washington Post*, June 13, 1990, b03. Shortly after Kennedy entered the White House, McGeorge Bundy had visited Harvard to seek Schelling's views on how to deal with a possible Soviet move on West Berlin (R. Dodge, *The Strategist* [Hollis, NH: Hollis, and Singapore: Marshall Cavendish, 2006], 88), and Schelling wrote a paper that Bundy noted, made a "deep impression" on the president. Richard Reeves, *President Kennedy: Profile of Power* (New York: Simon & Schuster, 1994).

41. Robert McNamara, letter to Robert Dodge, June 26, 2006.

42. Richard Ned Lebow and Janice Gross Stein, "Deterrence and the Cold War," *Political Science Quarterly*, Vol. 110, No.2(summer 1995), 170.

43. Sergei Khrushchev, e-mail to Robert Dodge, July 21, 2010.

44. Sergei Khrushchev, "How My Father and President Kennedy Saved the World," *American Heritage*, (October, 2002), 56–75.

45. Khrushchev, e-mail, July 21, 2010.

46. Ibid.

47. Sorensen, e-mail, Oct. 17, 2008.

48. Ibid.

49. Schlesinger, *A Thousand Days*, 818–819.

50. Sorensen, e-mail.

51. Khrushchev, "How My Father and President Kennedy Saved the World."

52. Sorensen, e-mail.

53. Ibid.

54. For a brief summary of the historiography of the evolving interpretation of Kennedy's motives and performance during the missile crisis see William J. Medland, "The Cuban Missile Crisis: Evolving Historical Perspectives," *The History Teacher,* Vol.23, No.4(August 1990), 433–447.

55. Khrushchev, e-mail.

56. Sorensen, e-mail.

57. CIA daily report, "The Crisis USSR/Cuba," October 27, 1962.

58. Sorensen, e-mail.

59. Ibid.

60. Khrushchev, "How My Father and President Kennedy Saved the World."

61. Thomas Schelling, interviewed by Robert Dodge, June 17, 2000.

62. Smith, "Missteps by U.S. Military Posed Threat during Cuban Missile Crisis."

63. For an analysis of the party-military falling out that occurred in the Soviet Union following Khrushchev's withdrawal from Cuba, see Benjamin S. Lambeth, *How to Think about Soviet Military Doctrine* (Santa Monica, CA: Rand Corporation, 1978), 18–19.

64. For a detailed transcription of the discussions that took place in the White House during the crisis see May and Zelikow, *The Kennedy Tapes*.

INDEX